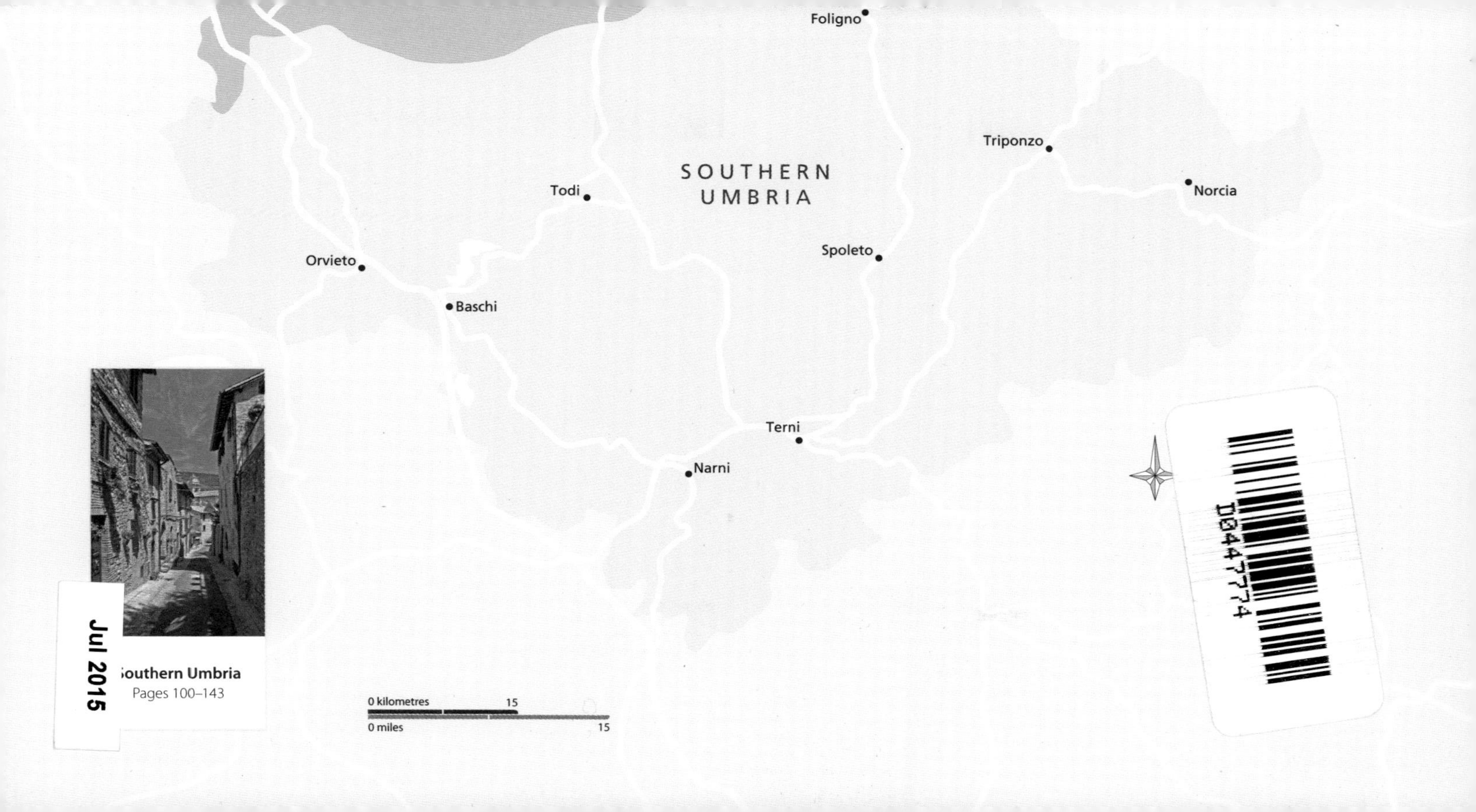

Norcia

Triponzo

Foligno

S O U T H E R N
U M B R I A

Spoleto

Terni

Narni

Todi

Baschi

Orvieto

0 kilometres 15

0 miles 15

Southern Umbria
Pages 100–143

Jul 2015

D0447774

EYEWITNESS TRAVEL

UMBRIA

EYEWITNESS TRAVEL

UMBRIA

LONDON, NEW YORK,
MELBOURNE, MUNICH AND DELHI
www.dk.com

Produced By Fabio Ratti Editoria Srl, Milan, Italy

Project Editors Mattia Goffetti, Silvia Riboldi
Editor Marina Beretta
Designers Modi Artistici, Tiziano Perotto

Contributors
Giovanni Francesio, Marina Dragoni, Patrizia Masnini

Photographer
Ghigo Roli

Illustrator
Elisabetta Mancini

Cartography
Laura Belletti

Dorling Kindersley Limited
Publishing Managers Fay Franklin, Kate Poole
Senior Art Editor Marisa Renzullo
Translator Fiona Wild
Editor Emily Hatchwell
Consultant Jeffrey Kennedy
Factchecker Leonie Loudon
Production Sarah Dodd

Printed and bound in China

First American Edition, 2004
15 16 17 18 10 9 8 7 6 5 4 3 2 1
Published in the United States by DK Publishing,
345 Hudson Street, New York, New York 10014.

Reprinted with revisions 2006, 2008, 2011, 2015

Copyright © Mondadori Electra SpA 2003.
Published under exclusive licence by Dorling Kindersley Limited.
English text copyright © Dorling Kindersley Limited 2004, 2015.

A catalog record for this book is available from the Library of Congress.

ISSN 1479-344X
ISBN 978-1-46542-738-0

Floors are referred to throughout in accordance with European usage; ie the "first floor"
is the floor above ground level

MIX
Paper from
responsible sources
FSC™ FSC™ C018179
www.fsc.org

**The information in this
DK Eyewitness Travel Guide is checked regularly.**
Every effort has been made to ensure that this book is as up-to-date as possible
at the time of going to press. Some details, however, such as telephone numbers,
opening hours, prices, gallery hanging arrangements and travel information are
liable to change. The publishers cannot accept responsibility for any consequences
arising from the use of this book, nor for any material on third party websites, and
cannot guarantee that any website address in this book will be a suitable source of
travel information. We value the views and suggestions of our readers very highly.
Please write to: Publisher, DK Eyewitness Travel Guides, Dorling Kindersley,
80 Strand, London, WC2R 0RL, UK, or email: travelguides@dk.com.

Front cover main image: Palazzo dei Consoli, Gubbio

◀ Stunning landscapes stretching over the fascinating town of Assisi

Contents

Dispute in the Temple, detail, Cappella
Baglioni, Spello

Introducing
Umbria

Streetside café on Piazza del Comune, in
the heart of Assisi

The imposing tufa platform supporting Orvieto

Mosaic by Solsternus adorning the façade of Duomo

Duomo's Gothic doorway, unfinished pulpit and papal statue

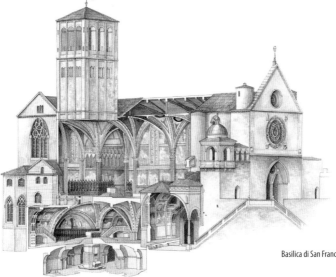
Basilica di San Francesco, Assisi

HOW TO USE THIS GUIDE

This guide helps you to get the most out of your visit to Umbria by giving detailed descriptions of sights, practical information and expert advice. *Introducing Umbria* sets the region in its geographical, cultural as well as historical context.

Umbria Area by Area describes the main sightseeing areas, with maps, detailed illustrations and photographs. Hotels, restaurants and shops are covered in *Travellers' Needs*, while the *Survival Guide* contains invaluable practical advice.

Umbria Area by Area

Umbria has been divided into two sightseeing areas, each with its own colour-coded thumb tab: a key to the colours used is on the inside front cover. Each area has its own chapter, which opens with a Regional Map with a numbered list of the sights described. There is a Road Map and a key to symbols inside the back cover.

Each area has a colour-coded thumb tab.

1 Introduction
The landscape, history and character of each region is described here, showing how the area has developed over the centuries and what it offers to the visitor today.

A locator map shows the area in relation to the region as a whole. It is identified by its colour-coding.

2 Regional Map
This gives an illustrated overview of the whole area. All the sights covered in the chapter are numbered and there are also useful tips on getting around by car and public transport.

Features and story boxes highlight special aspects of an area or sight.

3 Detailed Information
All the important towns and other places of interest are described individually. They are listed in order, following the numbering on the Regional Map. Within each entry there are details on the important buildings and other major sights.

4 Major Towns
All the important towns are described individually. Within each entry there is further detailed information on all the main sights. The Town Map shows their location.

A Visitors' Checklist provides the practical details needed to plan a visit, including local transport and details for the local tourist office.

The Town Map shows all the key sights, along with train and bus stations, car parks, churches and tourist offices.

5 The Top Sights
All the most important sights have two or more pages devoted to them. Historic buildings and churches are dissected to reveal their interiors, and museums and galleries have colour-coded floorplans.

Stars indicate the features you should not miss.

6 Areas of Natural Beauty and National Parks
Parks and nature reserves are described in detail and illustrated with a pictorial map. Roads are shown, together with scenic routes, picnicking areas and campsites.

The scale bar makes it possible to judge distances. The compass shows due north.

Verification of the Stigmata, detail, Upper Church of the Basilica di San Francesco, Assisi ▶

INTRODUCING UMBRIA

DISCOVERING UMBRIA

The following tours have been designed to take in as many of Umbria's highlights as possible, while keeping long-distance travel to a minimum. Our first tour covers two days in Perugia, followed by five days spent exploring Northern Umbria. These two itineraries can be followed individually or combined to form a week-long tour.

Next comes two days in Terni and its environs, and five days exploring Southern Umbria, which, again, can be combined to give a seven-day tour. Extra suggestions are provided for those who want to extend their stay. Pick, combine and follow your favourite tours, or simply dip in and out and be inspired.

Lake Trasimeno
The setting of the lake is idyllic, with a lush cypress belt and hills draped along the turquoise waters. This is Italy's fourth-largest lake and the spot where Hannibal destroyed the Roman army in 217 BC.

Città di Castello
Montone
Umbertide
Tevere
Isola Maggiore
Castiglione del Lago
Isola Polvese
Lago Trasimeno
Perugia
Torgiano
Deruta
Tevere
Chiani
Todi
Orvieto
Lugnano in Teverino
Amelia

5 Days in Northern Umbria

- Be captivated by **Assisi**, its history and its wondrous buildings, like the **Duomo**.

- Marvel at the scenery of the **Parco Regionale del Monte Subasio**.

- Walk through Gubbio's **Via Gabrielli**, a street lined with gorgeous medieval houses.

- Visit **Città di Castello's Pinacoteca Comunale,** one of Umbria's finest art galleries.

- Take a leisurely boat trip from Castiglione del Lago on **Lake Trasimeno** to Isola Maggiore and Isola Polvese.

- Spend two days hiking along the **Franciscan Path of Peace** from Assisi to Gubbio.

Key

━━ 5 Days in Northern Umbria

━━ 5 Days in Southern Umbria

Assisi
A picturesque view of the centre of the fascinating town of Assisi. This UNESCO World Heritage Site has a string of magnificent churches and timeless scenic beauty.

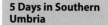

5 Days in Southern Umbria

- Visit the huge fortress sitting on top of a hill overlooking the ancient town of **Narni**.

- Explore **Amelia** with its ancient Mura Poligonali (Polygonal Walls).

- Head for the spectacular white and grey **Piazza del Duomo** in **Orvieto**.

- Admire **Pozzo di San Patrizio** in Orvieto, a deep well with a 248-step spiral staircase.

- Witness the well-preserved medieval architecture of **Palazzo dei Priori, Palazzo del Popolo** and **Palazzo del Capitano** in Todi.

- Enjoy dinner in one of **Spoleto**'s sophisticated restaurants in the buzzy **Piazza del Mercato**.

Amelia
Reconstructed in Baroque style in the 17th century, the cathedral in Amelia bears important works of art including a panel with *Madonna and Child* attributed to Antoniazzo Romano.

0 kilometres   15

0 miles   15

Parco Regionale del Monte Cucco

Gubbio

Gualdo Tadino

Nocera Umbra

Assisi
Eremo delle Carceri
Cortona
Parco Regionale del Monte Subasio

Spello

Bevagna
Foligno

Montefalco
Trevi

Fonti del Clitunno

Parco Nazionale dei Monti Sibillini

Nera

Norcia

Spoleto
Cascia

Acquasparta

Carsulae
San Gemini
Ferentillo

Terni
Parco Fluviale del Nera

Narni

Visciano

Narni
A typical old street in the unspoilt, medieval hill town of Narni.

Todi
Aerial view of red-tiled rooftops, Palazzo del Populo and Duomo in the centre of this well-preserved medieval town.

2 Days in Perugia

The largest city in Umbria, Perugia is notable for its Romanesque churches, monuments, museums and the famous Jazz Music Festival, Umbria Jazz.

- **Arriving** International and domestic flights arrive at the Aeroporto Regionale Umbro di Sant'Egidio daily. The airport is 12 km (7 miles) from Perugia and Assisi. Buses and taxis operate from outside the terminal.

- **Transport** The city's main sights can be visited on foot. There are buses around the city and to the suburbs.

Day 1

Morning A good place to begin touring **Perugia** (pp88–95) is **Piazzale Partigiani** (p88), where the bus terminal and car park are located. Take the escalator to Piazza Italia and follow Perugia's elegant main street, the Corso Vannucci to **Palazzo dei Priori** (pp90–91). This imposing 1293 building houses the splendid **Galleria Nazionale dell'Umbria** (pp92–3). Spend a couple of hours here admiring exquisite masterpieces such as St Anthony Polyptych and the San Domenico of Fiesole Altarpiece. Don't miss Sala dei Notari and its fabulous frescoes. Take the stairs down to Piazza IV Novembre, stopping at Fontana Maggiore, one of Italy's most important Romanesque monuments.

People walking outside the main entrance of the Palazzo dei Priori

Afternoon Stop for lunch at a restaurant around Piazza IV Novembre, and move on to the Piazza Danti dominated by the **Duomo** (p93). Visit the amazing engineering structure, **Etruscan Well** (p94), in Palazzo Bourbon-Sorbello. Next, head for the Palazzo del Capitano del Popolo on **Piazza Matteotti** (p94) and look out for the covered market, where you can see the piazza's foundations. Explore the narrow streets of Porta Sole quarter until you reach the church of **San Severo** (p94), home to one of Raphael's most famous frescoes, the Holy Trinity and Saints (1507–8). Follow the medieval Corso Garibaldi to see the 5th century church of **San Michele Arcangelo (Sant'Angelo)** (p95).

Day 2

Morning The well-preserved Benedictine church of **San Pietro** (p89), dating from the early Christian period (6th century AD), is your first port of call. Admire the splendour of its Romanesque and Renaissance styling. Head along Corso Cavour until you reach the huge church of **San Domenico** (p89). Venture inside to see its magnificent stained-glass window, the second largest in Italy. Behind the church is the **Museo Archeologico Nazionale dell'Umbria** (p88).

Afternoon After lunch around Corso Cavour, take the short walk to **Rocca Paolina** (p88) fortress and its striking Etruscan Porta Marzia archway before exploring Giardini Carducci and the Giardini del Campaccio gardens. Follow the city wall to **Oratorio di San Bernardino** (pp94–5), known for its Renaissance architecture and sculptures, and its piazza dominated by the church of **San Francesco al Prato** (p94).

> **To extend your trip…**
> Visit the ancient burial site, Ipogeo dei Volumni, 7 km (4 miles) southeast of **Perugia**, and the futuristic new district Fontivegge

5 Days in Northern Umbria

- **Arriving** Assisi, like Perugia, is served by the Aeroporto Regionale Umbro di Sant'Egidio.

- **Transport** The main sights of Assisi can be visited on foot.

Day 1

Morning Assisi (pp72–85) is one of the best-preserved cities in the world. Start the day at the **Duomo (San Rufino)** (pp74–5) where St Francis was baptized. Spend some time admiring its magnificent 12th-century façade and rose windows. Next, make your way along Via San Rufino to the Corso Mazzini, and on to the **Basilica di Santa Chiara** (p73) to see its collection of frescoes. Head back to the **Piazza del Comune** (p75) for lunch with a little detour to the **Santa Maria Maggiore** (p83), the city's first cathedral.

Fontana Maggiore flanked by the Palazzo dei Priori and the Duomo

For practical information on travelling around Umbria, see pp178-9

A grand view of Basilica di San Francesco, Assisi

Afternoon Walk down **Piazza del Comune** (p75), a handsome square lined with palazzos. In the middle is the **Temple of Minerva** (p75), which once marked the heart of the city. Continue on to **Basilica di San Francesco** (pp76–7), a 13th-century structure built to celebrate the life of St Francis. Inside, you will see important frescoes and the tomb of the saint. Spend the night in **Assisi**.

Day 2
Morning Take the road from Assisi (pp72–85) to **Nocera Umbra** (p69), but not before taking a short detour to **Parco Regionale del Monte Subasio** (pp70–71) to see the centuries-old friars' hermitage, the **Eremo delle Carceri** (p70). Stop a while to admire the park's natural scenery. From Nocera Umbra, continue on to the ancient town of **Gualdo Tadino** (pp68–9). Tour its churches and palazzos.

Afternoon Visit the **Rocca Flea** (p68), a hilltop fortress dominating **Gualdo Tadino** (pp68–9). It has an interesting small museum and an art and ceramics gallery. Later, take the road to **Gubbio** (pp62–5), your overnight stop, which passes through the scenic **Parco Regionale del Monte Cucco** (pp66–7).

Day 3
Morning Explore the ancient city of **Gubbio** (pp62–5), at the foot of Monte Ingino. Start with the **Roman Ruins** (p62) and

then follow the city wall to Porto Castello gate, where you can enter Gubbio's old quarter. Look out for **Via Gabrielli** (p63), a street lined with gorgeous medieval houses, the church of **San Domenico** (p63) and **Palazzo dei Consoli** (p64), one of Gubbio's most impressive buildings housing Museo Civico.

Afternoon A leisurely lunch in the old quarter might precede a visit to the **Duomo** (p65) and the restored **Palazzo Ducale** (p65). Don't miss the Ducale's archaeological area on its lower level, where ancient remains can be seen. Other attractions include the Gothic **San Giovanni Battista** (pp62–3), the medieval Porta Romana and the shop-lined **Corso Garibaldi** (p65), all worthy of a visit.

Day 4
Morning Leaving Gubbio (pp62–5), head for **Città di Castello** (pp58–9). Take the scenic route through mountains and valleys, or opt for a faster road, both routes pass through the ancient towns of **Montone** (p60) and **Umbertide** (p61).

Afternoon Explore **Città di Castello** (pp58–9), including its 11th-century **Duomo** (p58), its museum and the **Palazzo Comunale** (p58), or town hall. The **Pinacoteca Comunale** (p59), one of Umbria's finest art galleries, will occupy you until the evening. You can enjoy dinner as busy Città di Castello unwinds.

Detail of fresco of Madonna of the Quercia, Church of San Giovanni Battista

Day 5
Morning Leaving Città di Castello, make your way to **Lake Trasimeno** (pp96–7) via Perugia or by following a scenic mountain route. Explore the perimeter of the lake until you reach **Castiglione del Lago** (p98), from where you can bring your tour of Northern Umbria to a close with a leisurely boat trip to the islands, **Isola Maggoire** (p96) and **Isola Polvese** (p97).

> **To extend your trip...**
> Explore Umbria's villages and small towns: **Torgiano** (p86), **Bettona** (pp86–7) and **Deruta** (p87), or hike along the Franciscan Path of Peace from Assisi to Gubbio (2 days).

Beautiful frescoes above the entrance to Duomo Santa Maria Assunta

2 Days in Terni

Terni, with a compact historic centre, has many famous sights to visit that include Roman ruins, churches and museums.

- **Arriving** Terni is served by the Aeroporto Regionale Umbro di Sant'Egidio on the outskirts of Perugia. The A1 and S204 motorways, along with a good rail network, link the two capital cities.
- **Transport** The main sights of Terni can be visited on foot, while its environs are served by bus and road.

Day 1
Morning Begin your tour of **Terni** (pp122–3) with a visit to Piazza Duomo, a busy square dominated by the 17th-century **Duomo (Santa Maria Assunta)** (pp122–3). Look out for the intricate animal and bird reliefs on the main door. You can see the **Roman Amphitheatre** (p123) here. Next, make your way to the Romanesque church of **Sant'Alò** (p122), and on to the church of **San Salvatore** (p123) in Piazza Europa. Refresh yourself with coffee and delicious *pan nociato*, a sweet bread roll filled with pecorino cheese, walnuts and raisins.

Afternoon Head for the 14th-century church of **San Pietro** (p123) adorned with colourful frescoes. Walk down to the **Museum of Modern and Contemporary Art** (p122), where you can admire works by artists such as Picasso and Chagall. If studying fossils is your passion, visit the **Mostra Permanente di Paleontologia** (p123). Its exhibits tell Umbria's ancient history through mammals' remains.

Day 2
Morning Begin your day early with a visit to the **San Francesco** church (p122) before driving to Marmore, around 8 km (5 miles) away. Marvel at the spectacular **Cascata delle Marmore** (p126), the highest man-made waterfalls in Europe. You are now in Terni's **Parco Fluviale del Nera** (p127), which is a natural park that follows the valley of the River Nera. Continue along the road to **Montefranco** (p127) and on to the attractive town of **Ferentillo** (p127) for lunch. Many restaurants here have stunning views of its medieval castle.

Afternoon The Benedictine abbey of **San Pietro in Valle** (p119), 20 km (12 miles) from **Ferentillo** (p127), is breathtaking. The abbey, one of the most powerful in the land, contains frescoes considered among the finest in Italy. Don't miss the elaborate tomb of Faroaldo. Return to Terni for dinner.

> **To extend your trip…**
> The **Parco Fluviale del Nera** (p127) is famous for its excellent rafting, nature trails and rock climbing.

5 Days in Southern Umbria

- **Arriving** Southern Umbria is served by the Aeroporto Regionale Umbro di Sant'Egidio on the outskirts of Perugia.
- **Transport** The main sights of Southern Umbria can be explored by road.

Day 1
Morning Begin your tour of Southern Umbria in the unspoilt, ancient hill town of **Narni** (pp124–5). Its main sights, including its **Duomo** (p124), dedicated to its patron saint San Giovenale, can be found around Via Garibaldi. Don't miss its huge fortress that sits on top of the hill overlooking Narni. Continue until you reach the highway and follow signs to **Orvieto** (pp138–43), your overnight stop. There are a number of detours you might like to consider along the way. **Visciano** (p125) with its heavily frescoed church, the walled town of **Lugnano in Teverina** (p131) or **Amelia** (p130–31) with its ancient **Mura Poligonali** (p130).

Afternoon Orvieto (pp138–43) has a wealth of attractions so waste no time. Visit the spectacular white and grey structure that dominates this city, the **Duomo** (pp140–41). Inside, there is a breathtaking collection of paintings and frescoes, including the **Cappella della Madonna di San Brizio**

(p141). Around the piazza are a number of museums: **Museo Archeologico Nazionale** *(p138)*, **Museo dell'Opera del Duomo** *(pp138–9)*, **Palazzo Soliano and Museo Emilio Greco** *(p139)*, and **Palazzo Faina** *(p139)*, which houses Museo Civico and Museo Claudio Faina.

Day 2

Morning Start your day with a visit to **Sant'Andrea** *(p142)*, one of the oldest structures in **Orvieto** *(pp138–43)*. Look out for its unusual 12-sided tower. Next, head for the **Piazza dei Popolo** *(p142)*, passing the **Torre del Moro** *(p142)*, and on to the **Pozzo di San Patrizio** *(pp142–3)*, a deep well with a 248-step spiral staircase. Before leaving Orvieto, take a little time to admire the **Rocca dell'Albornoz** *(p143)* castle.

Afternoon Head for **Todi** *(pp134–7)*, passing through the Parco Fluviale del Tevere. Wander around its medieval square, the Piazza del Popolo. Here, you can see three palaces, **Palazzo dei Priori** *(p134)*, **Palazzo del Popolo** *(p134)* and the **Palazzo del Capitano** *(pp134–5)*, which are remarkable for their authentic, well-preserved architecture. The square also has the impressive Gothic-style **Duomo** *(p135)*. Join locals for a stroll along the **Corso Cavour** *(p136)*.

Day 3

Morning Leaving **Todi** *(pp134–7)*, your next stop is **Spoleto** *(pp114–17)*. En route take a short detour to the medieval towns of **Acquasparta** *(p133)* and **San Gemini** *(p132)*, or the ruined Roman town of **Carsulae** *(pp132–3)*. In Spoleto, begin your tour in the Piazza Garibaldi, which is dominated by the church of **San Gregorio Maggiore** *(p114)*, and take the Via dell'Anfiteatro to the historic centre.

Afternoon Around the elevated Piazza del Duomo in Spoleto, you will discover the **Santi Giovanni e Paolo** *(p115)* church, famed for its frescoes, along with the **Palazzo**

The steep, spice sellers' street, Corso Cavour in medieval Todi

Arcivescovile *(p116)* that tells the story of the city, and the **Duomo** *(p117)* itself, which has a lavish Baroque interior. Don't miss its frescoes by Pinturicchio and views of the La Rocca d'Albornoziana. Enjoy dinner in **Piazza del Mercato** *(p116)*.

Day 4

Morning An early start could see you visiting Spoleto's restored 1st century AD **Teatro Romano** *(p115)* theatre, followed by an hour or two in the Museo Archeologico before heading to the ancient town of **Trevi** *(p110)* for lunch, via the **Fonti del Clitunno** *(p111)* springs.

Afternoon Trevi's historic centre sits atop a hill with roads spiralling down to more modern quarters. At the summit is the

cathedral of **Sant'Emiliano** *(p110)* with the super **Palazzo Lucarini Contemporary** *(p110)* exhibiting contemporary Italian paintings.

Day 5

Morning Drive 16 km (10 miles) or so to **Spello** *(pp104–5)*, passing by the charming old towns of **Foligno** *(pp106–7)*, **Bevagna** *(p108)* and the hilltop wine-producing centre of **Montefalco** *(pp108–9)*. Once in Spello, take Via Centrale Umbria to the archaeological site where you can see the ruins of this once prosperous Roman city. Nearby, is the city's amphitheatre, along with **San Claudio** *(p105)*, one of Spello's most charming churches.

Afternoon Explore the medieval part of **Spello** *(pp104–5)*. Enter the city through the Roman gate, the **Porta dell'Arce** *(p105)*, and ascend to the **Piazza della Repubblica** *(p104)*. Here, both within walking distance, is the **Pinacoteca Civica** *(p104)* art gallery and the splendid church of **Santa Maria Maggiore** *(p104)* with its frescoes by Pinturicchio. Round off your stay with dinner in the medieval heart of the Spello.

> **To extend your trip...**
> Explore **Parco Nazionale dei Monti Sibillini** *(pp112–13)*, along with the nearby ancient towns of **Norcia** *(p120)* and **Cascia** *(p121)*.

Ruins of the ancient Roman town, Carsulae

Putting Umbria on the Map

Of all the regions that make up the Italian peninsula, Umbria is the only one to be totally landlocked. The region covers 8,450 sq km (3,260 sq miles), of which three-quarters belongs to the province of Perugia and one-quarter to the province of Terni. Plains make up less than one-tenth of the total area, the rest being taken up with hills and mountains. The main river is the Tiber (il Tevere) and the highest peak is Monte Redentore, at 2,450 m (8,050 ft). Lake Trasimeno, west of Perugia, is the largest inland lake in central Italy.

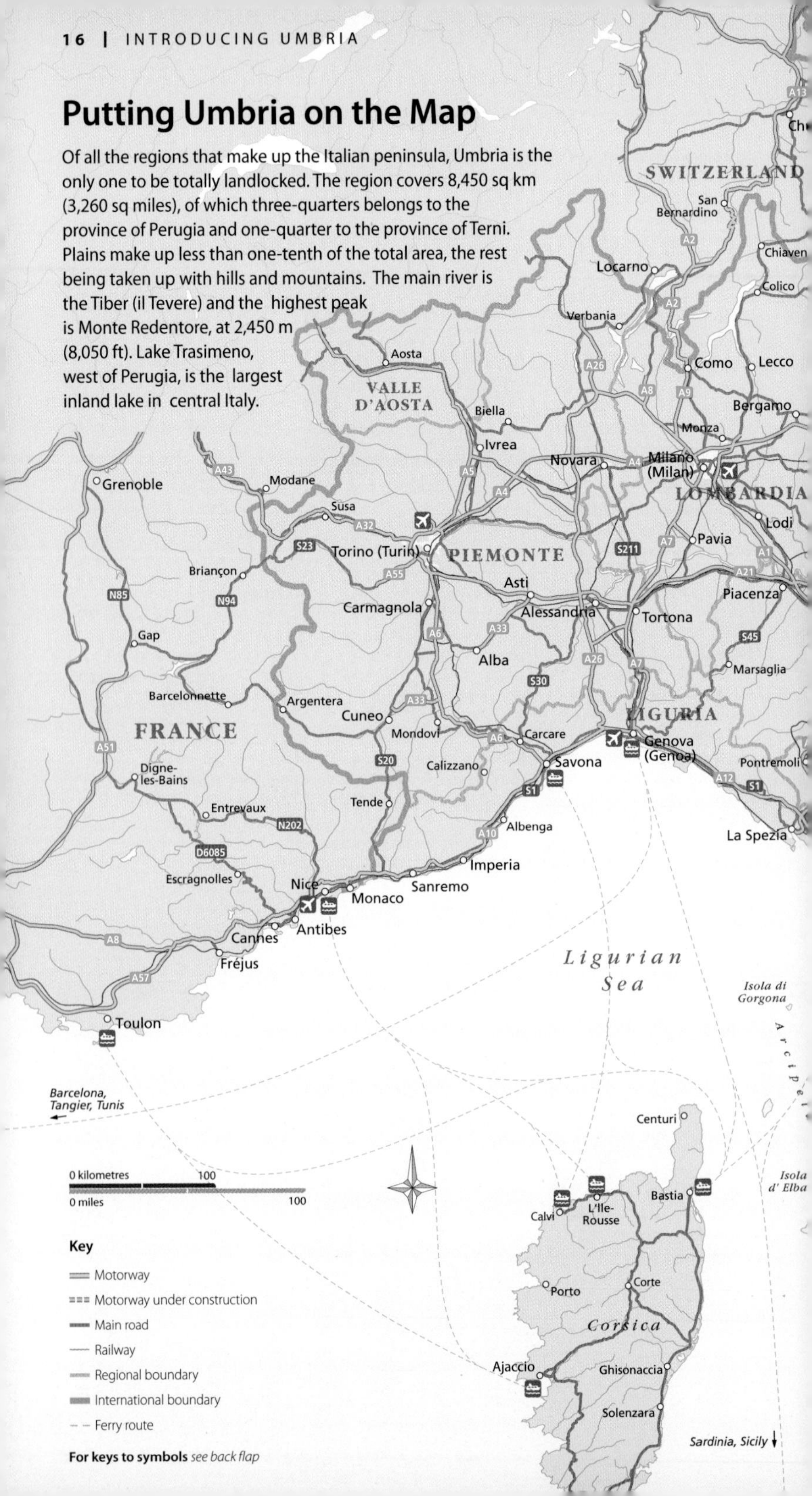

SWITZERLAND
San Bernardino
Chiaven
Colico
Locarno
Verbania
Aosta
Como
Lecco
VALLE D'AOSTA
Biella
Bergamo
Monza
Ivrea
Novara
Milano (Milan)
LOMBARDIA
Grenoble
Modane
Susa
Lodi
Torino (Turin)
PIEMONTE
Pavia
Briançon
Asti
Piacenza
Carmagnola
Alessandria
Tortona
Gap
Alba
Marsaglia
Barcelonnette
Argentera
Cuneo
LIGURIA
FRANCE
Mondovì
Carcare
Genova (Genoa)
Savona
Pontremoli
Digne-les-Bains
Calizzano
Tende
Entrevaux
Albenga
La Spezia
Imperia
Escragnolles
Nice
Sanremo
Monaco
Antibes
Cannes
Fréjus
Ligurian Sea
Isola di Gorgona
Toulon
Barcelona, Tangier, Tunis
Centuri
Isola d' Elba
Bastia
Calvi
L'Ile-Rousse
Porto
Corte
Corsica
Ajaccio
Ghisonaccia
Solenzara
Sardinia, Sicily
A13
A2
A26
A8
A9
A43
A5
A4
A32
S23
A55
S211
A7
A1
A21
N85
N94
A33
A6
S45
A26
S30
A51
S20
S1
A12
N202
A10
D6085
A8
A57
0 kilometres 100
0 miles 100
Key
Motorway
Motorway under construction
Main road
Railway
Regional boundary
International boundary
Ferry route
For keys to symbols see back flap

A PORTRAIT OF UMBRIA

Umbria is a land apart, with its own singular character and identity.
At the geographical centre of Italy, it is known, thanks to its lushness, as
the peninsula's "Green Heart"; its rolling hills and fertile plains are studded
with picturesque towns, castles and monasteries, recalling millennia of
human habitation.

Small in comparison to its neighbouring regions, at just 8,450 sq km
(3,260 sq miles), with barely a million
inhabitants, Umbria nevertheless radiates
a powerful image, both in Italy and
abroad. Elemental features of its
reputation are its unspoilt landscape,
its inimitable art and architecture, and,
perhaps most significantly, its deeply
mystical heritage. Add to that the region's
famously fine cuisine and exuberant
festivals and it is no wonder that Umbria
has developed a cachet all its own.

Recent decades have witnessed the
arrival of a breed of "New Umbrians",
neo-settlers who have migrated here,
maybe from Milan, Manchester or
Manhattan. It is not unusual, while

exploring the region's splendidly
scenic roads and byways, to come
across American couples enjoying
the view, monks with typically Nordic
features, or Italian ex-urbanites who
have chosen a new, more relaxed way
of life in this idyllic, largely rural setting.

Timeless Landscapes

Umbria's pristine natural loveliness
is certainly a major enticement. The
landscape ranges from the great green
slopes and peaks of the Monti Sibillini
and the mountain chains that border
Le Marche to the gentle hills and plains
around Assisi and Perugia; from the
roaring waters of the Cascata delle
Marmore to the subtle sibilance of the

The hamlet of Castelluccio, in a spectacular spot within the Monti Sibillini

◀ People taking part in La Corsa dei Ceri or Race of the Candles, an exciting candle race festival held in Gubbio

Piece of traditional Umbrian fabric

Umbria's cities and towns are among Italy's most gorgeous. Perugia, Assisi, Gubbio, Orvieto, Spoleto, Todi – the very names are synonymous with the perfection of the medieval hill town. They are approachable, human in scale, but also filled with world-class masterpieces of architecture and art in recognizably Umbrian style. Some of Italy's finest palaces and civic structures are here, as well as some of its most resplendent churches, while Umbrian painters such as Perugino helped set the standard for sheer beauty in the High Renaissance.

Lying at the crossroads between Rome and Florence, the region has been embellished by the works of many renowned artists, including Cimabue, Giotto, Piero della Francesca, Simone Martini, Fra Angelico, Filippo Lippi, Luca Signorelli, Ghirlandaio, Raphael and Gian Lorenzo Bernini. At the same time, venerable Umbrian crafts, especially ceramics and textiles, have been famous for centuries.

Nor should the ancient remains be overlooked. Throughout Umbria, the Romans left behind superb gates, towers, bridges and even a still-

wind among the reeds on the shores of Lake Trasimeno. Green – the colour which has, in effect, become the region's popular "trademark" – is very much a reality here and dominates the scenery. However, the beauty of the environment alone could never fully account for Umbria's undeniable mystique. The fields, the olive groves, the forests of beech, holm oak and chestnut are inevitably set off by evocative vestiges of a long-standing human presence.

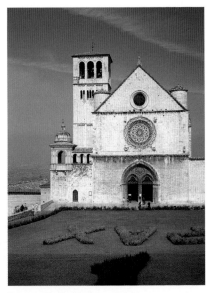
Umbrian potter at work

Sublime Architecture and Art

Whether in the form of a town, a village or a medieval monastery, an ancient farmhouse, a dry-stone wall or a ruined church, architecture is essential to the region's spirit. Whether grand or rustic, Roman, Romanesque or Renaissance, such architectural heritage conveys a timeless feel that is distinctively Umbrian. It evokes a symbiosis of man and nature that has flourished since the days of the primordial Umbri and Etruscans, and later the Romans, right down to modern Italians.

The renowned Basilica di San Francesco in Assisi

A snapshot of daily life in Assisi, a city visited by millions of tourists every year

functioning theatre or two, while the archaeological finds dating back to Etruscan times and beyond are immensely rich and displayed in beautifully appointed museums.

One insightful observer of Italian life wrote, "With its millennia of infiltration, art has saturated the soul – everyone here lives art, whether they know it or not." This is nowhere more true than in Umbria.

A Place of Spirituality

Most appealing to many modern newcomers is Umbria's glowing spiritual legacy. The birthplace of St Francis, St Clare and Jacopone da Todi has become the home of many spiritual centres and teachers of every persuasion. Retreats here are not only Christian, but are affiliated with all beliefs, everyone apparently drawn by the ineffable meditative power of the place. Overwhelmingly, it is a venue of peace, as embodied in the Marcia per la Pace (Walk of Peace) from Perugia to Assisi, which takes place every other autumn. Many global spiritual leaders have promoted greater understanding here, including the Dalai Lama.

Inviting Hospitality

Visitors attracted more by earthly pleasures are well satisfied, too. Umbria's robust and tasty cuisine consists of dishes that combine the best of local culinary traditions, while taking full advantage of the produce and game of the region – highlighting wild mushrooms, black truffles and wild boar (cinghiale).

Hospitality is an art form here, too. Every city, town or village proudly rivals its neighbours with its age-old festivals, as well as its gastronomic specialities. In the countryside, agriturismi (farm lodgings) have become a reliable alternative to standard hotel accommodation, offering a delightful first-hand taste of authentic Umbrian life.

Decades of modernization have tested the traditional values of the region, and the disastrous earthquake of 1997 has left its mark in others, but the quintessential allure of Umbria remains intact.

Apparition at Arles, Upper Church, Assisi

The Landscape of Umbria

The mountains of Umbria are of comparatively recent origin. The fact that the region's topography developed relatively late, together with the presence of still-active powerful tectonic forces, means that there is a heightened risk of earthquakes in Umbria. Once cultivated up to fairly high altitudes, the mountains have now been largely abandoned by farmers. Rolling hills made up of fertile but often fragile terrain border the highest peaks; centuries of cultivation have given them their current shape. In Umbria's southwestern corner, and around Orvieto, the land is of volcanic origin. Lake Trasimeno, in the northwest, is the most important lake in central Italy.

A bright field of sunflowers, widely cultivated in Umbria

The Mountains

The average height of the mountains in Umbria is around 1,000 m (3,280 ft). Most of the range consists of karst limestone and is riddled with caves and subterranean galleries and rivers. The vegetation most characteristic of this environment is beech forest and upland pasture. Among the wildlife found in the mountains are birds of prey, wildcats and several kinds of wolf.

The Hills

The climate in the hills is milder than that at higher altitudes, and is also less polluted than on the plain. For this reason, the hills of Umbria have been settled and cultivated since ancient times. In areas not given over to farmland and olive groves there are oaks, holm oaks and, lower down, mixed woodland and scrub.

Wolves became extinct in Umbria in the 18th century but have reappeared in the protected Monti Sibillini. There is a greater chance of seeing them in winter, when they come down to the valley.

The wild boar is one of the most common mammals in the hills. Its meat is prized.

Acorns

This Apennine edelweiss lives on calcareous crags. Similar to alpine edelweiss, it is distinguished by its spathulate leaves (that is, wide at the tip and narrow at the base).

The olive is one of the most important agricultural products in Umbria. Olives produced in the area around Trevi *(see p110)* are especially highly regarded.

Cultivation of the Plains

The few areas of plain found in Umbria lie along river courses and include the Valle Umbra (between Assisi and Spoleto), the Valle del Paglia (in the southwest), and the plains of Terni and Gubbio. Reclamation in these areas in the years after World War II has created very fertile land, where farming is now carried out on an industrial scale (where possible, producing forced and cash crops), although man has been present here since ancient times. The plants found are those commonly seen in cultivated fields.

The corn cockle *(Agrostemma githago)* was once widespread on cultivated land. It is now rare, owing to the use of herbicides by farmers. It's also poisonous.

Lapwings form flocks in cultivated fields and in pastureland during the winter season.

The Plains

In general, every area of flat ground in Umbria occupies the site of an ancient lake or marsh, and is therefore especially fertile. These plains are now primarily given over to cultivation (grapevines and olives, for example). As a consequence, the land is not known for its varied wildlife, although rodents and small predators, such as foxes, are common.

Grain was once grown as animal fodder, while today, increasingly, it is grown in industrial quantities.

The fox is a highly adaptable mammal which manages to live in all kinds of habitat. In cultivated fields, foxes find shelter among the hedgerows.

Lakes, Rivers and Marshland

Lake Trasimeno is a place that has a fascinating history, with a tradition of fishing going back to ancient times. Rivers in Umbria include the Tiber (il Tevere), the Velino and the Nera; the last boasts the spectacular manmade waterfall, the Cascata delle Marmore, and some particularly fine scenery. Freshwater fish and other species abound in the wild.

A trout is camouflaged among the stones on the riverbed thanks to its marbled colouring.

Freshwater crabs live in reedbeds and are active mainly at night. Their presence indicates good water quality.

Nature Reserves in Umbria

Although nature plays a fundamental role in the overall image of the region, Umbria has been rather slow to set up protected parks and reserves. The creation of parks has frequently been opposed at a local level (the inhabitants are exceedingly passionate about hunting), and their establishment has been achieved largely by balancing the demands of nature with those of the development of the economy and the tourist trade.

Together with the Umbrian portion of the Parco Nazionale dei Monti Sibillini (part of a great series of protected areas in the Apennines, safeguarding the principal mountain masses in the chain), Umbrian parks today protect around seven per cent of the terrain in the region. These parks can be divided into two categories: "mountain parks", which are those along the border with Le Marche, and "water parks", which are focused around the lakes and watercourses of the region.

The Parco Regionale del Lago Trasimeno *(see pp96–7)* covers 13,200 ha (32,600 acres) and includes the lake shores – thereby safeguarding the water and banks – but not the tourist resorts around the lake. The perimeter of Lake Trasimeno measures around 60 km (37 miles).

Lago di Alviano *(see p131)* is an ecosystem that serves as a breeding ground for numerous species of water birds, as well as an important source of food for rare birds such as cranes, wild geese and ospreys.

The Parco Fluviale del Tevere *(see p137)* extends from the gates of Todi as far as Alviano, along the banks of the longest river in central Italy, the Tiber. The park protects some 7,925 ha (19,585 acres), over a length of 50 km (31 miles).

Città di Castello

Umbertide

Lake Trasimeno

Perugia

Orvieto

Lago di Corbara

Todi

Alviano

Narni

S221 · S257 · S219 · S3bis · S75bis · S599 · S220 · S317 · S71 · S397 · S3bis · S79bis · S448 · S205

0 kilometres 15
0 miles 15

Key

Regional Park

National Park

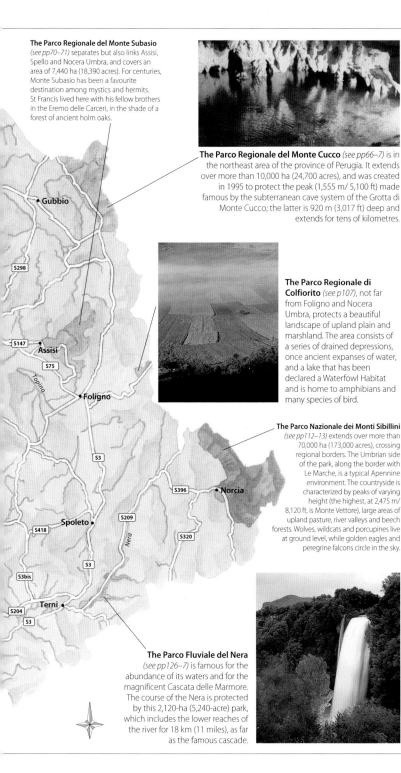

The Parco Regionale del Monte Subasio *(see pp70–71)* separates but also links Assisi, Spello and Nocera Umbra, and covers an area of 7,440 ha (18,390 acres). For centuries, Monte Subasio has been a favourite destination among mystics and hermits. St Francis lived here with his fellow brothers in the Eremo delle Carceri, in the shade of a forest of ancient holm oaks.

The Parco Regionale del Monte Cucco *(see pp66–7)* is in the northeast area of the province of Perugia. It extends over more than 10,000 ha (24,700 acres), and was created in 1995 to protect the peak (1,555 m/ 5,100 ft) made famous by the subterranean cave system of the Grotta di Monte Cucco; the latter is 920 m (3,017 ft) deep and extends for tens of kilometres.

The Parco Regionale di Colfiorito *(see p107)*, not far from Foligno and Nocera Umbra, protects a beautiful landscape of upland plain and marshland. The area consists of a series of drained depressions, once ancient expanses of water, and a lake that has been declared a Waterfowl Habitat and is home to amphibians and many species of bird.

The Parco Nazionale dei Monti Sibillini *(see pp112–13)* extends over more than 70,000 ha (173,000 acres), crossing regional borders. The Umbrian side of the park, along the border with Le Marche, is a typical Apennine environment. The countryside is characterized by peaks of varying height (the highest, at 2,475 m/ 8,120 ft, is Monte Vettore), large areas of upland pasture, river valleys and beech forests. Wolves, wildcats and porcupines live at ground level, while golden eagles and peregrine falcons circle in the sky.

The Parco Fluviale del Nera *(see pp126–7)* is famous for the abundance of its waters and for the magnificent Cascata delle Marmore. The course of the Nera is protected by this 2,120-ha (5,240-acre) park, which includes the lower reaches of the river for 18 km (11 miles), as far as the famous cascade.

Gubbio

S298

S147
Assisi

S75

Topino

Foligno

S3

S396 Norcia

Spoleto

S209

S418

Nera

S320

S3

S3bis

S204
Terni

S3

Outdoor Activities

Given the beauty of the landscape in Umbria, nature and the great outdoors should feature in every visitor's trip to the region. Furthermore, open-air sports are increasingly well catered for, and in every part of the region. Just as pilgrims flock to Assisi from all four corners of the globe, it is equally easy to encounter a whole range of languages among a crowd of canoeists sweeping its way down the Nera or the Tiber, or among the hang-gliding community taking off from Monte Cucco or from the windswept uplands of the Monti Sibillini.

More everyday activities should not be forgotten either, particularly as they constitute one of the best ways of seeing and appreciating this beautiful region: consider going on a long bicycle ride through the hills, past farms and ancient abbeys, or on a gentle horse-ride through one of the greenest, most fascinating and relaxing landscapes in Italy.

Hiking in one of the magnificent valleys of the Monti Sibillini

Horse-riding just outside the historic town of Spello

Horse-riding

In Umbria there are many stables and farm holiday (*agriturismo*) businesses that can organize horse-riding trips. As well as being an enjoyable sport, riding offers a closer and more natural view of the countryside than is possible with conventional means of transport.

Many Umbrian horse-riding stables belong to national associations, such as ANTE (Associazione Nazionale Turismo Equestre), and can offer trekking in all the most beautiful areas of the region, including the hills around Assisi, Città della Pieve and Bettona, the shores of Lake Trasimeno, the slopes of Monte Subasio and the steep bridle paths of the Valnerina. Treks that last for several days or more are available from various equestrian clubs, or you can apply directly to ANTE.

Walking and Cycling

No equipment is required to enjoy walking: all you need is a good view, decent weather, paths to follow and a destination, whether it be historical or natural.

The Monti Sibillini national park, to present the most enticing example, has always been one of the best-loved destinations among walkers in Umbria (along with neighbouring park areas in the nearby region of Le Marche). In the colder seasons, however, it is also possible to find routes at lower altitudes, such as the bridle paths that link the towns and villages.

The routes that connect Umbria's most famous towns and villages are very popular with cyclists: the gradients are not excessive and the varied landscape provides plenty of interest along the way. Bridle paths and footpaths at higher altitudes are also used by mountain bikers. There are now more than 600 km (373 miles) of mountain-biking trails in the region. Brochures and information about walking and cycling are available from tourist offices.

Rock Climbing, Caves and Gorges

Not all that long ago, all that one had to choose from was mountaineering. Today, various rock-climbing sports are popular in Italy, and there are all kinds of cliff faces to use. In Umbria, any visitor in search of a vertical cliff face will feel at home on certain cliffs in the Monti Sibillini and in the village of Ferentillo, where there are numerous suitable sites: rock climbing is such a big thing here that there is even a climbing guide dedicated to the area. Umbria is also a place that finds much favour among speleologists. The biggest attraction is the cave system beneath Monte Cucco, on the border with Le Marche (not far from that region's famous caves, the Grotte di Frasassi). There are also caves worth visiting in the mountains near Terni.

A sport that has taken hold in Umbria, which developed out of speleology – the equipment used is much the same – is "torrentismo", or canyoning, the sport of navigating steep-sided gorges. The most famous and popular sites are found in the Valnerina (Fosso di Rocca Gelli and Forra del Casco), on Monte Cucco (Forra di Riofreddo), and in the hills surrounding Lake Corbara (Gole di Prodo).

It is important to make clear that all of the above are extreme sports, and that they can all be exceedingly dangerous. Anyone trying them out for the first time should ensure that they are accompanied by an expert.

An Umbrian cave, and one of many visiting speleologists

Hang-gliding and Cross-country Skiing

Wind, unlimited vistas and serious gradients are the three ingredients necessary for hang-gliding and paragliding. Umbria has plenty of all three. Famous locations for this exciting but daredevil sport are Monte Cucco and the Monti Sibillini, where the isolated, high-altitude village of Castelluccio di Norcia is now one of the most popular destinations for hang-gliding

Hang-gliding on the slopes of Monte Vettore

aficionados, who come here from all over the world.

The topography of the Umbrian mountains does not much favour downhill skiing, however; few of the slopes are steep enough, and the lower altitudes are not suitable for the building of ski lifts or ski resorts of any great size. To compensate, the great Apennine uplands provide perfect cross-country territory. Skiers can follow the beaten tracks or, better still, ski along snow-covered bridle paths and footpaths.

Shooting Rapids

In spring, the many rivers and watercourses that cross Umbria, almost all of them torrential, are an irresistible attraction for canoeists from all over Europe. As the water rises and the rapids swell, canoes, kayaks and rubber rafts appear as if from nowhere along the banks of the rivers Nera and Tiber.

The Nera offers a range of experiences and caters to various levels of difficulty, up to the highest level, requiring considerable

skill and expertise. This river also offers the extraordinary sight of the Cascata delle Marmore (see pp126–7), which is the principal starting point for rafting trips. The stretch of the Tiber below Todi is one of the most popular routes for river rafting and other excursions, but you can also join the Tiber further north, at Città di Castello, allowing you to cross virtually the entire region.

A non-competitive descent from Todi to Rome takes place every year from the end of April to early May. It is open to everyone and is very popular. There are also good river-rafting sites from the Monti Sibillini down to the Valnerina.

Sailing on the Lakes

Lake Trasimeno is clearly the most obvious place for holidaymakers in landlocked Umbria to go sailing and windsurfing. Visitors can bring their own boats or make use of the craft available for hire. There are numerous regattas. Other stretches of water that are at least partially equipped for sailing, windsurfing and other watersports include Lago di Piediluco and Lago di Corbara, both in southern Umbria.

Shooting the rapids on the Nera

You can also go water-skiing on Lake Trasimeno, but you must first apply for a permit from the office of the Provincia di Perugia.

Sailing boats manoeuvring on Lake Trasimeno

In the Footsteps of St Francis

Francis was born in Assisi in 1181–82, and grew up to be a bright, cultured and even ambitious youth. A military career was chosen as the means by which he could rise up through the social hierarchy, and he enrolled in the army that Walter of Brienne was preparing for the Crusades. However, illness brought Francis back to Assisi, where he experienced his conversion and where he began his charity work. The story of his life, marvellously illustrated in the frescoes in the Upper Church at Assisi, provides us with a picture of a man drawn to nature, poverty and prayer. They also inspire us to go and explore the many places in Umbria that retain the memory of St Francis's presence.

Francis found refuge with the Spadalonga family of Gubbio after his departure from his father's house. The saint also spent time in the small monastery of the Vittorina (*see p85*), along the road between Gubbio and Assisi. It was here, according to historians, that he tamed a wolf.

Isola Maggiore, on Lake Trasimeno, was the home of one of the first communities of the Friars Minor at the beginning of the 13th century. St Francis spent a long Lenten period with them here.

Città di Castello

Arezzo

Tiber

Gubbio

S3bis

S298

Lake Trasimeno

S75b

Perugia

Sant Mari degli Ange

Cannara

Bevag

Nestore

Tiber

Chiani

Paglia

Lake Corbara

Lake Alviano

S204

R

Santa Maria degli Angeli was erected in the 15th century, in order to shelter the old monastery of the Porziuncola (*see p84*), in whose infirmary St Francis died on 4 October 1226. What is left of that room is kept in the Cappella del Transito. Above, *The Poor Clares mourn the dead saint*.

One of the most famous episodes in the life of the saint is undoubtedly his preaching to the birds. The stone on which the scene is said to have taken place is in the church of San Francesco in Bevagna (*see p108*). Right, *Francis preaches to the birds*.

On Monte Subasio *(see pp70–71)*, cloaked in holm oaks, the monastery of the Eremo delle Carceri was built around the little church and the caves where Francis and his companions would gather in prayer. A trail from the hermitage goes through the surrounding woods and passes a series of sites dear to the saint's tradition because they were places of prayer and meditation.

Every church, every corner of Assisi bears traces of the life of the saint. He was baptized in the font in the cathedral of San Rufino; next to the church of San Giorgio was his school; and the Chiesa Nuova was constructed on the very spot where Francis is thought to have been born. Right, *St Francis gives his cloak to a poor man*, with a view of Assisi in the background.

At Vecciano, not far from Montefalco *(see pp108–9)*, is the small church of San Rocco. Under the name of Santa Maria della Selvetta, this was the first seat of the Franciscan Order. To the left, *Innocent III approves the saint's Order*.

0 kilometres 20
0 miles 20

The monastery of Sacro Speco *(see p125)*, near Narni, was founded by St Francis in 1213. You can still see the small hollow where the saint used to pray.

Key

Near the Fonti del Clitunno *(see p111)*, in the church of San Pietro di Bovara, is a Crucifix which spoke to St Francis. (The more famous talking Crucifix is in the Basilica di Santa Chiara, *(see p74)*. Above, *The Saint in Ecstasy*.

- Trail of St Francis
- Other roads
- River

Montefalco
Vecciano
Bovara
Spoleto
Terni
Narni

Art in Umbria

The region of Umbria as it is defined today was established only after the unification of Italy in 1861. In the preceding centuries, Umbria's towns and cities formed part of a political and artistic mosaic which extended from Tuscany to the Adriatic coast, without precise boundaries. In art, as in politics, there was plenty of opportunity for contacts and exchanges with other regions. Two crucial highlights stand out in the long history of art in Umbria: the founding and construction of the Basilica of St Francis in Assisi – with the contribution of great artists, from Umbria and from other parts of Italy – and the golden age of the city of Perugia. UNESCO has recognized various sites and structures in the towns of Assisi and Spoleto, with splendid artistic presence, as World Heritage Sites.

Tempietto del Clitunno, detail of the front

Cast of stone with Umbrian inscription, 2nd century BC

Origins

Umbria was populated from the sixth millennium BC. Interesting ceramic finds from that time have been discovered near Norcia and Parrano (outside Orvieto). With the passing of the millennia, a community of shepherds – part of what scholars describe as the Apennine civilization – developed in the mountains. Around the 16th century BC, they started to produce elegant pottery, decorated with geometrical motifs. The burial site at Monteleone di Spoleto dates back to these very early civilizations. Archaeologists discovered a bronze cart here, and this is now in the Metropolitan Museum in New York. During the first millennium BC, Umbrian land was divided between two very different peoples: the Etruscans, who settled on the west bank of the Tiber, with the key towns of Perugia and Orvieto, and the Umbri, about whom little is still known, who were on the Tiber's east bank and in the Apennine mountains.

The Romans

The Roman conquest of Umbria was slow but inexorable. If one had to choose a symbolic historical date for the arrival of the Romans in Umbria, it would be 219 BC, the year in which the Via Flaminia was opened. This Roman road became the main communication route through the region for centuries. The presence of the Romans led to a great push in building and civil engineering: theatres, public works as well as roads were built. In terms of sculpture dating from the Roman age, many marble and some bronze statues survive. The latter include the extraordinary statue of Germanicus, found in Amelia and returned there only recently after

Male statue, 1st century AD

a long and controversial residence in Perugia (see p130). One can also see well-preserved Roman buildings, such as the amphitheatre in Gubbio (see p62) and the Temple of Minerva in Assisi (see p75).

Christianity reached Umbria in around the 3rd and 4th centuries AD. Of particular interest from this period are the church of San Salvatore in Spoleto (see p119) and the little temple at the Fonti di Clitunno (see p111), both of which show clearly how early Christian architecture was inspired by the Roman and classical traditions. Another important church from the Early Christian era in Umbria is San Michele Archangelo, or Sant'Angelo, in Perugia (see p95), which was influenced by Byzantine architecture.

The Middle Ages

Politically split between Byzantium (on the west bank of the Tiber) and the Lombard dominion (on the east bank), Umbria was subject to a range of influences in the field of art. Even though few works of art have survived from the second half of the first millennium, and even though the buildings that remain have often been extensively remodelled, it is known that the 9th century was a period of significant development in Umbria. Cathedrals were founded all over the region and were often adorned with great pictorial cycles (now mostly lost). The main centre for this boom was the Lombard stronghold of Spoleto (see pp114–19), where even today you can admire the reliefs on the façade of San Pietro and the frescoes in the churches of San Gregorio and San Paolo inter Vineas.

The cloister of the abbey of Sassovivo, near Foligno, was built using Roman columns and arches.

Detail of the façade of San Pietro in Spoleto

Assisi

In 1228, less than two years after the death of St Francis, and at the wishes of Frate Elia (who took it upon himself to hide the body of the saint), construction of the Basilica of San Francesco in Assisi (see pp76–7) began. This was a truly crucial moment, since the work on the basilica was to influence the art and architecture of both Umbria and nearby regions for centuries to come. The Basilica in Assisi is still one of the most important monuments of Western art today.

The first frescoes were commissioned in 1254 from an anonymous Umbrian artist, known as the Maestro di San Francesco, who is regarded as having operated a workshop of the highest quality. Then,

Giotto

Presumed self-portrait

Born in 1267, Giotto di Bondone probably trained at the Florentine workshop of Cimabue. It was accepted that the cycle of the Life of St Francis was not Giotto's work but that of Roman painters, but restored frescoes in the basilica of St Francis in Assisi beared his initials. Giotto's great works include a Last Judgment and Stories from the Life of the Virgin in the Cappella degli Scrovegni in Padua and the bell tower for the Duomo in Florence, a project that he directed up to his death in 1337.

from the end of the 13th century, great masters were summoned from outside the region – among them Cimabue and Giotto – to decorate the walls of the upper and lower churches. Their work would become a model for Umbrian painters later on. Work on the two basilicas continued for more than two centuries, with contributions by other great names from the history of Italian art, including Simone Martini and Pietro Lorenzetti. In parallel with the spreading of the Franciscan

Painted Cross, Maestro di San Francesco, 1272

faith, so too the pictorial style created in Assisi gained ground, and was imitated and reproduced in many new Franciscan churches all over Italy.

On 26 September 1997 this immense inheritance risked being lost forever. The entire complex was badly damaged by a violent earthquake, and parts of the vault in the upper church collapsed. Through the extraordinarily hard work of restorers, fragments of frescoes were saved and reinstalled where possible. The basilica remains magnificent but tarnished.

Vault of the Evangelists, Cimabue (1240–1302), Basilica of Assisi

Perugino

Pietro Vannucci, or Perugino, was born in Città della Pieve in 1452 and died in Fontignano in 1523. He was influenced by the work of Piero della Francesca and Verrocchio, in whose workshop the painter trained early on. Works in Rome include *Handing the Keys to St Peter* in the Sistine Chapel (1481), in the Vatican. In Florence are a *Lamentation* (Palazzo Pitti, 1494) and a *Crucifixion* (Santa Maddalena de'Pazzi, 1493). He also painted frescoes

Epiphany, 1475–8, detail

in the Sala dell'Udienza in the Collegio del Cambio, Perugia. His work can be found in several of the smaller towns of Umbria, particularly near Lake Trasimeno *(see p99)*. While still young, Raphael was apprenticed to Perugino, who exerted great influence over the former's works.

came here, including: Piero della Francesca, Fra Angelico (who contributed to the decoration of the cathedral in Orvieto), Filippo Lippi (who would later be called to Spoleto to fresco the cathedral apse), and also Agostino di Duccio. A cycle of frescoes (1498–1500) painted by Perugino in the Collegio del Cambio was to exert a great influence over painters such as Pinturicchio and the young Raphael, who produced some of his early work in Perugia.

In this same period – in Perugia as well as in other cities in Umbria – a new style of architecture began to change the look of the old medieval city spaces, with new palaces being erected for noble merchant families. Influences in this field came from Rome, Urbino or from the great cities of nearby Tuscany.

An example of Umbrian art by the Maestro di Città di Castello

Perugia's Golden Age

The position of Perugia, on the Via Flaminia and Via Amerina, at the junction of routes of communication between Rome and the Adriatic coast, made the city vulnerable to conquest. After invasions by the Goths and Lombards, the foundation of the cathedral (by the 10th century) marked the first stage in Perugia's rebirth in the Middle Ages.

For around three centuries, the commune of Perugia grew in power, riches and possessions. Signs of this prosperity are the thick walls and city gates, though an even greater indication is the aqueduct, which brought water to the

city centre and was one of the first of its kind to be built in Italy. To celebrate this magnificent achievement a fountain was built in Piazza IV Novembre, featuring sculptures by Nicola and Giovanni Pisano *(see p91)*.

The 16th Century in Perugia

Towards the middle of the 15th century, the city of Perugia was rich and cosmopolitan. The great Italian painters of the age

The Umbrian School

It was because of the influence of the great artists who were attracted to Umbria in the second half of the 15th century that a

Polyptych, Niccolò di Liberatore known as l'Alunno, 1471

regional school developed in its own right, liberated from the Gothic models that had influenced art in the previous centuries. The principal artists to learn lessons from the Florentine Renaissance were, besides Perugino, Niccolò Alunno, Antonio Mezzastris, Matteo da Gualdo, from around Foligno, and Benedetto Bonfigli, of Perugia. In the first half of the 16th century, the most representative name is that of Giovanni di Pietro, or Spagna. The Umbrian school lost its originality and died out rapidly with the advent of Mannerism.

Coronation of the Virgin,
1511, Spagna

The Domination of Rome

When the power of the communes *(see pp46–7)* gave way to papal rule, great military structures were built: Antonio da Sangallo the Younger designed Perugia's Rocca Paolina *(see p88)* and the Pozzo di San Patrizio in Orvieto *(see p142)*. Vignola worked on the Castellina in Norcia *(see p120)*.

By the end of the 16th century all the major artists of the time were working in Rome – not only Italians, but also Flemish artists such as Van Mander, Stellaert and Loots. Umbrian towns were totally dependent on the Church. In Todi, the construction of Santa Maria della Consolazione *(see pp136–7)*, worked on

by Baldassarre Peruzzi, Vignola and Ippolito Scalza, inaugurated a new concept of religious architecture. In 1569, on the plain below Assisi, work began on the great church of Santa Maria degli Angeli *(see p84)*, intended as a home for the Franciscan chapel of the Porziuncola. Designed by Galeazzo Alessi with Vignola as consultant, it was finished only in 1679.

Umbria's noble families, often important figures in administration and in the ranks of Roman power, built palazzi and villas in their native cities.

18th–19th Centuries

The following centuries, dominated by papal rule right up to the unification of Italy in 1861, did not really produce great works of art in Umbria.

Statue in Santa Maria della Consolazione

The dominant influence was Rome, and the examples of Baroque and Rococo in the region are not of great importance. A moment of regional pride came with the brief period of splendour of Perugia's Accademia di Belle Arti, which championed the Neo-Classical style. It is certainly no coincidence that the artist Canova, who stayed at San Gemini (near Todi), took up contact with the great families of Perugia.

The 19th century saw the cities of Umbria becoming stages on the set routes followed by travellers on the Grand Tour. Admiration for the art of the Middle Ages became the cult of the time and *medievalismo* took hold in Perugia and led to the restoration – sometimes rather ingenuously – of ancient buildings.

Applied Arts

Along with most of Italy, Umbria has long been famous as a treasure trove of art, sculpture and architecture. However, it has also produced a great many master craftsmen of skill and stature. In the many museums of Umbria's towns, old and new, one can find pieces of rare beauty, in particular ceramics and textiles, worked by hand over the centuries. The production of these objects continues today, and no tourist in Umbria should miss the opportunity to visit one of the numerous handicrafts workshops in the region.

Majolica jug, 16th century

Besides ceramics, for which Deruta *(see p87)* is particularly renowned, and fabrics, which are still woven by hand, look out for the embroidered tulle of Panicale (near Lake Trasimeno) and the delicate lace of Assisi, as well as painted stuccoes and woodcarving.

Antique fabric, manufactured in Todi in the 14th century

Architecture in Umbria

Even though the most significant impact on the towns of Umbria occurred during the centuries of the Middle Ages and the Renaissance, monuments from all periods of history are found in the region. From the time of the Etruscan city state to the era of Roman domination, from the rise of Romanesque architecture to the advent of Neo-Classicism, every people, every era, every architectural style and every artistic movement has left its traces, thanks to the work of the major artists of the time. The influence of the Roman Catholic Church has been a constant.

A bas-relief, frequently used to decorate churches and palazzi

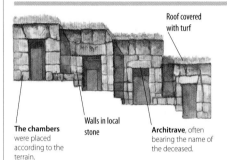

Roof covered with turf

The chambers were placed according to the terrain.

Walls in local stone

Architrave, often bearing the name of the deceased.

The necropolises are the most tangible sign of the Etruscan presence in Umbria. In general, they consisted of a series of tomb chambers lined up along cemetery roads. Inside, the deceased lay on a funeral bench.

Antiquity

While the Umbri left few traces of the form of their cities, the imposing polygonal walls of Amelia and Spoleto owe their existence to this Italic people. The Etruscans left necropolises and tombs, such as those near Orvieto (Necropoli del Crocifisso del Tufo) or the extraordinary monumental burial site of the Ipogeo dei Volumni at Perugia. There are impressive Roman monuments such as the Temple of Minerva in Assisi, the theatres of Gubbio, Spoleto and Terni, the great cisterns of Amelia and Todi, and the city gates of Spello and Todi. Not forgetting the Via Flaminia, which still links Rome with the Adriatic coast, as it did 2,300 years ago.

The Middle Ages and the Renaissance

After a period of Byzantine and Lombard domination, architecture was rejuvenated by the birth of the Romanesque style. Town squares lined with public buildings – a sign of temporal and communal power – were being built, as were cathedrals, a tangible and potent symbol of spiritual power.

The building of commercial towns in contact with outside markets brought about the arrival of the Gothic style during the 14th century. Especially fine examples of this style are Orvieto cathedral *(see pp140–41)* and the decoration in the Sala delle Arti Liberali e dei Pianeti in Palazzo Trinci in Foligno *(see p106)*, from the early years of the 15th century.

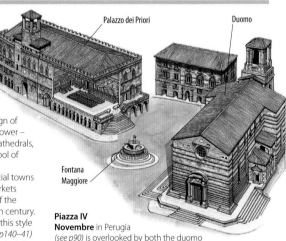

Palazzo dei Priori

Duomo

Fontana Maggiore

Piazza IV Novembre in Perugia *(see p90)* is overlooked by both the duomo (cathedral) and the Palazzo dei Priori, a sign of the political power of the medieval commune. Between the two stands the Fontana Maggiore, decorated between 1275 and 1278 by Nicola Pisano and his son, Giovanni.

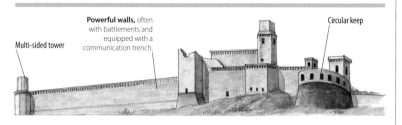

Multi-sided tower

Powerful walls, often with battlements and equipped with a communication trench.

Circular keep

The Rocca Maggiore at Assisi *(see p83)* was rebuilt in 1356 on the foundations of a feudal fortification built by Frederick Barbarossa. Its restoration was the work of Cardinal Albornoz, the papal legate who studded Central Italy with these strongholds of the faith.

The Age of the Fortresses

The conquest of Umbrian towns by the papacy brought about profound changes in the urban layout. The new power, aiming to increase military control and to diminish the importance of the traditional social space of the town square, commissioned a series of imposing fortresses which, although they have been modified over the centuries, have come down to us today virtually intact. These include the fortresses of Orvieto (begun in 1364 and then rebuilt in 1450), Narni (built from 1367–78), Assisi (rebuilt in 1356) and Spoleto (built in 1359).

Tympanum in classical style

Mirrored windows

Colonnade inspired by the entrance to a classical temple.

Palazzo della Regione *(see p94)*, in the Fontivegge quarter of Perugia, was part of a town plan by the architect Aldo Rossi. From 1982 to 1989 he rebuilt this area of the regional capital in Post-Modern style, with classical references.

Modern Architecture

Outside the encircling walls of Umbria's medieval towns, large and small, modern suburbs have developed, usually on the flat land just below the hilltop towns. Building styles have not always been particularly respectful of the artistic beauty of the old town, but there are some successful examples of modern architecture, such as the quarter of Fontivegge in Perugia. The countryside, too, has had to accept change. Many medieval groups of houses and farms have been converted for modern use, for example as hotels.

Romanesque Churches in Umbria

Around the 11th century, when medieval society was developing and the Church was re-creating its own autonomy, a style of religious architecture developed which, with simple linear forms, attempted a direct link with local cultures. In the 19th century, this style was defined as "Romanesque", after its derivation from the Christian basilica of the Roman era. The Romanesque church presents a harmonious façade, featuring arches and one or more rose windows. From the three doorways access is gained to the three-aisled interior, at the end of which is a presbytery, raised to allow the construction of a crypt. Examples of the style, since reworked, are San Lorenzo di Arari in Orvieto and the cathedrals of Spoleto, Assisi and Todi.

Three-mullioned window in a square frame

Large rose window (13th century)

San Michele (1195) in Bevagna has a beautiful doorway in which Romanesque elements and Roman finds are combined.

UMBRIA THROUGH THE YEAR

All year round in Umbria there are feast days, religious celebrations and pagan festivals linked to the farming year, including the harvest, or to popular and historical traditions of the ancient communes. Some of these events are famous worldwide, but every small village in Umbria has its own festival or saint's day worthy of wider renown. Besides the traditional events that have taken place for decades or centuries, there is also a full calendar of cultural events, such as the Festival of Spoleto and Umbria Jazz, not to mention historical re-enactments, and cinema and theatre seasons.

Spring

Umbria has no sea coast. As a result, the spring climate can be cool and windy. On higher ground, the snow may remain until March or April, while on the hills and high plains spring flowers are emerging. The main religious events during this season are those that fall during the Easter period, but there are also important feast days in May.

Women in medieval costume at the Calendimaggio in Assisi

March

Benedictine celebrations, Norcia *(third week of Mar)*. Includes a torchlit procession and a crossbow competition.

April

Antiques fair, Todi *(mid- to late Apr)*. Held in the Palazzo delle Arti.
Wine week, Montefalco *(Easter)*. Large trade fair of DOC wines.
La Desolata, Perugia *(Holy Week)*. Exciting staging of the Passion.
Tableaux Vivants, Città della Pieve *(Holy Week)*. Scenes from the Passion.

Processione del Cristo Morto, Assisi, Tuoro sul Trasimeno and Norcia *(Holy Week)*.
Via Crucis, Alviano and Amelia *(Good Friday)*.
Processione della Rinchinata, Bastia Umbra and Cannara *(Easter)*. Staging the meeting of Christ and the Madonna.
Coloriamo i Cieli, Castiglione del Lago *(late Apr to early May)*. A colourful biennial kite festival.
Corsa all'Anello, Narni *(late Apr to mid-May)*. Costumed knights spear a ring *(anello)* with a lance.

May

Cantamaggio, Terni *(May)*. Folk festival celebrating the advent of spring. Parade of floats with allegorical scenes.
Festa del Calendimaggio, Assisi *(first week)*. Three days of fun, including a costumed re-enactment of medieval stories, in which two of the town's districts compete.
Corsa dei Ceri, Gubbio *(15 May)*. Three guilds challenge each other to carry towering candlesticks *(ceri)* on their shoulders up to the basilica of Sant'Ubaldo.
Palio della Balestra, Gubbio *(last Sun)*. In Piazza della Signoria, the crossbowmen of Gubbio and Sansepolcro (Tuscany) challenge each other in a Palio.
Festa di Santa Rita, Cascia *(21–22 May)*. A torchlit procession towards the Santa Rita basilica, then a historical procession with the saint's remains and the staging of scenes from her life.
Festa della Palombella, Orvieto *(Pentecost)*. Similar to the Scoppio del Carro in Florence, in which an artificial "dove" sets light to a cart of fireworks.

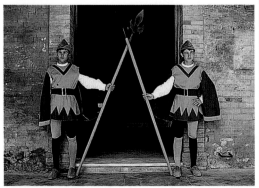
Opening of the Corsa all'Anello festival in Narni

Average Daily Hours of Sunshine

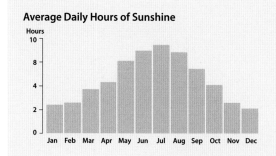

Hours

Sunshine
In summer the days are long and sunny, and it can become very hot in the towns. In September and October the days are still sunny, and often pleasantly warm, as they are also in the spring – perhaps the best time to visit Umbria.

Summer

Umbria can be very hot and humid in July and August, so many summer events are held outside, and in the evening. Festivals take place in squares, parks and gardens, and attract locals and tourists alike.

June
Festa della Fioritura, Castelluccio di Norcia. Ancient feast marking the return of flocks of sheep to the mountains.
Mercato delle Gaite, Bevagna *(second half of Jun)*. Medieval fair with splendid costumes and stalls.
Infiorata, Spello *(Corpus Christi)*. Procession along a flower-strewn route. Floral carpet competition.
Procession, Orvieto *(Corpus Christi)*. Procession in historical costume.
Festa del Voto, Assisi *(22 Jun)*. Re-enactment of the expulsion of the Saracens.

Piazza IV Novembre in Perugia, crowded with jazz fans

Rockin' Umbria, Perugia and Umbertide *(last ten days of Jun)*. Rock music festival, with up-and-coming bands, as well as photography and comic exhibitions.
Biennale di Scultura, Gubbio. A biennial exhibition of works by contemporary Italian artists.
Festa delle Acque, Piediluco and at the Cascata delle Marmore *(late Jun)*. Processions of boats, canoe races and fireworks.

July
Festival di Spoleto *(end Jun to mid-Jul)*. A major international event dedicated to theatre, dance and music.
Umbria Jazz, Perugia *(mid-Jul)*. Theatres, gardens and squares are taken over by some of the world's great jazz artists.
Gubbio Summer Festival *(Jul–Aug)*. Chamber and symphony music in the open air.

Floral decorations in the street during the Infiorata, Spello

Palio delle Barche, Passignano sul Trasimeno *(last week in Jul)*. Town districts compete in a boat race, for which participants wear medieval costume.

Historical costume

August
Palio dei Terzieri, Città della Pieve. Archery competition and all manner of street entertainment, including acrobats and a procession featuring costumes derived from the works of Perugino.
Palio dei Quartieri, Nocera Umbra. Popular historical re-enactment in costume.
Palio di San Rufino, Assisi. Crossbow competition.
Rassegna Internazionale del Folklore, Castiglione del Lago. Folklore festival.
Festival delle Nazioni *(late Aug to early Sep)*, Città di Castello. Festival of chamber music.

Average Monthly Rainfall

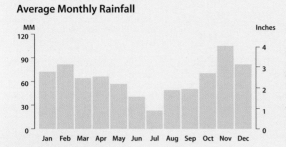

Rainfall
Late autumn is the time of year when rainfall is at its heaviest. In winter heavy snowfalls are common in the Apennines, while storms may occur in spring and late summer.

The Joust of the Quintana in Foligno, September

Autumn

The end of the summer heralds the grape harvest, followed by the olive harvest. These are two very important occasions for the customs and culture of the region. Summer festivals and tourist events are usually over by this stage, and this is the start of a season of festivals linked to the gastronomy and history of the region.

September
Cavalcata di Satriano, Nocera Umbra *(first Sun)*. Knights in medieval costume retrace the last journey of St Francis, from the hermitage at Nocera to his native Assisi.
Giostra della Quintana, Foligno *(second Sun)*. In this joust, competing knights attempt to spear a ring held by a wooden puppet. The streets are filled with historical processions.
Giochi delle Porte, Gualdo Tadino *(last week of Sep)*. Includes archery and catapult competitions, donkey and donkey cart races all around the town. There are also historical re-enactments.

Festa dell'Uva *(end Sep)*, Montefalco. Celebration of the grape harvest.
Segni Barocchi, Foligno *(Sep–Oct)*. Musical and theatrical performances, all with a Baroque theme.

October
Giostra dell'Arme, San Gemini *(late Sep to mid-Oct)*. Costumed knights from two town districts compete in a jousting tournament.
I Primi d'Italia, Foligno *(late Sep to early Oct)*. National food festival celebrating the first dishes of Italy.
Palio dei Terzieri, Trevi *(first Sun of Oct)*. Cart race and historical parade.
Festival Eurochocolate, Perugia *(mid- to late Oct)*. Chocolate stands and superb chocolate sculptures fill the historic centre.
Festa di San Francesco, Assisi *(2–4 Oct)*. Important religious celebration on the anniversary of Francis's death.
Marcia per la Pace, Perugia to Assisi *(biennial)*. Groups and movements from around the world participate in an

international march for peace.
Rassegna Antiquaria, Perugia *(end Oct to early Nov)*. Antiques fair. Includes displays of antique textiles.
Ottobre Trevano, Trevi. Gastronomic feasts and historical re-enactments performed in costume.
Mostra del Tartufo, Città di Castello *(late Oct to early Nov)*. Taste white truffles and all sorts of other woodland delicacies.

November
Fiera dei Cavalli, Città di Castello *(third Sun of Nov)*. Cattle markets and horse fairs.
Wine Tasting, Torgiano *(late Nov)*. World-famous wine-tasting competition of Umbrian and other Italian wines.
Festa dei Ceramisti, Deruta *(25 Nov)*. Festival for Deruta's older ceramicists, plus displays of ceramics. Dedicated to Santa Caterina d'Alessandria, patron saint of ceramicists.
Rassegna Cinematografica di Assisi *(Oct/Nov/Dec)*. Film festival dedicated to Italian cinema.

Flag-waving display at the Giochi delle Porte in Gualdo Tadino

Average Monthly Temperature

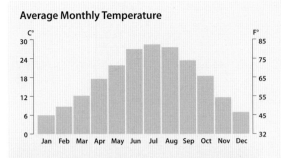

Temperature
The Umbrian climate is temperate, though temperatures are much cooler in the Apennines. Autumn and spring, when the days are not too hot, are the most pleasant seasons. The summer months are hot and humid, especially in the towns.

The Nativity in Città di Castello, one of Italy's most important festivals

Winter

This season can be very cold and windy, and snow often falls at higher mountain altitudes. There are festivals celebrating the chestnut harvest, for instance, but Christmas is the focus of the season. At Christmas, living nativity scenes are staged, a popular tradition dating from the Middle Ages.

National Holidays

New Year (1 Jan)

Epiphany (6 Jan)

Easter Sunday

Anniversary of Liberation (25 Apr)

Labour Day (1 May)

Festa della Repubblica (2 Jun)

Ferragosto (15 Aug)

All Saints (1 Nov)

Immaculate Conception (8 Dec)

Christmas (25 Dec)

Santo Stefano (26 Dec)

December

Ri Fauni or Festa delle Campane (9 Dec). Commemorating the transporting of the Madonna of Nazareth to Loreto (9 December 1921).
World's largest Christmas tree, Gubbio (from 7 Dec). Lights transform Monte Ingino into a giant Christmas tree.
Living Nativity, Attigliano, Alviano, Acquasparta, Calvi, Giove, Monteleone, Petrignano, Lugnano in Teverina, Perugia and Rocca Sant'Angelo (24 Dec).
Christmas in Assisi. Concerts and formal celebrations in the basilica and other churches.
Monumental nativity, Città della Pieve (Christmas to Epiphany). This is displayed in the Palazzo della Corgna.

January

Umbria Jazz Winter, Orvieto (end Dec to early Jan). Winter version of the Perugia jazz festival. Concerts and musical events.

February

Carnevale. Parades and events throughout Umbria.
Festa dell'Olivo and **Sagra della Bruschetta**, Spello (penultimate Sun of Carnevale). Olive and bruschetta festivals, with parades, feasts and music.
Mascherata, San Leo di Bastia (first Sun of Carnevale). A masked procession through the village.

Norcia black truffles

Festa di San Valentino, Terni (Feb). Events all month, but 14 Feb is the focus. Betrothed couples exchange vows of love in the basilica of St Valentine.
Sagra del Tartufo Nero e dei Prodotti Tipici della Valnerina, Norcia (Feb). Tastings and sales of produce, including truffles.

Gospel singing in Orvieto cathedral during Umbria Jazz Winter

THE HISTORY OF UMBRIA

Wedged between powerful neighbours like Tuscany, Le Marche and Lazio (especially Rome), the territory of Umbria has been an area of conquest, transit and trade for millennia. Its regional identity today dates back to the creation of a unified Italy in the 19th century, although the towns and cities of Umbria nonetheless have many characteristics in common.

The first populations date back to the Neolithic age – evidence remains of ceramics from the 6th and 5th millennia BC. Later, the Apennine civilization occupied Umbria's hills and mountains, and lived off agriculture and stock raising. They left behind decorated vases and tools of stone, bone and metal.

The golden age of prehistory in central Italy coincided with the development of the Villanovan culture in the 9th and 8th centuries BC. This people used iron for tools and arms, and had complex funerary rituals. The cities of many Italic peoples developed from the settlements of this era. They had a turbulent relationship with the emerging economic and military powers of the Etruscans and the Romans, and would manage to remain independent for only a few more centuries.

Until the Romans arrived, the Umbrian territory was divided into two areas of control: on the west bank of the Tiber was a series of rich Etruscan cities, while on the east bank the Umbri held control. The little that is known about the Umbri comes from the famous Eugubine Tablets (*see p64*). Discovered in 1444, these seven bronze slabs were written in the 2nd century BC in the Umbrian language, using the Etruscan and then the Latin alphabet. The text describes religious rites and also Gubbio's political system. Other cities founded by the Umbri include Todi, Assisi, Spello and Gualdo Tadino.

Confrontation between Rome and the Etruscans reached crisis point in 295 BC, when Roman legions defeated the Umbri, the Sannites, Gauls and Etruscans, opening up territory for conquest. The cities changed sides quickly, and the opening in 219 of the Via Flaminia from Rome to the Adriatic confirmed Rome's power. Rome suffered one of its most bitter defeats, however, on the shores of Lake Trasimeno. In 217 BC the Roman army clashed with Hannibal and the Carthaginians to the west of the lake. The Carthaginians laid a trap to surprise the enemy on the lake shore and Hannibal's army wiped out two-thirds of the Roman forces.

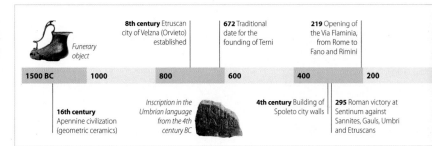

Funerary object

8th century Etruscan city of Velzna (Orvieto) established

672 Traditional date for the founding of Terni

219 Opening of the Via Flaminia, from Rome to Fano and Rimini

1500 BC	1000	800	600	400	200

16th century Apennine civilization (geometric ceramics)

Inscription in the Umbrian language from the 4th century BC

4th century Building of Spoleto city walls

295 Roman victory at Sentinum against Sannites, Gauls, Umbri and Etruscans

◀ *Fortitude and Temperance*, Perugino (1448–1523), Collegio del Cambio in Perugia (detail)

Roman Umbria

After the defeat of the Etruscans and the Italic peoples allied to the Umbri, Rome consolidated its domination of Umbria in the 1st century BC, when Emperor Augustus created Region VI (Umbria), which included all the cities and municipal towns on the west bank of the River Tiber. Region VII (Etruria) took in territory and settlements on the east bank of the river. The Romans, who were great civil engineers, undertook a series of urban projects in the 1st and 2nd centuries AD, including aqueducts, cisterns, theatres and walls that would feature in the lives of Umbrian towns for centuries. Via Flaminia and Via Amerina would become the main communication routes in the region for hundreds of years to come.

The Villa di Plinio (Pliny's Villa) at San Giustino would have been very grand at one time. This shows one of many hypothetical reconstructions.

Lake Trasimeno was the scene of a battle between the Romans and Carthaginians *(see p97)*. Today, there is little to be seen of the encounter: just the names of a river and a hill – Rio Sanguineto (bloody river) and Monte Sanguigno (Mount Blood) – and several ditches dug to cremate the corpses of Hannibal's soldiers.

Roman Umbria

This map shows the administrative shape of Umbria under the Romans, as well as the busy network of Roman roads planned and built over the centuries. The Via Flaminia was of particular importance to Umbria. Construction began at the end of the 3rd century BC, and a number of towns of importance developed along its length, among them Spoleto. The road maintained its role in the centuries following Roman domination.

The site of Carsulae *(see p132)* is one of the most important in Umbria, and many of the objects discovered here now feature in the museums of the region. The site was abandoned in 27 BC, when commercial traffic moved to the eastern side of the Via Flaminia.

Via Amerina was the second main artery road.

The baths at Otricoli were built on the site of natural springs. Baths were an important feature of Roman civilization.

San Giustino

VIA TIBERINA

Tifernum Tiberinum (Città di Castello)

Tuoro al Trasimeno

Lake Trasimeno

Perusia (Perugia)

Region VII

VIA ORVIETANA

VIA AMERINA

VIA CASSIA

VIA NOMENTRANA

Tuder (Todi)

Carsulae

Volsinii Veteres (Orvieto)

Paglia

River Tiber

Ameria (Amelia)

Narnia (Narn

Ocriculum (Otricoli)

The Mausoleum of Pomponio Grecino, near Gubbio, demonstrates that the city was an important political and religious place at the time of Region VI.

The bronze statue of Germanicus, found near Amelia, is now on view in the town's archaeological museum (*see p130*). For a long time the famous statue was held in Perugia's Museo Archeologico Nazionale dell'Umbria (*see p88*), which is probably the best in Umbria for the wealth and importance of its Roman and Etruscan collections.

The Via Flaminia was the main route through Umbria, built along the axis of the towns of Narnia, Spoletium, Carsulae and Fulginiae. Traces of the original paving stones can be seen in many towns.

The Temple of Minerva (*see p75*) in Assisi was built in the 1st century AD, on a set of terraces representing the centre of the Roman city. The temple performed different functions over the centuries until, in 1456, it finally became the church of Santa Maria sopra Minerva.

The paving of Roman roads was famous for its solid construction. Various stretches are still visible today, including at Spoleto.

Region VI

● **Asisium (Assisi)**

● **Hispellum (Spello)**

● **Fulginiae (Foligno)**

● **Tribiae (Trevi)**

Region IV Nursia (Norcia)

● **Spoletium (Spoleto)**

● **Interamna Nahars (Terni)**

Theatres and amphitheatres were built by the Romans in Umbria. They can be seen in many parts of the region, several still in good condition, such as the one at Spoleto (*see p115*), from which the above mosaic comes. It is now used for events and concerts.

Norcia was a prefecture and then a municipium of Region IV.

0 kilometres 10

0 miles 10

Cisterns were large underground reservoirs for storing water, built by the Romans and still visible today in some towns, along with their wells. Amelia's reservoirs are particularly impressive; they consist of ten parallel tanks with a capacity of four and a half million litres.

Key

-- Today's regional boundary

— Roman boundary

The Late Middle Ages

The ending of Roman rule in Umbria was a heavy blow to a region that depended on trade and agriculture. Communication routes ceased to be secure, apart from the road linking Rome with Amelia, Narni, Perugia and Gubbio. The townspeople had built houses on the plain in the quest for more space during the years of the *pax romana* (as can still be seen today in Gubbio), but they were forced to return to the hills to protect themselves from the aggressive barbarians – the Goths and Huns – coming from the north. The towns became crowded and unsanitary, plague and famine wrought havoc in many areas. The Umbrian population declined noticeably and the ordered farms of the Roman era rapidly became fragmented into numerous small plots of land. Feudal power held sway virtually everywhere, typically dominated by local families who ruled over small areas from a castle or a fortress. In 553, a narrow strip of Umbrian land passed into Byzantine hands, but of far greater significance was the arrival of the Lombards, who set up a principality that included much of Umbria. From the 570s onwards, the so-called Duchy of Spoleto developed into a political entity of some weight. When either historians or geographers referred to

Frederick Barbarossa flanked by his sons Enrico il Severo and Frederick, 12th-century miniature

Lombard sword hilt

"Umbria" at this time, and indeed for centuries to come, they generally meant the lands of the Duchy of Spoleto and therefore only the east bank of the Tiber. In the centuries prior to the year 1000, small monasteries and convents appeared all over the region, albeit scattered and often in inaccessible places. Under the Lombards, who adopted many of the customs of the local people, there was a flowering of art and architecture.

The end of the first millennium signalled a change in the tendency to build hill fortresses. During this phase, lower, flat ground gradually began to be reoccupied, as trade became more significant. New towns (which sometimes kept Roman elements in their names, such as Villa Nova) were built,

300 A.D.	400	500	600	700	800

4th century Construction of the basilica of Santo Salvatore in Spoleto

553 End of the war with the Goths: part of Umbria comes under Byzantine domination

756 Pepin the Short gives Perugia and the Duchy of Spoleto to Pope Stephen II

c.480 Birth of St Benedict (San Benedetto) in Norcia

St Benedict in a miniature

6th–7th centuries Invasion of the Lombards. The Duchy of Spoleto includes Terni, Foligno, Spello and Assisi.

populated by ordinary peasants, now freed from their feudal obligations. This led to the birth of early forms of self-government, which would later develop into the communes of the 11th and 12th centuries.

At the request of the papacy, the Franks (under Pepin the Short and then Charlemagne), drove the Lombards and the Byzantines out of Umbria. Charlemagne won the title of Holy Roman Emperor from the papacy in exchange for territory, but relations soured. When Barbarossa, Holy Roman Emperor, arrived in Italy in the 1150s, he destroyed Spoleto and a number of other towns.

Artisans and farm labourers at work in the era of the communes

The Rise of the Communes

Eventually, economic progress and demographic growth made it essential to expand the towns, too restricted now inside their old walls. In 1244 construction began of the new walls in Todi, and in 1296 Spoleto enlarged its city walls. The emphasis on ambitious public works, such as town halls and cathedrals, demonstrated a lively spirit of initiative on the part of the town populations. It was certainly no coincidence that they elected to adopt a form of autonomy in the 11th and 12th centuries, leading to the rise of the communes *(see pp46–7)*. By 1111, Pope Pasquale II was complaining that Umbrian towns did not recognize the authority of the Church of Rome. In Umbria, meanwhile, the communes flourished: Perugia's Palazzo

dei Priori, Orvieto cathedral and the basilica in Assisi date from this time. In addition, the Franciscan influence started to spread from Assisi, encouraging the use of the Gothic style in new churches. The years of architectural, social and political triumph of these autonomous towns were, however, also years of constant battles for regional or local domination, and plagues and earthquakes badly affected the towns and countryside. The end of the era of the communes coincided with a push by the papacy to regain control. Between 1350 and 1370 the figure that the Umbrians feared most was Egidio Albornoz, cardinal and papal legate, creator of the great fortresses which were to watch over Umbrian towns on behalf of Rome for the next five centuries.

Montefalco, an example of a fortified city commune, in a painting by Benozzo Gozzoli (1420–1497)

Pasquale II, pope from 1099 to 1118	**1155** Frederick Barbarossa destroys Spoleto	**1277** Cimabue starts work on the frescoes in the basilica of Assisi	**1290** Orvieto: Nicholas IV blesses the first stone laid in the building of the cathedral
900 ... **1000**	**1100**	**1200**	**1300**
11th–12th centuries The Umbrian communes are set up: in 1111 Pasquale II realizes that none of the Umbrian towns respect the authority of the pope		**1226** On 4 October, St Francis of Assisi dies	**1354** Beginning of the papal campaign to reconquer Umbria

The Communes of Umbria

The communes *(comuni)*, or independent city states, and their organizational structures spread rapidly throughout central Italy in the 11th–12th centuries. The independence of the communes – which were frequently at war with one another – developed at a time when central power was weakening. Despite the reaction of the papacy and of the Holy Roman Empire, the 12th century marked the rise of the commune, asserting the autonomy of the city-state and enabling the arts and economy to flourish. The political master was no longer a feudal lord but an urban bourgeoisie growing rich through manufacturing and trade. Textile industries were established, as were the first banks (which later led to the creation of the great Italian banks of subsequent centuries). In the meantime, merchants from the communes developed trade relationships with the rest of Europe and the Mediterranean, and, thanks to the Crusades, with the Far East, too.

Palazzi Comunali (town halls), symbols of the communes, were built in Umbria during the 13th and 14th centuries. In many towns and cities, they are still the seat of the town hall.

The Torre del Popolo remains a landmark in Assisi's Piazza del Comune.

One of the first signs of the birth of communal civilization was population growth, which required cities to increase available housing. City walls were enlarged and rebuilt in all the main town centres in Umbria, among them Spello, shown above.

Increasingly imposing cathedrals (left is the cathedral of Foligno) were often built facing the centres of temporal power. After centuries of fortified towns criss-crossed with narrow streets, the era of the commune saw the building of town squares that functioned as meeting places as well as centres of power.

St Francis was the subject of a book by St Bonaventure, written in the same century that the saint died.

The Temple of Minerva, still visible in Assisi's Piazza del Comune, is clearly recognizable, even in this stylized rendering.

The town fountain was a celebration of the wealth of a city – the years when the communes flourished signalled the return of water supplies to many towns. After centuries of abandonment, ancient aqueducts were restored and rebuilt. This is the famous Fontana Maggiore in Perugia (*see p91*).

Population growth meant that urban centres were forced to expand upwards as well as outwards. This is how multi-storey houses and porticoes arose.

Homage of a Simple Man

St Bonaventure, a 13th-century Franciscan monk, tells the story that one day, in Assisi, Francis met "a simple man". Inspired by God, the man laid his own cloak down before the saint. This episode begins the story of the life of St Francis in the cycle of frescoes in the Basilica in Assisi. The work is of great importance because, with great attention to detail and careful observation, the artist has created a perfect picture of the medieval centre of Assisi at the end of the 13th century. A picture that is not so different from that visible in Piazza del Comune today.

Clashes and battles between the Umbrian communes were continual. Some cities had troops of soldiers, such as the crossbowmen, that formed exclusive companies. They are commemorated today in numerous historical processions.

The citizen in the era of the communes, like the one present in this scene, was expected to maintain a dignified demeanour in public squares; swords should never be unsheathed. Crimes committed in this place were severely punished.

Impressive fortresses, like the one at Spoleto, pictured here, dominate Umbrian towns. They were built by the papacy, from the end of the 14th century, in order to consolidate the power of the Church. The construction of such strongholds, often under the watchful eye of Cardinal Albornoz, heralded the end of communal power.

Perugia, as depicted in a fresco by Benedetto Bonfigli in the mid-15th century

The Centuries of Decline

The conquest of Umbria by the papacy coincided with the effects of the great plague that had devastated Europe in 1348.

At the end of the 15th century, the term "Umbria" began to appear in the works of scholars and academics: the clergyman Innocenzo Malvasia, in his *Italia Illustrata* drawn up for Pope Sixtus V, defined Umbria as the land of the Duchy of Spoleto, while he described the remainder of the region as being part of Etruria, and Gualdo and Gubbio as dependencies of the Duchy of Urbino.

Following centuries of development, 16th-century Umbria found itself in a tricky situation. The cities, peripheral dominions of the state gravitating around Rome, were declining, while craftsmen and industries were diminishing in number and quality. The heads of the great aristocratic families abandoned the cities and returned to the land and agriculture.

Town and Countryside

A fundamental instrument in the development of the new Umbrian economy was the "*mezzadria*", or sharecropping system, and the gradual colonization of the hills and plains, on partly reclaimed land in some cases. One very noticeable effect of the agricultural revival was the gradual depopulation of the cities. The historian Cipriano Piccolpasso wrote of Assisi: "…it is a badly composed city, with many derelict and unoccupied houses next to inhabited ones, so that it seems more like the residue of a city than a completed one…". The move to the country was not the only factor to alter the appearance of the cities: during the 16th and 17th centuries, nobles invested some of the profits from their farms in town projects.

Politically, the 17th century saw important new developments: in 1624 the della Rovere family ceded the Duchy of Urbino to the pope, and the following year Pope Urban VIII put the University of Perugia under episcopal control.

Urban VIII, pope from 1623 to 1644

From Papal Rule to the Unification of Italy

By now an agricultural, rural region, Umbria became one of Rome's "bread baskets" and a major producer of olive oil. Mills multiplied, as did the frequency of country fairs, which took the place of town markets in the economy of the countryside.

1416–24 Braccio da Montone becomes lord of Perugia

1472 In Foligno, 300 copies of The *Divine Comedy* are printed: the first book published in Italian in Italy

Paul III, pope from 1534 to 1549

| 1400 | 1500 | 1600 | 1700 |

1444 The Eugubine Tablets are discovered

1508 Building begins on Santa Maria della Consolazione, near Todi

1540 Perugia comes under the papal rule of Paul III

1656–1701 The population of Umbria falls from 317,000 to 280,000

Perugia's Rocca Paolina, destroyed on 14 September 1860

Modern Umbria

Following a plebiscite, the province of Umbria was created in 1861, as part of a unified Kingdom of Italy. It included all the current provinces (plus Rieti), with a population of 500,000. The economic situation in the closing decades of the 19th century was, however, woeful: agriculture was languishing and farmers were increasingly forced into seasonal migration towards the Maremma and the countryside around Rome. Even so, the Industrial Revolution did not leave Umbria behind: in 1866 the railway line that links Rome, Terni and Foligno was completed, and between 1875 and 1887 arms factories and the Terni steelworks (the first – and only – really major employer in the region) were founded. In 1881 the population of Umbria numbered 611,000 in 1911 it was 767,000.

With the end of the 18th century came the Napoleonic revolution. As part of the Roman Republic created in 1798, Umbria was divided into the two departments of Trasimeno and Clitunno. In the imperial era the division was dissolved, and Umbria became a single territory, with Spoleto as its capital. This confirmation of a common identity would be returned to without much alteration by the unified state after 1860.

In line with the Romantic movement elsewhere, the 19th century saw a rise in interest in the Middle Ages. The discovery of the remains of St Francis (1818) and Santa Chiara (1850) caused a sensation. In 1859, a great popular uprising in Perugia against the papal troops resulted in a brutal massacre, which became known as the "Stragi di Perugia". In September 1860 soldiers entered the town, and the local population immediately set about destroying the Rocca Paolina fortress, which had become a much detested symbol of the power of the Roman Catholic Church.

World War II saw the bombing of Umbria's industries, and recovery in the postwar period was slow. The development of light industry, cottage industries and especially tourism has helped boost the region's fortunes, though the earthquakes that strike periodically have affected certain areas of Umbria badly. The worst happened in 1979, in Valnerina, but the quake that struck Assisi, Foligno and Nocera Umbra in 1997 received broader coverage around the world because of the damage done to the art-packed St Francis basilica.

Santa Chiara in Assisi, which holds the remains of Santa Chiara

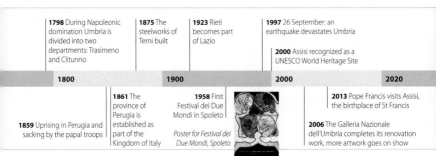

1798 During Napoleonic domination Umbria is divided into two departments: Trasimeno and Clitunno

1875 The steelworks of Terni built

1923 Rieti becomes part of Lazio

1997 26 September: an earthquake devastates Umbria

2000 Assisi recognized as a UNESCO World Heritage Site

1800   1900   2000   2020

1859 Uprising in Perugia and sacking by the papal troops

1861 The province of Perugia is established as part of the Kingdom of Italy

1958 First Festival dei Due Mondi in Spoleto

Poster for Festival dei Due Mondi, Spoleto

2013 Pope Francis visits Assisi, the birthplace of St Francis

2006 The Galleria Nazionale dell'Umbria completes its renovation work, more artwork goes on show

UMBRIA
AREA BY AREA

Umbria at a Glance

The region of Umbria is not particularly large, but it has numerous towns, villages, parks and other places of great interest. Northern Umbria includes the upper valley of the River Tiber (Alta Val Tiberina), the Apennine regional parks (Monte Subasio and Monte Cucco), the medieval towns of Perugia, Assisi and Gubbio and the great expanse of Lake Trasimeno. The southern half of the region revolves around the towns of Todi, Narni, Terni and Orvieto, on the border with Tuscany, within the area once occupied by the Etruscans. Completing this picture of southern Umbria are the great mountains of the Monti Sibillini national park and the Valnerina (the valley of the Nera River), with its famous waterfalls, the Cascata delle Marmore.

NORTHERN UMBRIA
(see pp54–99)

Città della Pieve
Famous as the birthplace of the artist Perugino (some of his works are here), this small town near the Tuscan border is a good departure point for visiting the area south of Lake Trasimeno.

| 0 kilometres | 15 |
| 0 miles | 15 |

Todi
Perched on a hill above the Tiber, Todi was for centuries a border town between the land of the Etruscans and territory occupied by the Umbri. It has a lovely historic quarter, centred around Piazza del Popolo.

◀ Panoramic view of the medieval town of Orvieto

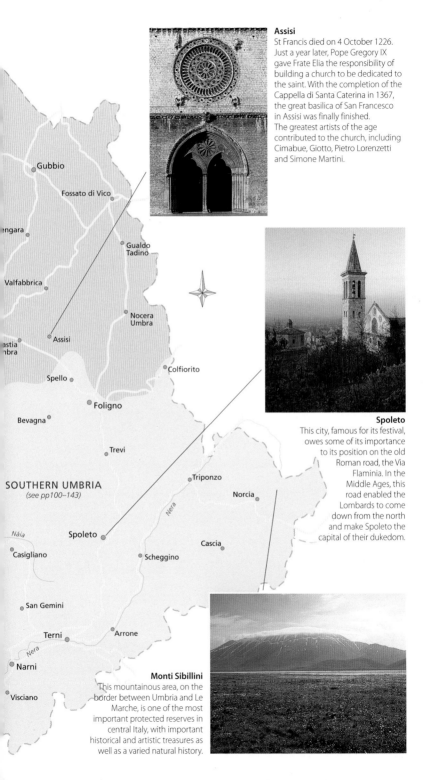

Assisi
St Francis died on 4 October 1226. Just a year later, Pope Gregory IX gave Frate Elia the responsibility of building a church to be dedicated to the saint. With the completion of the Cappella di Santa Caterina in 1367, the great basilica of San Francesco in Assisi was finally finished.
The greatest artists of the age contributed to the church, including Cimabue, Giotto, Pietro Lorenzetti and Simone Martini.

Gubbio

Fossato di Vico

engara

Gualdo
Tadino

Valfabbrica

Nocera
Umbra

astia
nbra

Assisi

Spello

Colfiorito

Foligno

Bevagna

Trevi

Triponzo

SOUTHERN UMBRIA
(see pp100–143)

Norcia

Nera

Náia

Spoleto

Cascia

Casigliano

Scheggino

San Gemini

Terni

Arrone

Nera

Narni

Visciano

Spoleto
This city, famous for its festival, owes some of its importance to its position on the old Roman road, the Via Flaminia. In the Middle Ages, this road enabled the Lombards to come down from the north and make Spoleto the capital of their dukedom.

Monti Sibillini
This mountainous area, on the border between Umbria and Le Marche, is one of the most important protected reserves in central Italy, with important historical and artistic treasures as well as a varied natural history.

NORTHERN UMBRIA

Northern Umbria consists of three distinct geographical areas: the first is the Alta Val Tiberina (the Upper Tiber Valley), the second is the area around Lake Trasimeno, and the third is the easterly Apennine region around Gubbio and the Via Flaminia. These three regions, laden with history and culture, meet at northern Umbria's two most important towns, Perugia and Assisi.

Perugia is the capital of the region and one of the main cities in central Italy, both culturally and economically. Assisi is visited every year by thousands of tourists and pilgrims, who come to retrace the steps of St Francis and admire the fresco cycles in the basilica.

The three aforementioned areas have differing histories. The Alta Val Tiberina, as well as delineating the border between the Etruscans (to the west) and the Umbri (to the east), has long been of commercial importance, with its direct lines of communication with the north. The entire area of Lake Trasimeno, on the other hand, has always been of great strategic and military significance, as can still be seen today from the many fortifications scattered around the lake. The lakeshore was the setting for one of the battles of the Second Punic Wars (217 BC), which culminated in the victory of Hannibal over the Romans. To the east, in contrast,

hermitages that were refuges for entire populations in the time of barbaric invasions cling to the Apennines. Northern Umbria's fortunes became allied to those of the rest of the region with the ending of the Duchy of Spoleto.

Despite the bombardments of World War II and the earthquake of 1997, which struck the area along the border with Le Marche, splendid testimony remains to the region's history, including Etruscan and Roman buildings and finds. The legacy of the Middle Ages and the Renaissance can be seen in churches, palazzi, town halls and castles, as well as in works by the great artists of the day, among them Perugino, a native of Città della Pieve.

The varied and well-preserved landscape of the northern region includes two national parks, Monte Cucco and Monte Subasio, where the "song of nature" that so struck St Francis of Assisi can still be sensed.

A patchwork of ordered fields carpeting the hillsides of northern Umbria

◀ View of San Gerolamo Monastery in Monte Cucco Park

Exploring Northern Umbria

Città di Castello is the first main town on the road into Umbria from neighbouring Emilia-Romagna, along the old trade route which then continues down through the Upper Tiber Valley. At Umbertide, a road heads off eastwards to Gubbio and beyond to the Via Flaminia, which skirts the Apennines on its route south towards Assisi. West of Assisi lies the province of Perugia and the regional capital itself. Further west again, bordering Tuscany, is Lake Trasimeno and the homeland of Perugino.

Castello di Petroia, between Gubbio and Assisi

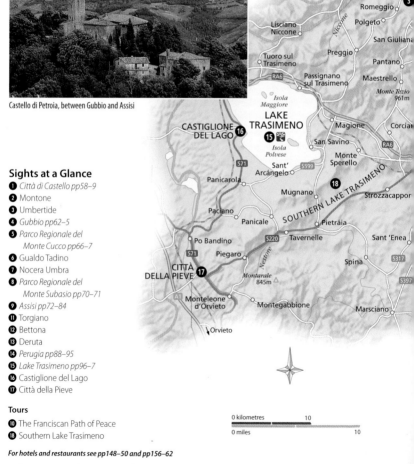

Sights at a Glance

Tours

For hotels and restaurants see pp148–50 and pp156–62

The famous silhouette of the basilica in Assisi

Getting Around

Lake Trasimeno and Perugia can be reached from the Autostrada del Sole (A1) by following Superstrada 75bis, a motorway spur that heads east from the exit Val di Chiana, Bettole-Sinalunga. Further south, the Fabro exit from the A1 is just a few kilometres from Città della Pieve. The state roads 3 and 3bis, which link Umbria with Le Marche and Emilia-Romagna, are also major routes. Two railway lines run from Perugia: north to Sansepolcro and northwest to Florence, with trains running at least daily. Coach and bus services are good, in particular around Lake Trasimeno (where there are also ferry services) and in and around Perugia.

Key

- ═══ Motorway
- ═══ Major road
- ≡≡≡ Major road under contruction
- ━━━ Secondary road
- ⋯⋯ Minor road
- ━━━ Scenic route
- ┅┅┅ Main railway
- ──── Minor railway
- ═══ Regional border
- △ Summit

Market stalls under the arcades in Gubbio

For keys to symbols *see back flap*

❶ Città di Castello

The town that is today the most important centre in the Upper Tiber Valley, the gateway to Umbria for anyone approaching from the north, was originally a settlement of the ancient Umbri. Situated as it was between Le Marche and Tuscany, and not far from Emilia-Romagna, the town was in a perfect position as far as trade was concerned. It became a commune in the Middle Ages, when it was in almost perpetual conflict with the nearby city-states. Even so, the former "Civitas Castelli" grew in power and riches, thanks to the flourishing commercial activity, including printing, which is still an important part of the city's economic fabric today. Following a period of rule by nobles installed by the Church, Città di Castello was completely redesigned under the rule of the Vitelli family, in the 16th century, as can be seen by the various palazzi bearing its name.

Exploring Città di Castello

The town is built on the right bank of the River Tiber, at the northernmost edge of Umbria. The architecture displays Tuscan influences, thanks to the work of the Florentine architects Antonio da Sangallo and Giorgio Vasari, brought in by the Vitelli family in the 16th century.

The tour described here begins in Piazza Gabriotti. Visitors are advised to leave their cars in the car park in Viale Nazario Sauro and then take the escalator up to the piazza. The monuments seen at the beginning of the tour date from the period prior to that of the Vitelli.

⛪ Duomo

Piazza Gabriotti. **Open** daily.

It is immediately apparent that the cathedral exterior has undergone more than one remodelling. The round bell tower formed part of the original 11th-century building, but the body of the church reveals two successive rebuildings, in the 14th and then the 15th–16th centuries. The unfinished Baroque façade dates from 1632–46. The interior has a single nave and contains a wooden choir and a *Resurrection* by Rosso

Fiorentino (1529), in the chapel on the right-hand side. In the **Museo del Duomo,** objects on display map the evolution of the church in the Middle Ages.

🏛 Museo del Duomo

Piazza Gabriotti.
Tel 075 855 4705.
Open Apr–Sep: 10am–1pm, 3:30–6pm Tue–Sun; Oct–Mar: 10am–12:30pm, 3–5pm Tue–Sun.

⛪ Palazzo Comunale

Piazza Gabriotti.

In the same piazza as the Duomo (typical of a medieval town) is the Palazzo Comunale, or town hall. This 14th-century building is the work of Angelo da Orvieto and shows how the Florentine influence on the town's architecture pre-dates the arrival of the Vitelli family: in particular, the use of rusticated stone echoes the style of the

Paliotto, c.1144, Museo del Duomo

Palazzo Vecchio in Florence.

In front of the palazzo, on the other side of the piazza, stands the **Torre Civica**, also 14th-century and once called "del Vescovo" (the bishop's), because it stood next to the bishop's palace (Palazzo Vescovile). From the top of the tower (open daily, entrance fee), there are good views over the town and the surrounding countryside.

⛪ Palazzo del Podestà

Corso Cavour.

The 14th-century Torre Civica

From the east of the piazza runs Corso Cavour, home to the Palazzo del Podestà. The façade facing the street dates from the same era as the Palazzo Comunale, and it may be that the original design was also by Angelo da Orvieto. The eastern side is Baroque and leads on to Piazza Matteotti, where **Palazzo Vitelli "in Piazza"** stands.

⛪ San Francesco

Via D Albizzini. **Open** daily.

The street that cuts the city in half from north to south is made up of Via XX Settembre, Via Angeloni and Corso Vittorio Emanuele. Halfway along Via Angeloni, near the corner of Via Albizzini, stands the church of St Francis, of 13th-century origin, to which the famous Florentine painter and architect Giorgio Vasari contributed in the 1500s. He was responsible for the Cappella Vitelli as well as an altar with a *Coronation of the Virgin* (1564).

⛪ Palazzo Vitelli a Porta Sant'Egidio

Piazza Garibaldi.

A short distance from San Francesco is this Vitelli palace (1540), one of many that the family had built in the town in an effort to impose some stylistic unity. The façade is symmetrical and there is a pretty garden inside.

The Work of Alberto Burri

Alberto Burri, a major figure in 20th-century Italian art and known all over the world, was born in Città di Castello in 1915 (he died in Nice in 1995). A doctor by profession, he turned to art during World War II. His work is often large-scale and makes use of innovative materials: particularly famous is the *Cretto* at Gibellina Vecchia, in Sicily, a huge carpet of white cement covering the ruins left by the 1968 earthquake. Città di Castello has a good collection of his work in Palazzo Albizzini and the former tobacco drying house, Ex Seccatoi del Tabacco.

Great Iron Sextant, 1982, on show in Città di Castello

Collezioni Burri: **Tel** 075 855 46 49. Palazzo Albizzini: Via Albizzini. Ex Seccatoi del Tabacco: Via Pierucci. **Open** 9:30am–12:30pm, 2:30–6:30pm Tue–Sat; 10:30am–12:30pm, 3–7pm Sun & public hols (check website for details) **Tel** 075 855 9848. **Closed** Mon, 1 Jan, 25 Dec. 🖭 **fondazioneburri.org**

by Antonio da Sangallo (1521–32) with the assistance of Vasari, who was responsible for part of the frescoed friezes.

Among the many works are an *Enthroned Madonna and Child* by the Maestro di Città di Castello (early 14th century); a *Martyrdom of St Sebastian* by Luca Signorelli (1497–8); a *Gonfalone della Santissima Trinità* by Raphael (1499); and a *Coronation of the Virgin* attributed to the workshop of Ghirlandaio (early 1500s). There is, also, a remarkable *Assumption of the Virgin* in terracotta from the workshop of Andrea della Robbia (early 16th century).

⬆ San Domenico
Largo Monsignor Muzi.
Open daily.
Between Piazza Garibaldi and the Pinacoteca is the church of San Domenico, the largest in the town. It was built by the Dominicans in the 15th century and later reworked, although the façade remains unfinished. Frescoes from the 15th century line the nave.

🏛 Pinacoteca Comunale
Via della Cannoniera 22.
Tel 075 855 4202.
Open 10am–1pm, 2:30–6:30pm Tue–Sun. 🖭 🖭 🖭
The Pinacoteca, one of the region's top art galleries, is housed in the **Palazzo Vitelli alla Cannoniera**, the most notable of the various Vitelli palazzi. It was built

Coronation of the Virgin, detail, Ghirlandaio workshop

Città di Castello Town Centre

① Duomo
② Palazzo Comunale
③ Palazzo del Podestà
④ San Francesco
⑤ Palazzo Vitelli a Porta Sant'Egidio
⑥ San Domenico
⑦ Pinacoteca Comunale

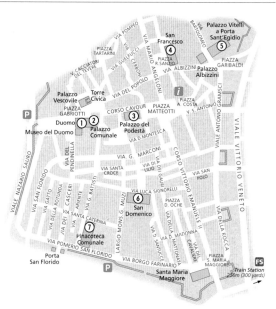

0 metres 250
0 yards 250

View of the verdant Upper Tiber Valley, from the medieval village of Montone

❷ Montone

Perugia. **Road Map** C2. 👥 1,500.
🚆 Umbertide, 13 km (8 miles), FCU
Perugia–Sansepolcro line. 🚌 ℹ️ Pro
Loco, Piazza Fortebraccio 1, 075 930
7019. 🌐 montone.info

Montone, 10 km (6 miles) from
Città di Castello, is one of the
most beautiful villages in Italy.
Built on two hilltops on the left
bank of the Tiber, it is the first
town of historical interest on the
road running south through
the Upper Tiber Valley. Founded
as a fortified site in the Middle
Ages (probably in the 11th
century), Montone is still enclosed
within a powerful circle of walls.
These are pierced by three gates:
Porta del Verziere, Porta di Borgo
Vecchio and Porta del Monte.
The names correspond to the
districts into which the castle
was once divided.

Montone was the birthplace
of Braccio Fortebraccio, better
known as Braccio da Montone
(1368–1424), who became
perhaps Umbria's greatest
condottiere (leader of a
mercenary army). He created
a genuine state, with Perugia as
its capital.

The medieval village is
beautifully preserved and,
furthermore, offers superb views.
There are several buildings of
interest. On the road leading
up to the centre of Montone
from the south is the church of
the **Madonna delle Grazie**
(16th century), as well as the
oldest church in the village,
the Romanesque **Pieve di San
Gregorio**, dating from the
11th century.

Beyond the walls, it is worth
visiting the Gothic church of
San Francesco (14th century),
at the top of the village. Along
with the attached monastery,
this is now home to the **Museo
Comunale**. The fine doorway is
made of inlaid wood (1519).
Inside, the single-nave building
contains several valuable works
of art by Bartolomeo Caporali.

Above the votive altar are frescoes
of the Fortebraccio family and
also a painting depicting the
Madonna del Soccorso.

The church, which contains
a splendid wooden choir dating
from the 16th century, once
housed a *Madonna in Gloria* by
Luca Signorelli. This is now in
the National Gallery in London.
The former monastery also
houses an ethnographic museum.

Students of Italian history
should consider visiting the
Archivio Storico Comunale, one
of the most important historical
archives in Umbria, with papal
bulls and other important
documents. It is housed in the
former convent of Santa Caterina,
at the southern end of the village.

🏛️ **Museo Comunale &
Museo Etnografico**
Ex Convento di San Francesco.
Tel 075 930 6535. **Open** Apr–Sep:
10:30am–1pm, 3:30–6pm Fri–Sun
(Jun–Sep: from 4pm); Oct–Mar:
10:30am–1pm, 3–5:30pm Sat & Sun.
Closed 1 Jan, 25 Dec 🐾 📷 ♿ 📷

Environs

The countryside around Montone
offers plenty of opportunities for
walking, particularly along the
course of the **Torrente Carpina**,
which skirts the village to the east
and joins the Tiber at Umbertide.
On its banks, 4 km (2 miles)
northwest of Montone, is the
splendid **Rocca d'Aries**, a fortress
with Byzantine origins. It was
renovated in the Renaissance
era and restored in the 1990s,
and is now open for concerts and
exhibitions. It offers marvellous
views over the Valle del Carpina.

A narrow, paved street in the heart of Montone

❸ Umbertide

Perugia. **Road Map** C2. 🚗 17,000.
🚆 FCU Perugia–Sansepolcro line.
🚌 ℹ️ IAT Alta Valle del Tevere, Via
Cibo 26, 075 941 7099.
🌐 **comune.umbertide.pg.it**

One of the principal centres
of the Upper Tiber Valley,
Umbertide is of ancient origin,
dating back to the 6th century
BC, and was probably founded
by the Etruscans. The town,
skirted to the west by the Tiber,
frequently found itself at the
centre of wars and suffered
the resulting destruction and
sackings. In 1863, the town's
traditional name of Fratta
was replaced by the name
Umbertide in honour of the
sons of Umberto Ranieri,
who rebuilt the city after the
devastation caused by the
Lombard invasions of AD 790.

Much more recently,
the centre of the old
town was badly
damaged by
bombardments
during World War II
(1944). Even so, many
important buildings
survive. Two of these
overlook the vast
Piazza Mazzini,
northwest of the
town centre: **La Rocca** (1385),
a fortress inserted into the
walls and now a centre for
contemporary art, and the
church of **Santa Maria della
Reggia**, begun in the second
half of the 16th century and
built on an octagonal plan.
The design was by Galeazzo
Alessi and Giulio Danti. Inside,
among the canvases that
decorate the tambour

The square and circular towers of the Rocca of Umbertide

The octagonal Santa Maria della Reggia

(the wall below the dome),
note the one above the organ,
an *Ascension to Heaven* by
Pomarancio (1578).

Other important works
to be found in the town's
churches include a fresco
by Pinturicchio (1504), in
the lunette of the
doorway to the church
of **Santa Maria
della Pietà** (north
of the old town,
outside the walls),
and, in particular,
a *Deposition* by Luca
Signorelli in the
Baroque church of
Santa Croce, in
the southern (and
oldest) part of the town, in
Piazza San Francesco. Due
to the importance of the
Signorelli painting – it is
the only one by the Cortona
artist still to be found in its
original setting – the church is
now a museum. In the same
square are two other churches:
San Francesco (13th–14th
centuries) and San Bernardino
(18th century).

🏛 **Santa Croce Museum**
Piazza San Francesco. **Tel** 075 942
0147. **Open** 10:30am–1pm, 3–5:30pm
Fri–Sun. **Closed** 1 Jan, 25 Dec. 🐾 📷

Environs

The countryside around
Umbertide is scattered with
fortifications, lasting evidence
of the region's great strategic
military importance. Along the
road to Preggio, 15 km (9 miles)
southwest of Umbertide, is
the **Rocca di Preggio**, one of
the principal strongholds in
the area, dating from the
10th century. Also of note
along this route are the castles
of **Romeggio and Polgeto**.

A short distance east of
Umbertide, towards Gubbio,
look out for the privately-owned
Castello di Civitella Ranieri
(15th century), which is one of
the most complete and best-
preserved examples of military
architecture in the area. Nearby,
but higher up, is the splendid
Castello di Serra Partucci.

Just north of Umbertide,
along the Città di Castello road,
you can see the tall tower of
another castle, the **Castello
di Montalto**.

A couple of kilometres
south of town, along the
River Tiber, a road climbs up
to the **Badia Monte Corona**,
a Romanesque abbey with
a beautiful underground
crypt. Climbing still higher,
you reach the 16th-century
hermitage and pretty village
of **San Giuliana**, set in a
panoramic position, and
restored to its medieval
appearance.

The churches of Santa Croce and San Francesco in Umbertide

❹ Gubbio

The sight of Gubbio, built from local stone at the foot of Monte Ingino, is one of the most famous images of medieval Umbria. Founded by the Umbri, the town holds the famous Eugubine Tablets, seven bronze slabs that survived from the ancient city of Iguvium; they were engraved in the 2nd century BC with text in the local language describing rites and sacred sites. Under the Romans the town spread onto the plain, but after the Lombards invaded the people returned to the slopes, where they could defend themselves more effectively. A walled city, including the monumental Palazzo dei Consoli, was built here in the Middle Ages. At the end of the 14th century, the city, by now powerful and rich, passed to the Montefeltro of Urbino. In 1624 Gubbio, like the Duchy of Urbino, came under papal rule.

The well-preserved 1st-century arcades of the Roman theatre

Exploring Gubbio

The easiest route into Gubbio is by the road from the south, which also provides a chance to admire the town as a whole, as it spreads out in horizontal swathes against the slopes of Monte Ingino. Before climbing up to explore one of the best-preserved medieval cities in the world, take a look at the ruins of the Roman city, which, during the stability of the *pax romana*, developed on the flat land below the slopes.

🏛 Roman Ruins

Via del Teatro Romano.
The first Roman monument that you see as you arrive in Gubbio from the south is a mausoleum, a monumental tomb of which the burial chamber has survived with its barrel vault. Further on, not far from Piazza Quaranta Martiri, are the ruins of the Roman theatre (Teatro Romano), which dates from

the 1st century. It could accommodate around 6,000 spectators, and was faced in squared and rusticated blocks. Among other works uncovered over the last two centuries of excavations are some beautiful mosaics.

🏛 Piazza Quaranta Martiri

This broad square is the principal point of arrival in Gubbio, as well as the best place to leave a car. It is dedicated to the 40 local people executed by the Germans in 1944 in an act of vengeance against the partisans. The lowest point in Gubbio, the piazza is a good place from which to gaze upwards to admire the full extent of the town.

Gubbio's finest church, **San Francesco**, dominates the piazza. Its construction was begun in the mid-1200s and continued at least until the end of that century (though the façade was never finished).

Inside are three aisles without a transept. There is a fresco cycle by Ottaviano Nelli in the apse chapel on the left (*Scenes from the Life of Mary*, c.1408–13). The frescoes in the central apse, by an unknown artist, can be dated to around 1275, but they are badly damaged.

On the opposite side of the piazza is the **Antico Ospedale** (Old Hospital) of Santa Maria della Misericordia, a 14th-century building, with a long portico in front, surmounted by a loggia, added in the 17th century by the wool merchants' guild, which used the premises for some of its processing. Nearby stands the church of **Santa Maria dei Laici**, dating back to 1313 and now restored.

🏛 San Giovanni Battista

Via della Repubblica. **Open** daily.
From Piazza Quaranta Martiri, the steep Via della Repubblica leads to the base of the great structure supporting Piazza Grande (*see p65*). Heading up this street, visitors enter the oldest part of the medieval city, where the first cathedral, dedicated to San Mariano, is believed to have stood. What is now the church dedicated to San Giovanni Battista (St John the Baptist) probably occupies the site of the old cathedral.

This church, built in the 13th and 14th centuries, has a Gothic façade with a Romanesque bell tower. The Gothic style continues inside, with characteristic

Gubbio, clinging to the lower slopes of Monte Ingino

The church of San Giovanni Battista, with Palazzo dei Consoli behind

VISITORS' CHECKLIST

Practical Information
Perugia. **Road Map** D2.
🏛 32,000. 🛈 Piazza Oderisi 6,
075 922 0693. 🎭 Corsa dei Ceri,
15 May; Palio della Balestra, last
Sun in May.

Transport
🚈 Fossato di Vico, 20 km
(12 miles), Roma–Ancona line,
892 021. 🚌

coupled columns and great arches in stone. The single -nave church culminates in a squared apse.

🏛 San Domenico
Piazza G. Bruno. **Open** daily.
Returning to Piazza Quaranta Martiri, turn into Via Cavour to enter the old quarter of San Martino, which is built on both sides of the River Camignano.

At the heart of this district, in Piazza Bruno, is the church of San Domenico, which was built by the Dominicans in the 14th century on the site of a 12th-century church dedicated to San Martino. The appearance of the interior dates primarily from a period of restoration during the 18th century, but 16th-century frescoes from the Gubbio school remain; there is also a fine lectern decorated with inlaid wood.

🚏 Via Gabrielli
This street, lined with medieval houses, runs north from Piazza Bruno to Porta Metauro. Near the end is the small but impressive **Palazzo del Capitano del Popolo**, whose façade curves in line with the road. Adorned with a series of small Gothic windows, the palazzo is a typical Gubbio construction from the late 13th century. Nearby is the park attached to the **Palazzo Ranghiaschi Brancaleoni**. Laid out in the mid-1800s, the garden extends south along the slopes of Monte Ingino as far as the Palazzo Ducale. There is a Neo-Classical temple here.

Sculpture on the tower of Palazzo Ranghiaschi Brancaleoni

Gubbio Town Centre

① Roman Ruins
② Piazza Quaranta Martiri
③ San Giovanni Battista
④ San Domenico
⑤ Via Gabrielli
⑥ Largo del Bargello
⑦ Palazzo dei Consoli
⑧ Palazzo Pretorio
⑨ Duomo
⑩ Palazzo Ducale
⑪ Via XX Settembre
⑫ Corso Garibaldi

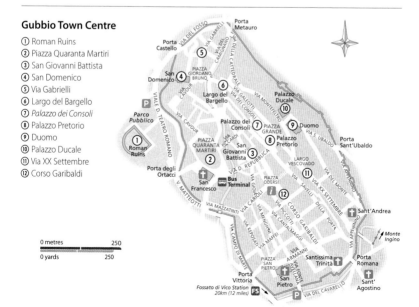

0 metres 250
0 yards 250

Fossato di Vico Station
20km (12 miles) 🚈

For keys to symbols see back flap

Gubbio: Palazzo dei Consoli

This superb building, begun in 1332, lords it over Piazza Grande and is supported on the west side by an impressive row of arched buttresses. The entrance doorway, approached by a fan-shaped flight of steps, is a masterly example of the Gothic style and is decorated with a lunette representing the *Madonna and Saints John the Baptist and Ubaldo*, patron saint of the city. The palazzo houses the Museo Civico and an art gallery. From the loggia there are fine views over the city and countryside around.

VISITORS' CHECKLIST

Practical Information
Piazza Grande. **Tel** 075 927 4298.
Open 10am–1pm, 3–6pm (Nov–Mar: 2:30–5:30pm) daily. **Closed**
1 Jan, 13–15 May, 25 Dec.

The tower is crowned with battlements and has four apertures echoing the form of the windows below.

Madonna and Child
This fresco by Mello da Gubbio from 1340–50 is one of the works on display in the Pinacoteca Civica (art gallery) on the first floor.

Arches, supporting the palazzo on the hill

The windows are set in pairs and decorated with a toothed cornice, which runs above the arches and unifies them.

Museo Civico, situated on the ground floor

In the Sala dell'Arengo, a magnificent room which occupies the entire floor area of the building, popular assemblies were held in the 14th century. Today fragments and stone tablets are displayed here.

Eugubine Tablets
These inscriptions in the old Umbrian language are on display in the Museo Civico. They provide crucial evidence of life in the region before the Roman conquest.

The Fontana dei Matti in Largo del Bargello

🏛 Largo del Bargello

About halfway along Via dei Consoli, which connects the San Martino quarter and Piazza Grande, the street broadens out to form Largo del Bargello, the centre of the ancient quarter of San Giuliano. In front of the 14th-century palazzo, after which the square is named, is the small **Fontana dei Matti**: tradition has it that in order to be defined as mad (*matto*), people had to run around the fountain three times bathing themselves in the water.

🏛 Piazza Grande

Via dei Consoli follows the route of the old Umbrian fortifications before suddenly opening out into Piazza Grande. Quite apart from the importance of the buildings found here, the square is an extremely impressive piece of engineering: it is, in fact, an artificial space supported by walls and embankments.

In front of the more famous and much larger Palazzo dei Consoli is the **Palazzo Pretorio** (closed to the public), which was erected in the mid-14th century and designed by the same architect, Gattapone. On the last Sunday in May the traditional Palio della Balestra (involving the crossbowmen of Gubbio and Sansepolcro, over the border in Tuscany), takes place between the two buildings.

🏛 Duomo

Via Galeotti. **Open** daily.

From Piazza Grande, Via Galeotti climbs in a series of steps to the cathedral. This was founded in 1229 and enlarged around a century later. The façade has an entrance with an ogival arch and an oculus with bas-reliefs which belonged to the previous church on the site. Inside, the single nave is covered by a very high and distinctive stone "wagon vault", a local architectural speciality. There are many frescoes and other paintings, as well as some fine stained-glass windows.

🏛 Palazzo Ducale

Via Federico di Montefeltro.
Tel 075 927 5872. **Open** 8:30am–7pm Tue–Sun. **Closed** 1 Jan, 25 Dec. 🎫

The restored Palazzo Ducale stands right in front of the cathedral. Locally known as the Corte Nuova, it was built by the Montefeltro family after they had taken possession of the town. The palazzo has an interesting archaeological area underground (where it is possible to see traces of the piazza that was here before the palazzo was built) as well as several rooms used for temporary exhibitions.

🏛 Via XX Settembre

From Piazza Grande, Via XX Settembre leads past palazzi and churches to the quarter of Sant'Andrea and the **Porta Romana**. This medieval town gate, with its high tower, houses a collection of majolica pottery and other pieces in various materials, as well as weaponry, maps and so on.

The medieval Porta Romana

Nearby, outside the walls, is the church of **Sant'Agostino**, which retains traces of frescoes dating back to the church's foundation (1294), as well as several works dating from the 14th century.

A short walk east of the church is the terminal for the funicular up to the **Basilica di Sant'Ubaldo**, which lies high above the town on Monte Ingino. The ride takes 8 minutes and offers lovely views on the way; there is also a path, if you prefer to go up on foot.

🏛 Corso Garibaldi

This street runs parallel with the quarter of Sant'Andrea and is the main thoroughfare through the San Pietro quarter, the busy centre of Gubbio. The narrow streets retain a village atmosphere and are lined with shops. On Corso Garibaldi itself look out for the churches of **Santissima Trinità** and of **San Pietro**, of 13th-century origin and built close to a large monastery complex.

The Festa Dei Ceri

The Corsa dei Ceri (candle race), considered within Umbria almost as great a spectacle as Siena's Palio, takes place every year on 15 May. The finishing line is the hilltop basilica of Sant'Ubaldo. The "candles" in question, three in all, are heavy wooden and papier-mâché structures in the form of superimposed prisms, 10 m (33 ft) high and 200 kg (440 lb) in weight. They bear the effigies of Sant'Ubaldo, St George and St Anthony Abbot, patron saints of masons and stonecutters, craftsmen and peasants respectively. The first drumroll is heard at dawn, but the *ceri* are not brought out until noon. The actual race, which attracts huge crowds, takes place in the evening.

The heavy wooden "candles" carried aloft over the crowd

❺ Parco Regionale del Monte Cucco

On the border with the neighbouring region of Le Marche, Monte Cucco is one of the most fascinating peaks in central Italy. Below ground are miles and miles of galleries and caverns, which form one of the most impressive cave systems in Italy: the Grotta di Monte Cucco. The higher altitudes can be reached from the village of Costacciaro, and the windswept terrain attracts devoted fans of hang-gliding. Within the park, which is centred around the village of Sigillo, various hiking trails have been marked out. There are also facilities for various open-air sports. Besides paragliding, the park can arrange exploration of the Forra di Riofreddo gorge (for experts only), and there are also mountain-bike trails and tracks for runners. Many palaeontological and archaeological finds have been discovered in the park, as well as ancient Roman settlements.

Scheggia

From this village of Roman origin it is possible to enter and explore the northern part of the park, with its Benedictine abbeys – in particular, Sant'Emiliano at Isola Fossara and the Hermitage of San Girolamo a Pascelupo.

Costacciaro

Unlike the other villages that surround the park, which are almost all of Roman origin, Costacciaro was built in 1250 by the citizens of Gubbio as a fortified town.

The "Natives" of Monte Cucco

Wildcat

Besides all kinds of opportunities for sport, the Parco Regionale del Monte Cucco is also one of the best places in the Apennines for observing wildlife. In fact, as well as being home to typically Apennine species (such as deer, wild boar, porcupines and martens), the park also harbours other species that are increasingly rare in central Italy, including the wolf, wildcat and golden eagle. Among other birds that can be seen in the park are partridges, quails, eagle owls and kingfishers. Crayfish can also be found in the rivers.

Golden eagle

0 kilometres   2
0 miles   1

Summit of Monte Cucco
At 1,566m (5,136ft), Monte Cucco is one of the highest peaks in Umbria. It can be reached fairly easily along the scenic Via del Ranco, which leads out of Sigillo.

Badia di Sitria ③

Isola Fossara

S360

Casacc ●

④

Montebollo ●

Pian delle Macinare

Monte Cucco 1,566m

Ranco ●

S3

jillo

Purello ●

Valico di Fossato

Perugia

Gualdo Tadino

VISITORS' CHECKLIST

Practical Information
Perugia. **Road Map** D2.
i Ente Parco, Via Matteotti 52, Sigillo, 075 917 7326. **W parks.it**

Transport
FS Fossato di Vico, Rome–Ancona line, 892 021.

Key
 Major road
Minor road
Scenic route

Grotta di Monte Cucco
This cave can be reached on foot from the car park just beyond Val di Ranco. The cave reaches the record depth of 922 m (3,024 ft) and the water that gathers within the mountain emerges, after a lengthy subterranean journey, at the Scirca spring near Sigillo.

KEY

① **At Scirca**, ruins of a large Roman settlement have been uncovered. In the village, the old church of Santa Maria Assunta is decorated with frescoes by Matteo da Gualdo.

② **La Valdorbia**

③ **The Badia di Sitria** is an abbey with an interesting Romanesque church (Santa Maria) with a single nave and a barrel vault. The crypt is held up at the centre by a Roman column with a Corinthian capital.

④ **The Forra di Riofreddo**, is a deep, narrow gorge, which can only be tackled by experienced climbers. It was formed after many centuries of erosion by streams coming down from the mountain top.

Sigillo
Home to the park administration, this village has visible Roman origins, in the bridges on the Via Flaminia and over the Scirca torrent. Of note are the church of Sant'Agostino, in the heart of the village, and Sant'Anna, near the cemetery, with frescoes by Matteo da Gualdo.

For keys to symbols *see back flap*

6 Gualdo Tadino

Perugia. **Road Map** D3. 🚗 15,000.
🚆 Foligno–Ancona line. 🚌 Piazza
Orti Mavarelli. ℹ️ Associazione Pro
Tadino, Piazza Martiri della Libertà,
075 9150 263.

Gualdo Tadino, a town
of ancient Umbrian and
Roman origins, endured
a tormented history of
defeats, destruction
and emigration until
the 12th century, when
it was resettled on its
present site. The name
is a combination of the
Roman name *Tadinum*
and the Lombard word
wald, meaning forest.

As a commune, the
village took shape in
the Middle Ages, but
was heavily modified
over the course of the
centuries and today
bears only a few traces of its
centuries-old history. Gualdo
suffered terrible damage during
the 1997 earthquake, but
has now been almost totally
restored. The town is still, as
it was in the Middle Ages and
later centuries, one of the
principal centres of majolica
manufacture in Umbria.

The only ancient gate to
survive in Gualdo is that of San
Benedetto, on the eastern side:
from here, Corso Italia (which
becomes Corso Piave) cuts
through the whole of the
historic centre. Walking along
this street, you reach Piazza XX
Settembre, home to the
churches of **San Donato** (12th
century) and **Santa Maria dei
Raccomandati** (13th century).
The latter contains a fine
triptych by Matteo da Gualdo
of the *Madonna with Child and
saints Sebastian and Roch*, but
is closed to the public.

Further along, on Corso Piave,
is the church of **San Francesco**,
built by the Franciscans in the
13th and 14th centuries. It has
a beautiful façade, with an
elegant Gothic doorway, and
inside are many frescoes, most
of which are the work of Matteo
da Gualdo (1435–1507), the
best-known artist native to
Gualdo Tadino, whose works

*Fresco on a palazzo
in the centre
of Gualdo*

can also be seen in Assisi and
Spoleto. The fresco on the first
pilaster on the left, of *St Anne,
the Virgin and Child*, is said to
be the oldest work by the artist.
You soon arrive at the central
Piazza Martiri della Libertà,
better known to the residents
of Gualdo as Piazza
Grande, and where the
town's most important
buildings are found.
Lording it over the
space is the **Palazzo
Comunale**. The
original, 12th-century
palazzo was rebuilt
after a terrible
earthquake in 1751,
so what is seen now is
its 18th-century form.
Most of the town's
medieval buildings
collapsed during the
same earthquake,
and the **Palazzo del
Podestà** (13th century), in
front of the Palazzo
Comunale, was also
badly damaged. An
international ceramics
exhibition and
competition is held
annually in the Palazzo
del Podestà, which
brings dozens of ceramic
workers back to Gualdo,
a centre for the
manufacture of lustreware.

The cathedral of **San
Benedetto** stands on the
eastern side of Piazza Martiri.
The façade, dating from the
13th century but carefully
restored after the earthquake,
has three doors – one for each
of the aisles inside – and a
beautiful rose window. The
interior was entirely rebuilt in
the 19th century, and has

*Detail of a
fountain*

20th-century frescoes. Outside,
to the left, stands a lovely
Renaissance fountain. The only
building that remained intact
after the earthquake, and that is
still visible in the piazza today,
is the **Torre Civica**.

In common with many other
villages in this part of Umbria,
Gualdo Tadino has a fortress at
the top of the hill. The origins
of the **Rocca Flea** date back to
the 10th century, when the
construction of fortifications
began on the site of a church,
of which several frescoes have
been uncovered. Today, the
sizeable fortress has more than
40 rooms – the result of a series
of enlargements and restoration work carried out over
the centuries. In particular, the
buildings show the influence
of Frederick II, who restored and
made improvements to the
castle during the 13th century,
and also of the Perugians,
who made changes in
the following century.
The Rocca, which has
reopened after several
years of closure,
houses a **Pinacoteca**
(art gallery), a ceramics
gallery and a collection
of archaeological finds.
The former has on
display detached
frescoes by Matteo da Gualdo
as well as works by Jacopo
Palma, Antonio da Fabriano
and Niccolò Alunno.

🏰 Rocca Flea

Piazza della Rocca. **Tel** 075 914 2445.
Open Apr, May & Oct–Dec:
10am–1pm, 3–6pm Thu–Sun; Jun–
Sep: 10am–1pm, 3–7pm Tue–Sun;
Jan–Mar: 10am–1pm, 3–6pm Fri– Sun.
Closed 1 Jan, 25 Dec. ♿ 📷

The fortified bulk of Rocca Flea, guarding the town

Environs

About 7 km (4 miles) north of Gualdo Tadino is **Fossato di Vico**, a town that is divided into two parts: Fossato Basso, the largely modern town along the road, and Fossato Alto, the remnants of a major medieval settlement perched on a rocky spur. It is worth stopping off along the road between the two parts, at the church of San Benedetto, in order to see the frescoes by Matteo da Gualdo.

In the heart of Fossato Basso are covered walkways and the Cappella della Piaggiola, with frescoes by Ottaviano Nelli and his school (early 15th century).

Nocera Umbra, devastated by the 1997 earthquake but being rebuilt

Porta Vecchia, ancient entrance to the old centre of Nocera Umbra

❼ Nocera Umbra

Perugia. **Road Map** D3. ⛰ 6,000.
🚆 Nocera Scalo, 3 km (2 miles), Rome–Ancona line. 🛈 Pro Loco, Via San Renaldo 9, 348 736 4629. 🎉 Palio dei Quartieri, first Tue in Aug.

The collapse of the Torre di Nocera Umbra, now rebuilt, during the earthquake of 1997 was an enduring image of that tragic natural disaster. The town has been hit by earthquakes on a number of occasions, but never with such ferocity. The structural damage affected the whole of the historic centre, formerly one of the best-preserved in the region. Even now, only a small number of inhabitants have returned. Yet Nocera Umbra is a hive of activity – houses are being rebuilt, while historic buildings

are gradually being restored. The symbolic tower has already been reconstructed.

High on a rocky outcrop that looms over fertile valleys drained by the Topino and Caldognola rivers, Nocera Umbra has always occupied a strategically significant location, thanks partly to the town's position on the border of Le Marche and to its proximity to the Adriatic Sea. Originally an ancient Umbrian town (called Nuokria), it was an important settlement under both the Romans and the Lombards. The waters that gush from the many springs in the area are known for their curative properties.

Most of the important buildings in Nocera Umbra are still closed for safety reasons, including the **Duomo**, on the top of the hill. The same is true of the historic centre, although visitors are allowed access to the heart of the old town, Piazza Caprera. The former church of

San Francesco, now home to the Pinacoteca Comunale and Museo Civico, can be found on this square at No. 5. It is open Tuesdays to Sundays from April to September, and at weekends during the rest of the year. It is also worth going as far as the western walls to the church of **San Filippo**, a Neo-Gothic structure from the late 19th century. This marks the start of the Portici di San Filippo, a covered walkway within the walls, which has apertures and arrow-slits that enable visitors to admire the views.

Environs

The peak of **Monte Pennino** (1,571 m/5,155 ft), on the Le Marche border, is reachable from Nocera Umbra by car along 20 km (12 miles) of tortuous road (asphalted, apart from the last stretch). This mountain, as well as being a very scenic place to visit, has facilities for hiking and skiing.

The Waters of Nocera

The therapeutic quality of the mineral water springs in the Nocera area has been known since the 16th century; in the 18th century the water was used as a benchmark for measuring the purity of other waters. However, it wasn't until the 20th century that the spring waters began to be exploited for economic and industrial use, through the building of bottling plants and spas. The two main springs are at Bagni di Nocera and at Schiagni (Fonte del Cacciatore). Their curative powers derive from the combination of a water that is particularly pure and mineral-rich in itself, and the clay typical of this terrain.

The modern spa at Bagni di Nocera

❽ Parco Regionale del Monte Subasio

In outline, Monte Subasio (1,290 m/4,230 ft) has a distinctively rounded form. It rises, isolated, between the historic centres of Assisi, Spello and Nocera Umbra and, since 1995, has formed the southern margin of a 7,442-ha (18,390-acre) regional park. As well as its own natural beauty, Monte Subasio offers superb views across to the high Appenines in the east. The park also includes many places of historic and religious significance. Subasio's distinctive rose-coloured stone was used to build much of Assisi, which lies right on the fringes of the park. The mountain was regarded as a sacred place in the 10th century BC, and its importance endured during the life of St Francis, who perhaps drew inspiration from these magical and mystical surroundings.

Monte Subasio
The summit of Monte Subasio is easily reached and seems to offer a view of the whole of Umbria. To the southeast are the sink-holes known as *"mortaro grande"* and *"mortaro piccolo"*, cavities which were once used for collecting ice.

Eremo delle Carceri
Around 4 km (2 miles) from Assisi, this small and peaceful hermitage is surrounded by dense woodland. The name (Hermitage of the Prisons) derives from the fact that Franciscan friars used to "lock themselves away" here in order to pray: there is still a 15th-century church here, as well as a cave where St Francis would go to rest. Beyond the hermitage is a bridge that leads to a wood containing a series of caves and hermitages used in the Middle Ages by the devout and by friars.

KEY

① **I Prati degli Stazzi**, on the road between the Eremo delle Carceri and the peak, offer fine views over Assisi. In May, the fields are carpeted in flowers.

② **The northern road**, leaves Assisi near Cà Piombino, base for the park administration. Before winding its way south towards Spello, the road goes through the small historic centres of Armenzano, San Giovanni and Collepino.

③ **The Abbey of San Silvestro**, dates from the 11th century. According to tradition, it was built by San Romualdo, founder of the Camaldolese order.

Piano di Pieve

Téscio

S444

Assisi

S147

Perugia

Monte Subasio (1,290m)

San Damiano

San Vitale

Road to the summit
Between Assisi and Spello the road retraces the route of an ancient cart track. A lovely scenic road, it leads almost to the peak of Monte Subasio. On the descent towards Spello, the road passes the sanctuary of the Madonna della Spella.

0 kilometres 2
0 miles 2

Key
▭ Minor road
▬ Scenic route

Rocca di Postignano
Within the park is the ancient fortification of Rocca Postignano, as well as several churches that were built on the site of places where hermits once prayed.

VISITORS' CHECKLIST

Practical Information
Perugia. **Road Map** C2. 🛈 Loc Cà Piombino, 06081 Assisi, 075 815 5290. Fax: 075 815 307. 🗔 **parks.it**

Transport
🚆 Santa Maria degli Angeli, Assisi, Foligno–Terontola line, 892021. 🚌 APM Assisi–Eremo delle Carceri, 800 512 141.

Wildlife on Monte Subasio

The slopes of the mountain are today covered with three different kinds of vegetation. Olive trees are grown on land stretching from Assisi as far as Spello. Other areas support mixed woodland, including oak, black hornbeam, ash, maple, beech and holm oak.

A pair of porcupines

Forests of resiniferous trees, the result of replanting, characterize the third type of vegetation, along with meadow pasture. This range of natural habitats does not support a wide variety of wildlife, however, despite a ban on hunting lasting several decades: the golden eagle has not been seen since the 1960s. Current wildlife sightings include the partridge, wood pigeon, magpie, jay, wildcat, squirrel, porcupine, badger, wolf, weasel, stone marten and wild boar. Birds of prey seen here include the buzzard and goshawk.

Bandita
Cilleni

Santa
Maria
Lignano

Castello di Armenzano
During the Middle Ages, this place was fortified because it occupied a strategic position. Today, the village offers peace and fine views.

Armenzano ●

Nocera Umbra

San Giovanni ●

③

Madonna della
Spella

Collepino ●

Spello

Collepino
About 10 km (6 miles) from the peak of Monte Subasio, this walled medieval village stands isolated near the source of the river Chiona.

For keys to symbols *see back flap*

ⓐ Assisi

Even without the churches, extraordinary frescoes and associations with St Francis, it would be worth coming to Assisi simply to witness a sunset. As the sun sinks, the medieval centre of Assisi, one of the best-preserved in the world, is bathed in a warm glow. Founded by the Umbrians, Assisi was prominent during the Roman era, but the town achieved greatest fame and importance during the era of the communes in the Middle Ages. By the time the Basilica of San Francesco was founded in the 13th century, Assisi, built using the reddish stone of Monte Subasio to which the town owes its distinctive coloration, had already taken shape. In the 14th century, when Assisi came under papal rule, two fortresses were built. Over the following centuries, the city changed little. Even today, the town has a timeless fascination.

View of the Basilica di San Francesco

Palazzo del Capitano del Popolo

Temple of Minerva

Basilica of San Francesco (see pp76–7)

VIA PORTICA

PIAZZA D COMUNE

Monastery of San Giuseppe

VIA BANDA DA QUINTAVAL

VIA PORTA MOIAN

Santa Maria Maggiore
This church was Assisi's first cathedral. Its Romanesque origins are clear from its formal simplicity.

Porta Moiano

Palazzo Vescovile is where Francis renounced all worldly goods. The bishop's palace was entirely rebuilt in the 17th century.

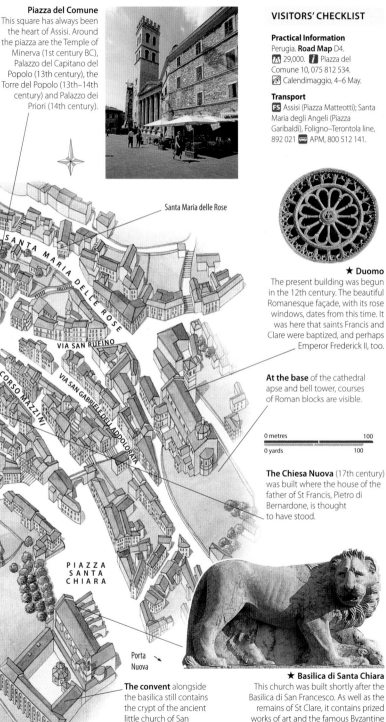

Piazza del Comune
This square has always been the heart of Assisi. Around the piazza are the Temple of Minerva (1st century BC), Palazzo del Capitano del Popolo (13th century), the Torre del Popolo (13th–14th century) and Palazzo dei Priori (14th century).

Santa Maria delle Rose

VIA SANTA MARIA DELLE ROSE

VIA SAN RUFINO

VIA SAN GABRIELE DELL'ADDOLORATA

CORSO MAZZINI

PIAZZA SANTA CHIARA

Porta Nuova

The convent alongside the basilica still contains the crypt of the ancient little church of San Giorgio, in the cloister.

VISITORS' CHECKLIST

Practical Information
Perugia. **Road Map** D4.
🚉 29,000. **ℹ** Piazza del Comune 10, 075 812 534.
📅 Calendimaggio, 4–6 May.

Transport
🚆 Assisi (Piazza Matteotti); Santa Maria degli Angeli (Piazza Garibaldi), Foligno–Terontola line, 892 021 🚌 APM, 800 512 141.

★ **Duomo**
The present building was begun in the 12th century. The beautiful Romanesque façade, with its rose windows, dates from this time. It was here that saints Francis and Clare were baptized, and perhaps Emperor Frederick II, too.

At the base of the cathedral apse and bell tower, courses of Roman blocks are visible.

| 0 metres | 100 |
| 0 yards | 100 |

The Chiesa Nuova (17th century) was built where the house of the father of St Francis, Pietro di Bernardone, is thought to have stood.

★ **Basilica di Santa Chiara**
This church was built shortly after the Basilica di San Francesco. As well as the remains of St Clare, it contains prized works of art and the famous Byzantine Crucifix of San Damiano.

Exploring Assisi

The draw of Assisi's famous Basilica can be overpowering, but there is much else to explore in the town. Motorists would do best to leave their car in the huge car park in Largo Properzio, just outside the walls, and to enter the historic centre through Porta Nuova, on the southeastern side of town. From here, Via Borgo Aretino leads to Assisi's first great building, the basilica of Santa Chiara. This lies in the heart of a medieval quarter, which is linked by steep streets to the upper town, dating from Roman times and home to the Duomo and Piazza del Comune. From this central piazza, continue along Via Seminario and Via San Francesco, lined with medieval buildings, to reach the great basilica of St Francis *(see pp76–7).*

Baptismal font in the cathedral of San Rufino

The door and rose window of the basilica of Santa Chiara

🔼 Santa Chiara

Piazza Santa Chiara. **Tel** 075 812 282. **Open** 6:30am–noon, 2–7pm (6pm in winter).

Assisi's second great church was begun in 1257, and consecrated eight years later by Pope Clement IV: the body of St Clare (declared a saint in 1255), founder of the order of the Poor Clares, was buried here in 1260.

The façade has a simple doorway with a rose window above, while the side that faces the street is supported by three vast buttresses. The church is distinctive because of the use of alternating layers of white and red stone, as seen in some Tuscan churches.

The interior is in the form of a Latin cross, simple and spare. In the right transept there is a cycle of frescoes depicting *Scenes from the Life of St Clare,* by an unknown artist called the Master of Santa

Chiara (late 13th century). Other interesting frescoes, from the 14th century, can be found on the left wall, while on the right, in the Oratorio delle Reliquie, there is the late 12th-century wooden Crucifix of San Damiano. According to the hagiography, this is the crucifix that famously spoke to Francis in San Damiano, asking him to "repair his church" *(see p84).*

🔼 Duomo (San Rufino)

Piazza San Rufino. **Tel** 075 816 016, 075 812 283. **Open** summer: 8am–1pm, 2–6pm daily; winter: 8am–1pm, 3–7pm daily (holy week, Aug & the day before public hols: 7am–7pm).

From Santa Chiara, a climb up stepped streets leads to the duomo, built on a Roman religious site in around 1029 by Archbishop Ugone, and then rebuilt in the 12th–13th centuries. The church was consecrated in 1253, the year construction was completed, by Pope Innocent IV.

Less well-known than the other basilicas of Assisi, the cathedral is worth a visit just for its splendid

façade, a masterpiece of Umbrian Romanesque. It is divided into three horizontal sections. At ground level are three doors decorated with lions, with bas-relief lunettes; above, divided from the lower level by a band of sculpted corbels, are three rose windows with symbols of the Evangelists. At the top is a triangular tympanum with a Gothic arch. To one side, rising above the scene, is the bell tower, part of the 11th-century church and with double-mullioned windows.

The interior, laid out on a rectangular plan, dates from the 16th century. It still has the old baptismal font where both St Francis and St Clare were baptized, a wooden choir dating from the 16th century and the underground Franciscan oratory, where the saint would withdraw before preaching to the crowd. The Cappella del Sacramento, by Giacomo Giorgetti, is a Baroque composition on the theme of the Eucharist.

View of Assisi, with its walls and fortifications, from Monte Subasio

Adjacent to the church is the **Museo della Cattedrale** (cathedral museum), which contains pieces from the original church, a series of frescoes from the Oratorio di San Rufinuccio and paintings from various churches in Assisi. To the left of the church are the ruins of a Roman theatre and, a little further north, those of an amphitheatre. In the church courtyard a plaque shows the site of the house where St Clare was born.

🔲 Piazza del Comune

From the cathedral, heading along Via di San Rufino, you reach the square that has always been the true heart of the city. It was created in its current form in the 13th century. The main focus of the piazza is the **Temple of Minerva**, built in the 1st century BC on a set of terraces that once marked the centre of the town. This beautifully preserved Roman temple has changed function at various times over the centuries: first a church, then a group of shops, then seat of the town hall until, in 1456, it finally became a church again, with the name of Santa Maria sopra Minerva.

On the left of the temple portico is the **Palazzo del Capitano del Popolo**, built in the 13th century and extensively restored in the 20th century. At the foot of the bell tower (Torre del Popolo), you can see the 14th-century measures for bricks, tiles and fabrics then in use in Assisi,

The late Renaissance façade of the Chiesa Nuova

set into the wall. On the opposite side of the piazza is the **Palazzo dei Priori**, begun in 1275 and completed in the late 15th century. On the right is the Arco della Volta Pinta, with 16th-century frescoes. The Fonte di Piazza, at the far end of the square, is an 18th-century fountain built on the foundations of a 13th-century water basin.

A brief descent through the Arco dei Priori leads to the 17th-century **Chiesa Nuova**, which was commissioned by Philip III of Spain to mark the spot where St Francis was said to have been born.

🏛 Temple of Minerva

Piazza del Comune. **Tel** 075 812 268. **Open** 7:15am–7pm Mon–Sat; 8:15am–7pm Sun & public hols. **Closed** 2–5:15pm Tue, Fri.

⛪ Chiesa Nuova

Piazzetta Chiesa Nuova. **Tel** 075 812 339. **Open** 6:30am–noon, 2:30–6pm (winter: 5pm).

🏛 Museo and Foro Romano

Via Portica 2. **Tel** 075 813 053. **Open** mid-Mar–mid-Oct: 10am–1pm, 2–6pm daily; mid-Oct–mid-Mar: 10am–1pm, 2–5pm daily. 🖼

On the corner of Piazza del Comune, beyond the Arco del Seminario – the ancient limit of the walled city in the Roman era – is a museum of Roman finds. From the museum, visitors can gain access to the ruins of what may have been the Roman forum, beneath the Piazza del Comune.

⛪ Via San Francesco

Heading towards the Basilica di San Francesco, you cover the whole length of Via del Seminario, which becomes Via San Francesco. Along the way you pass the **Palazzo Giacobetti** (17th century) and, opposite, the delightful **Oratorio dei Pellegrini** (15th century), once part of a

The Loggia dei Maestri Comacini, on Via San Francesco

Madonna in Maestà

pilgrim's hospice, followed by the arches of the Portico del Monte Frumentario, part of a 13th-century hospital. Next comes the Palazzo Vallemani, which is the temporary home of the **Pinacoteca Comunale**; the art gallery's most important work is probably the *Madonna in Maestà* (Giotto school), found near the entrance. A little further along is the **Loggia dei Maestri Comacini**, a 13th-century *palazzetto* which, according to tradition, was the seat of the Lombard rulers; it is adorned with 15th-century coats of arms. Nearby, the steep Vicolo di Sant'Andrea climbs up to the Piazza di Santa Margherita, from where there are classic views towards the Basilica di San Francesco. It is especially moving at sunset or at dawn.

⛪ Oratorio dei Pellegrini

Via San Francesco 13. **Tel** 075 812 267. **Open** 10am–noon, 4–6pm Tue–Sat.

🏛 Pinacoteca Comunale

Palazzo Vallemani, Via San Francesco 10. **Tel** 075 815 5234. **Open** mid-Mar–mid-Oct: 10am–1pm, 2–6pm; mid-Oct–mid-Mar: 10am–1pm, 2–5pm. 🖼

Assisi: Basilica di San Francesco

St Francis died on 4 October 1226. Just 18 months later Frate Elia, Vicar-General of the Franciscan Order, was charged by Pope Gregory IX with building a church dedicated to the saint. After the laying of the first stone, the Lower Church was the first part to take shape; the Upper Church was eventually built on top of it. The basilica was consecrated by Pope Innocent IV in 1253, though the chapel of Santa Caterina, the final stage in the basilica's construction, was not completed until 1367. Some of the greatest artists of the age, including Cimabue and Giotto, left their mark on the building. On 26 September 1997, a severe earthquake badly damaged the church: part of the vault collapsed and cracks appeared in the transept. Just two years later, however, the basilica reopened for visits and worship, the culmination of an exceptional feat of restoration.

★ **Quattro Vele**
The celebrated allegorical frescoes of the Quattro Vele (vault above the altar), in the Lower Church, represent *The Three Virtues of St Francis*. Long attributed to Giotto, they are now thought to be the work of one of his assistants. A detail of the *Allegory of Obedience* is shown here.

KEY

① **The Tomb of St Francis**, in the crypt, was discovered only in 1818. The exact location had never been revealed for fear that someone might want to seize such a precious relic. The remains of the saint were transferred here in 1230, before the basilica was finished.

② **The wooden choir**, situated in the apse and on the sides next to the crossing, is an example of Gothic Renaissance engraving and inlaid wood, the work of Domenico Indovini.

③ **The walls of the transept**, are decorated with an outstanding cycle of frescoes painted by Cimabue and his assistants. The Crucifixion in the left transept is superb.

④ **The façade**, is an example of Italian Gothic. It has a double rose window in Cosmatesque style and a double door.

⑤ **The Cappella di San Martino**, the first on the left in the Lower Church, was decorated by Simone Martini (1312–1320). His frescoes, depicting several saints and a cycle illustrating the *Life of St Martin*, are true masterpieces.

★ **Frescoes in the Crossing**
The left side of the crossing was decorated by Pietro Lorenzetti in 1515–20. This is one of two portraits of the *Madonna and Child*.

Frescoes in the Nave
The vault in the nave is decorated with frescoes by various masters, one of whom may have been the young Giotto. The vault in the first bay represents the Four Doctors of the Church working in their studies, each with an assistant. St Augustine is shown here.

VISITORS' CHECKLIST

Practical Information
Piazza San Francesco. **Tel** 075 819 001. **Open** Upper Church: 8:30am– 6:50pm (to 6pm Nov–Easter). Lower Church: 6:30am–6:50pm (Nov–Easter: 6pm). ✝ at the Tomb of St Francis: 7:15am Mon–Fri (075 819 0084 for bookings).
w **sanfrancescoassisi.org**

Interior of the Upper Church
The bright, soaring, single-nave Upper Church is typical of Franciscan monastic architecture. It takes the forms of French Gothic, but simplifies them and adds local elements. It was intended to symbolize the asceticism and spirituality that characterized the life of St Francis.

Entrance to the Upper Church

Entrance to the Lower Church

★ **Life of St Francis**
The frescoes on the lower walls of the nave (1290s), long thought to be by Giotto and his assistants, are now attributed by most specialists to a superb unknown artist, often referred to as the Maestro di San Francesco.

Assisi: The Frescoes in the Basilica

It was not without controversy that Frate Elia erected such a grandiose building to hold the relics of a saint who had preached poverty. It appears that two buildings, one above the other, were envisaged from the very beginning, although the exact date of the commencement of work on the Upper Church is not known. The Lower Church, both smaller and simpler, was to function as the saint's burial place and to accommodate pilgrims, while the Upper Church was for regular worship. The speed with which the work was carried out evidently did not allow for much sculptural decoration, and the vast plain walls seemed designed for impressive cycles of frescoes, on which the greatest painters of the age could work. Together they created one of the finest and most loved monuments in the history of Western art.

Lower Church

Austere and rather gloomy, the Lower Church shows the influence of the Romanesque style. The solemnity is lightened by the wonderfully rich pictorial decoration, which is less famous than the decoration in the Upper Church, but more representative of Italian art of the time, given the number and quality of the artists who worked here.

Detail from the *Deposition*, Pietro Lorenzetti

Main Frescoes in the Lower Church
Walls
Maestro di San Francesco.
Left: *Stories from the Life of St Francis*; Right: *Scenes from the Passion* (c.1260, much damaged, only half visible).
Quattro Vele (vault above the altar)
Maestro delle Vele.
Apotheosis of St Francis; Allegory of Obedience; Allegory of Poverty; Allegory of Chastity (c.1315–20).
Right Transept
Vaults:
Workshop of Giotto.
Infancy and Adolescence of Jesus (c.1315–20).
West and north walls:
Workshop of Giotto.
Posthumous Miracles of St Francis (c.1320).

East wall:
Cimabue. *Enthroned Madonna with Angels and St Francis* (c.1280); Giotto (?), *Crucifixion* (c.1320); Simone Martini, *Madonna with Child and two Magi Kings* (c.1321–6).
Cappella di San Nicola:
Simone Martini, Giotto.
Saints Francis, Louis of Toulouse, Elizabeth of Hungary, Clare and an Unknown Saint (c.1321–6).

Left Transept
Entirely frescoed by Pietro Lorenzetti and workshop (c.1315–20).
Barrel vault:
Entry into Jerusalem; The Last Supper; Washing of the Feet; Expulsion from the Temple; Ascent to Calvary; Flagellation; Crucifixion.
South wall:
Descent from the Cross; Deposition; Descent into Limbo; Resurrection.
East wall:
Crucifixion; Madonna and Child; St Francis and St John the Evangelist.
West wall:
Death of Judas; St Francis receives the stigmata.
Cappella di San Giovanni Battista:
Madonna with Child and Sts Francis and John the Baptist.
Cappella di San Martino di Tours (first on the left) Entirely frescoed by Simone Martini (c.1321–6). Figures of saints and cycle of frescoes depicting the *Life of St Martin.*

Upper Church

The Upper Church is as airy and light as the Lower Church is low and dark. Its pictorial decoration is divided substantially into two main blocks: the frescoes of the apse, transept and the crossing, by Cimabue and his school; and those of the nave and vaults, where the life of St Francis and episodes from the Old and New Testament are portrayed in one of the world's great masterpieces.

Madonna and Child, Pietro Lorenzetti, detail, Lower Church

◀ The interior of the Upper Church, Basilica di San Francesco, Assisi (pre-1997 earthquake)

Frescoes in the Apse and the Transepts
Cimabue and his school (1280).
Left Transept
Crucifixion; Scenes from the Apocalypse; Michael and the Angels.
Main Apse
Scenes from the Life of the Virgin Mary.
Right Transept
The Apostles.
Crossing
The Evangelists.

Detail, *Dream of the Throne*, from the Life of St Francis cycle

Frescoes in the Nave
Scenes from the Life of St Francis, either by Giotto or the Maestro di San Francesco; the upper register and vaults by Cimabue and others.

Detail from *Miracle of the Spring*, 14th scene, Giotto cycle

Life of St Francis

I	Francis honoured in the piazza
II	Gift of the Cloak
III	Dream of Arms
IV	Prayer in San Damiano
V	Renounces worldly goods
VI	Dream of Innocent I
VII	Approval of the Order
VIII	Apparition in Chariot of Fire
IX	Dream of the Throne
X	Expulsion of Demons from Arezzo
XI	Francis before the Sultan
XII	Francis in ecstasy
XIII	Celebration of Christmas
XIV	Miracle of the Spring
XV	Preaching to the birds
XVI	Death of the Knight
XVII	Prayer before Honorius III
XVIII	Apparition in Arles
XIX	Francis receives the stigmata
XX	Death of Francis
XXI	Apparition of the saint
XXII	Girolamo accepts the truth of the stigmata
XXIII	Poor Clares mourn the saint
XXIV	Canonization
XXV	Dream of Gregory IX
XXVI	Healing of the man from Ilerda
XXVII	Revival of the devout woman
XXVIII	Liberation of Pietro di Alife

Key to Frescoes in the Nave and Vaults

Old Testament
1 Creation of the World
2 Creation of Adam
3 Creation of Eve
4 Original sin
5 Expulsion from Paradise
6 The labours of Adam and Eve
7 Cain and Abel
8 Cain kills Abel
9 Noah builds the Ark
10 Boarding the Ark
11 Sacrifice of Isaac
12 Abraham and the three angels
13 Isaac blessing Jacob
14 Esau before Isaac
15 Joseph thrown into the well by his brothers
16 Joseph forgives his brothers

New Testament
17 Annunciation
18 Visitation
19 Nativity
20 Adoration of the Magi
21 Presentation at the Temple
22 Flight into Egypt
23 Christ among the Doctors
24 Baptism of Christ
25 Marriage at Cana
26 Resurrection of Lazarus
27 Capture of Christ
28 Flagellation
29 Ascent to Golgotha
30 Crucifixion
31 Lament over the dead Christ
32 Maries at the Sepulchre

Monastic Orders

Anyone visiting Umbria, and in particular Assisi, will be aware immediately of the many convents and monasteries belonging to different religious orders, direct descendants of the ministry of St Francis and St Clare. Monastic orders in Europe were born officially in the 6th century, with the drawing up of St Benedict's Rule. Reforms to the Benedictine Order instigated at Cluny in the 10th century gave a great boost to the monastic movement, as did the development of the Cistercian Order two centuries later. St Francis (1182–1226) broke new ground by reacting against the luxury and seclusion of old-fashioned monasticism, with its great abbeys, and instead invited his followers to live a life of poverty and renunciation, ministering to the urban poor. It was very hard to apply such a severe precept to a group, even of monks, which led to the the birth of other Franciscan orders. Three exist today.

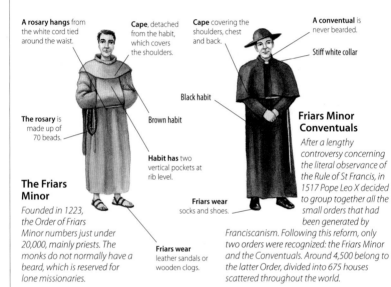

A rosary hangs from the white cord tied around the waist.

Cape, detached from the habit, which covers the shoulders.

Cape covering the shoulders, chest and back.

A conventual is never bearded.

Stiff white collar

Black habit

The rosary is made up of 70 beads.

Brown habit

Habit has two vertical pockets at rib level.

Friars wear socks and shoes.

Friars wear leather sandals or wooden clogs.

The Friars Minor

Founded in 1223, the Order of Friars Minor numbers just under 20,000, mainly priests. The monks do not normally have a beard, which is reserved for lone missionaries.

Friars Minor Conventuals

After a lengthy controversy concerning the literal observance of the Rule of St Francis, in 1517 Pope Leo X decided to group together all the small orders that had been generated by Franciscanism. Following this reform, only two orders were recognized: the Friars Minor and the Conventuals. Around 4,500 belong to the latter Order, divided into 675 houses scattered throughout the world.

Poor Clares, Franciscan Nuns and Capuchin Nuns

The cloister of the convent of San Damiano

The origin of the Order of Poor Clares (Clarisse) dates back to when St Clare (Santa Chiara) took the veil, celebrated by St Francis in 1212 at Santa Maria degli Angeli (see p84), when Clare was just a teenager. Having entered a traditional Benedictine convent, she left with a group of sisters and went to the church of San Damiano (see p84), where she decided to follow in the footsteps of St Francis by establishing a female Franciscan Order. The Rule of the Poor Clares was drawn up in 1224 by Francis himself and was observed with rigour by St Clare. Over time, the severity of the original Rule was slightly relaxed. In the 15th century, the establishment of the Reformed Franciscan Order of nuns signalled a return to the earlier, stricter observance, and in 1525 a female branch of the Capuchin Order was founded. The three orders survive to this day.

Robe of St Francis Traditionally regarded as the first robe worn by St Francis, this item of clothing reflects the saint's own rules of poverty and is in keeping with the description that history provides of his renunciation of worldly goods.

The Capuchin always has a beard, once unkempt, but today less neglected.

Pointed hood

There are two pockets within the sleeves.

Brown habit

Capuchin Friars

Seeking a return to the rigour of the traditional Rule of St Francis, in 1525 Matteo da Bascio founded the first house of the Capuchins at Camerino. The Order spread throughout Italy as well as abroad, but its members suffered persecution because of the character of the Friars' rule, which was considered to be too rigid and extreme. Currently, around 11,000 belong to this Franciscan Order (including 70 bishops, 7,300 priests and 3,500 lay members).

Exterior view of San Pietro showing its clean lines

🔼 San Pietro

Piazza San Pietro. **Tel** 075 812 311. **Open** Easter–Nov: 8am–7pm; Nov–Easter: 8am–6pm .

It is just a short walk from Basilica di San Francesco along Via Frate Elia to the church of San Pietro, which was founded, along with the adjacent monastery, by the Benedictines in the 10th century. The existing church dates from the same period as the Basilica of St Francis, and was consecrated in 1254.

The striking Romanesque-Gothic façade was originally decorated with a pediment, taken down in the 19th century. The interior, mainly Romanesque, contains no works of art of note. Its distinguishing features are its sober simplicity and the height of its nave.

🔼 Santa Maria Maggiore

Piazza del Vescovado. **Tel** 075 813 085. **Open** Easter–Nov: 8:30am–7pm, Nov–Easter: 8:30am–5pm.

Walking east from San Pietro, you eventually emerge into Piazza del Vescovado. This square was an important site in the Middle Ages, shown by the presence of the Palazzo Vescovile (Bishop's Palace) and the church of Santa Maria Maggiore, the city cathedral until 1020. The church was probably founded in the 10th century, but was rebuilt in Romanesque form around 1163. From the crypt, which is original, there is access to what is supposed to be the House of Propertius (Casa di Properzio) – "supposed", since the origins of the great Roman poet (c.50–16 BC) are anything but clear. In fact, at least three Umbrian cities – Assisi, Spello and Bevagna – have claimed to be the poet's birthplace.

🏛 Rocca Maggiore

Via Portica 2. **Tel** 075 815 5234. **Open** 10am–dusk daily. **Closed** 1 Jan, 25 Dec. 🏛

This well-preserved fortress stands at the northern edge of the city, reached by walking up Via di Porta Perlici from Piazza San Rufino. The panorama, overlooking the Valle del Tescio, the Valle Umbra and Assisi itself, with the façade of the duomo in the foreground, more than compensates for the effort of the climb.

The fortress was built in the 12th century and was used by Duke Corrado di Urslingen (who was tutor to the future Emperor Frederick II). It was destroyed and rebuilt more than once, including by Cardinal Albornoz in 1367, from which period most of what is now visible dates. Later additions include the polygonal tower (1458) and the round tower by the entrance (1553–8).

The fortress of the Rocca Maggiore, on the skyline above Assisi

For hotels and restaurants see pp148–50 and pp156–62

San Damiano, its formal simplicity suited to such a mystical place

⬆ Sanctuary of San Damiano

Via Padre Antonio Giorgi. **Tel** 075 812 273. **Open** summer: 10am–noon, 2–6pm (winter: 4:30pm); Vespers at 7pm (summer) and 5pm (winter).

From Porta Nuova, a walk of around 15 minutes leads to the Franciscan church of San Damiano, one of the most significant places in the life of St Francis. It was here that, in 1205, the saint said he heard the words: "Francis, go and repair my church which is falling down". According to the great chronicler of Francis' life, Tommaso da Celano, the words were spoken by the Crucifix which is now in Basilica di Santa Chiara (*see p74*). The building indicated by the crucifix was that of the church of San Damiano. Francis himself, together with a few faithful followers, undertook the restoration.

St Francis brought St Clare to San Damiano; she and her first followers congregated here, and founded the convent in which St Francis composed his *Canticle of the Creatures* (1225). Today, the convent is run by the Order of the Frati Minori Osservanti (Friars Minor).

Besides the spiritual value of the place, the sanctuary is worth a visit from both an architectural and artistic point of view, especially for the old convent rooms: the Oratorio di Santa Chiara, the cloister with frescoes by Eusebio da San Giorgio (1507) and the refectory. A good part of the 13th-century structure of the building can still be seen.

⬆ Santa Maria degli Angeli-Porziuncola

Santa Maria degli Angeli. **Tel** 075 805 11. **Open** summer: 6:15am–7:45pm (Jul–Sep: also 9–11pm); winter: 6:15am–12:30pm, 2–7:45pm; rosary and procession at 9:15pm Sat.

Another place that was dear to Francis is at the bottom of the hill (through Porta San Pietro). Built at the end of the 16th century, the church of Santa Maria degli Angeli (the seventh-largest church in the world) was, in fact, designed to accommodate the buildings of the 11th-century Porziuncola ("the little portion"), the chapel where St Francis lived and which was the centre of the early Franciscan Order. In 1569, Pope Pius IV laid the first stone of the vast Santa Maria, constructed to receive hordes of pilgrims. The project was given to Galeazzo Alessi, and work was concluded more than a century later with the building of the great cupola (1667) and one of the two bell towers. Inside the vast church, beneath the dome, is

The little oratory of the Porziuncola

the old oratory, known as the Cappella della Porziuncola; on the right is the Cappella del Transito, the old infirmary cell where the saint died on 4 October 1226; the door is original. This chapel contains a majolica statue of St Francis by Andrea della Robbia. Also of note is the Cappella del Roseto (chapel of the rose garden), with early 16th-century frescoes by Tiberio d'Assisi. The chapel takes its name from a legend, according to which St Francis rolled naked on the roses in the garden (to mortify his body), only to find that all the thorns immediately vanished.

In the convent there is a small museum, with a painted *Crucifix* by Giunta Pisano (mid-13th century) and a *St Francis* by an unknown artist who later passed into history as the Maestro di San Francesco.

Environs

About 5 km (3 miles) south of Assisi, on the road to Foligno, is the imposing **Santuario di Rivotorto**, built in 1854 in Neo-Gothic style on the site of a stone hut where the first community of Franciscan friars lived briefly, in 1209; St Francis wrote the first set of rules for his Order here. On the façade are the symbols of the Basilica di San Francesco. Also in Rivotorto is the peaceful British and Commonwealth "Assisi War Graves" cemetery.

⬆ Santuario di Rivotorto

Rivotorto di Assisi, 5 km (3 miles). **Tel** 075 806 5432. **Open** 6:45am–12:30pm, 2:30–7pm daily (from 7:30am Sun).

Crucifixion, 1561, fresco by Dono Doni in the duomo of San Rufino

❿ The Franciscan Path of Peace

There are many trails in the Umbrian hills, among them this one, established in the Jubilee year (2000). It retraces the journey taken by St Francis in 1206. Along the way, the saint decided to abandon his lay life and discovered the force of his spiritual conversion. The route, which is reasonably easy to walk, links Assisi and Gubbio and not only follows the physical paths trodden by Francis, but also recaptures the future saint's spiritual journey.

Tips for Drivers

ℹ️ Piazza del Comune 10, Assisi, 075 812 534. Length: 40 km (25 miles). Time needed: 2 days. Stopping-off points: Assisi, Valfabbrica, Gubbio. Lodgings at Vallingegno abbey, 075 920 158.

🇼 ilsentierodifrancesco.it

⑥ Abbey of Vallingegno
Another notable spiritual stopping place is the abbey dedicated to San Verecondo, a Benedictine centre from the 11th century, still in good condition. The church, cloister and crypt can be visited.

⑦ Gubbio
Just before the town is the "Vittorina", the church dedicated to Santa Maria della Vittoria, where it is said that Francis tamed the wolf. In Gubbio, the trail ends at the church of San Francesco.

⑤ Church of Caprignone
Foremost among all the churches that Francis built, stone by stone, during his life, this simple church sums up the austerity of the Order and marks the start of the history of the Franciscan movement.

④ Pieve di Coccorano
This is one of many chapels that Francis must have encountered on his journey, giving him the chance to stop and pray. The countryside here is particularly beautiful and tranquil.

③ Abbey of Valfabbrica
This may well have been the place where Francis stayed before continuing to Gubbio. Only the little church of Santa Maria remains today, with frescoes of the Umbrian school.

② Pieve San Nicolò
After a hilly journey from Assisi, you reach this village, which marks the divide between Assisi and Valfabbrica. Both towns can be seen from here, and, when the weather is good, you can even see as far as Gubbio.

① Assisi
The trail starts from Porta San Giacomo, probably the gate through which Francis passed when he left Assisi. It is near the Basilica di San Francesco, where the body of the saint now lies.

Umbertide

Ponte d'Assisi

Castiglione

Santa Maria di Colonnata
S298

Mengara

Biscina

Chiáscio

S219

S318

S318

Pianello

Rocca Sant'Angelo

Palazzo

Perugia

S147

Spello

Key

▬▬ Tour route

═══ Other roads

0 kilometres 3

0 miles 3

Vineyards belonging to the Lungarotti family, near Torgiano

❶ Torgiano

Perugia. **Road Map** C4. 🏔 6,000.
🚉 Perugia and Assisi stations, 5 km
(3 miles) and 8 km (5 miles), Foligno–
Terontola line. 🚌 ❓ Pro Loco, Corso
Vittorio Emanuele 23, 075 985 297.

The small town of Torgiano,
15 km (9 miles) south of
Perugia (just east of the main
road 3bis), occupies a lovely
position at the confluence of
the Tiber and Chiascio rivers.
Inhabited since the Roman
era, it was rebuilt during the
Middle Ages as a fortified site
to guard over the territory of
Perugia – as the Torre Baglioni
(probably 13th century) still
bears witness.

Torgiano is not an especially
remarkable town in itself, and
yet it is famous for the now
historic production of wine,
acknowledged in the town's
coat of arms and recorded in
the excellent **Museo del Vino
and Osteria**. Housed in the
17th-century Palazzo Baglioni,
this is a private museum
owned by the Lungarotti
family, probably the best-
known wine producers in
Umbria; the Rubesco Riserva
di Torgiano is one of Italy's
best red wines.

The 19 rooms illustrate
the history of oenology and
vine-growing since antiquity:
on display, with good notes
and explanations (including
in English), are the tools used
for the production of wine over
the centuries, as well as old
books and printed material
relating to wine. There is

also a valuable collection
of majolica pieces, among
them a plate by Maestro
Giorgio da Gubbio (1528) and
a tondo with Bacchus which
is attributed to Girolamo
della Robbia.

Next door to the
museum is the
Osteria del Museo,
where it is possible to
taste and buy wines
from the **Cantine
Giorgio Lungarotti**.

In an additional
demonstration of the
high esteem in which
local agricultural
products are held, the
Lungarotti Foundation
has also added a **Museo
dell'Olivo e dell'Olio**,
where displays relating to
olives and oil are housed in
attractively restored medieval
dwellings. High-quality olive oils
and balsamic vinegar produced
on the estate are offered for
sale in the winery shop.

🏛 **Museo del Vino
and Osteria**
Corso Vittorio Emanuele 31–33.
Tel 075 988 0200. **Open** Apr–Jun:
10am–1pm, 3–6pm Tue–Sun; July–
Sep: 10am–6pm daily; Oct–Mar:
10am–1pm, 3–5pm Tue–Sun.
Closed 25 Dec. 🎫 ⓦ **lungarotti.it**

🍷 **Cantine Giorgio Lungarotti**
Tel 075 988 661 (call ahead).

🏛 **Museo dell'Olivo e dell'Olio**
Via Garibaldi 10. **Tel** 075 988 0200.
Open Apr–Jun: 10am–1pm, 3–6pm
Tue–Sun; July–Sep: 10am–6pm daily;
Oct–Mar: 10am–1pm, 3–5pm Tue–
Sun. **Closed** 25 Dec. 🎫 ♿

❷ Bettona

Perugia. **Road Map** C4. 🏔 3,700.
🚉 Perugia and Assisi stations, 7 km
(4 miles) and 4 km (2 miles), Foligno–
Terontola line. 🚌 ❓ Pro Loco, Corso
Marconi, 075 997 5643.

It is worth taking the time to
travel the 6 km (4 miles) along
the Assisi road from Torgiano,
in order to visit the village of
Bettona. Apart from offering
lovely views over the
surrounding countryside,
Bettona is unusual historically:
it is among the extremely
rare centres of culture of
Etruscan origin found to the
east of the River Tiber. Evidence
of Etruscan beginnings is clear
from the huge blocks of stone
set into the medieval walls.

Significant sections of the
walls remain, dating from
the 4th century BC and
typically Etruscan in
design. The best
example is the 40-m
(131-ft) section at the
northwestern corner;
the other sections are of
medieval origin, but rest
on an Etruscan base. The
entire circuit of the outer
walls can be explored
on foot. Bettona has
largely kept its
medieval feel. It is
home to works of art
that some have
attributed to the school of
Perugino, while others believe
they are the work of the
master himself. The first is
a processional banner with
a Madonna and Child and St
Anne. Until recently, it was kept

St Anthony, by
Perugino

Bettona's village wall, with Etruscan and
medieval stonework

NORTHERN UMBRIA | **87**

with other important works in the church of Santa Maria Maggiore, erected in the 13th century but later rebuilt. Today, the work is on display in the **Pinacoteca Comunale**, a good art collection housed in the Palazzo del Podestà, on Piazza Cavour.

The gallery also has a *St Anthony of Padua* by Perugino, an *Adoration of the Shepherds* by Dono Doni (a masterpiece from 1543, once kept in the church of San Crispolto), and other works of importance by Jacopo Siculo, Niccolò Alunno, Tiberio d'Assisi and Fiorenzo di Lorenzo.

Pinacoteca Comunale

Palazzo del Podestà, Piazza Cavour 3. **Tel** 075 987 306. **Open** Mar–May, Sep & Oct: 10:30am–1pm, 2–6pm daily; Jun–Aug: 10:30am–1pm, 3–7pm daily; Nov–Feb: 10:30am–1pm, 2:30–5pm Tue–Sun. **Closed** 1 Jan, 25 Dec.

A work by Niccolò Alunno, in the Pinacoteca in Bettona

⑬ Deruta

Perugia. **Road Map** C4. 9,000. Pro Loco, Piazza dei Consoli 4, 075 971 15 59.

Heading out of Torgiano along road 3bis, you soon reach Deruta, just 6 km (4 miles) south. On a knoll overlooking the Tiber valley, Deruta has been inhabited since Neolithic times, and still bears traces of its history in part of the walls and in the three arches that give access to the old centre. The town's name may derive from the fact that it has been destroyed ("*distrutta*") several times.

The heart of Deruta is Piazza dei Consoli where, as in most medieval settlements, all the

The Ceramics of the Tiber

Umbria is famous all over the world for its ceramic production. Between the 15th and 16th centuries some extraordinary ceramicists emerged, including the locally born Giacomo Mancini and Francesco Urbini. Even today, ceramics manufacture is one of the most important aspects of the local economy for many towns along the Val Tiberina, and particularly in Deruta, which is full of workshops where craftsmen can be seen at work, and Gubbio. It is not just by chance that the vast majority of the main production centres for ceramics should have emerged and are still found along the Tiber: this is due to the fact that there is a greater availability of clay, malleable and at the same time fire-resistant, in the area, as well as the silica needed for the glazes.

Decorating a plate by hand

chief religious and civic monuments stand. **Palazzo dei Consoli**, housing the town hall and also the excellent Pinacoteca (art gallery), is here, as well as the Romanesque-Gothic church of **San Francesco**.

Residing in the former monastery of San Francesco, next door to the church, is the **Museo Regionale della Ceramica**, which highlights the importance of ceramics in Deruta. The production of jars, plates and other everyday items started in the Middle Ages and is documented in perhaps the most important museum of its kind in the region. On the ground floor, Room 5 is of most interest, with pieces of ancient pottery; on the first floor are fragments from the floor in the church of San Francesco. On the second floor are more valuable pieces, among them a series of Renaissance plates,

including one depicting the myth of Pyramus and Thisbe, from the late 16th century.

The production of ceramics is still a thriving industry in the town, and there are many workshops making and selling majolica pieces. Pottery is also the main attraction at the church of the **Madonna dei Bagni** (1657), 2 km (1 mile) south of Deruta. Its walls are covered in old ex votos made of Deruta pottery.

Museo Regionale della Ceramica

Largo San Francesco. **Tel** 075 971 10 00. **Open** Apr–Jun: 10:30am–1pm, 3–6pm daily; Jul–Sep: 10am–1pm, 3:30–7pm daily; Oct–Mar: 10:30am–1pm, 2:30–5pm Wed–Mon. **Closed** 1 Jan, 25 Dec, Jan–Aug: Mon & Tue; Sep & Oct: Mon.

Madonna dei Bagni

SS E45, exit Casalina. **Tel** 075 973 455. **Open** 8am–noon, 2:30–6:30pm daily **Closed** during Mass.

The fertile Umbrian countryside near Deruta

⓮ Perugia

Now with over 160,000 inhabitants, Perugia has always been the largest city in Umbria. The historic centre of the city has a medieval appearance but is based on an Etruscan layout. The old city occupies a strategic position on a hill dominating the Tiber valley, while the modern city, with flourishing clothing and food industries, developed down below. The Etruscans settled *Perusia* in the 5th century BC or earlier, and it was conquered by the Romans in 309 BC. Perugia saw its greatest splendour in the 13th and 14th centuries, after which civil strife undermined the city's stability; it came under the jurisdiction of the papacy in 1531. Modern Perugia has a distinctly young, cosmopolitan and artistic population and outlook that sets it apart from other cities in the region. It has a thriving Università per Stranieri (University for Foreigners), hosts Italy's top jazz festival, Umbria Jazz *(see p37)* and an annual chocolate festival, Eurochocolate.

Porta Marzia, set into the eastern bastion of the Rocca

Exploring Perugia

Visitors arriving by car are advised to leave their vehicle in the underground car park at Piazzale Partigiani, and from here to take the escalators or microtrain, which take about ten minutes to reach the historic centre, passing by the ruins of the Rocca Paolina and emerging in Piazza Italia.

🏛 Rocca Paolina and Porta Marzia

Built in 1543 and virtually destroyed in

Embossed bronze plate

1860, this fortress is a symbol of papal domination over Perugia. It was built on the orders of Pope Paul III Farnese, who sacked the city in 1540 and annexed it to the Church. Construction of the fortress was entrusted to Antonio da Sangallo, the great exponent of military architecture of the age. To make way for the Rocca, many other buildings were razed. This only increased the hatred of the people of Perugia towards the edifice, which was destroyed as soon as the city gained independence from the pope in the mid-1800s. The gap created was filled with Piazza Italia. Parts of the fortress survive, including the Porta Marzia, an astonishing Etruscan archway which Sangallo liked so much that he incorporated it into the wall of his own building. Beneath the archway is the entrance to the bizarre Via Baglioni Sotterranea, a medieval street once buried beneath the Rocca Paolina.

🏛 Museo Archeologico Nazionale dell'Umbria

Piazza G Bruno. **Tel** 075 572 7141. **Open** 8:30am–7:30pm Tue–Sun, 10am–7:30pm Mon (ticket office closes 6:30pm). **Closed** 1 Jan, 1 May, 25 Dec. 🎫 🏛 🅿 partial.

Along Corso Cavour is the Church of San Domenico and its attached monastery, now home to the Museo Archeologico. The collection underwent a major renovation and there is now much more to see than the original Etruscan and Roman finds. The Carri Etruschi di Castel San Marino is a particularly fine exhibit of 6th century BC bronze chariots. Another must-see is the Cippus Perusinus, an Etruscan boundary stone which bears one of the longest inscriptions in Etruscan ever found.

Perugia Town Centre

① Rocca Paolina & Porta Marzia
② Museo Archeologico Nazionale dell'Umbria
③ San Domenico

⛪ San Domenico

Piazza G Bruno. **Tel** 075 572 4136.
Open 8am–noon, 4pm–dusk daily.
🅿️ ♿ 📷 Sat, Sun am; 075 573 1635.

This huge church was built in the 14th century, to a design reminiscent of the Florentine churches of Santa Croce and

Detail from the polyptych, San Pietro

Santa Maria Novella. It was rebuilt in the Baroque style in the 17th century, but was never finished. Inside, note in particular the Cappella del Rosario, with statues by Agostino di Duccio (second half of the 15th century), and also the wonderful stained-glass window (1411), the second largest in Italy after the one in Milan cathedral.

⛪ San Pietro

Borgo XX Giugno. **Tel** 075 337 53.
Open 8am–noon Mon–Fri (also 3:30–6pm Tue & Thu).

Further along Via Cavour, beyond Porta San Pietro (14th–15th centuries, built with some help from Agostino di Duccio), is one of the oldest religious buildings in Perugia, the Benedictine church of San Pietro. The church was founded in the 10th century, but there is some evidence to suggest that, in this slightly elevated site,

VISITORS' CHECKLIST

Practical Information
Road Map C3. 🏠 168,000. 🛈
Piazza Matteotti 18, 075 573 6458.

Transport
🚆 Cortona–Foligno & Rome–Perugia lines, 892021; FCU line, 075 575 401.
🚌 APM, 075 9637 637.

there were underground passages. These rooms were used for burial first by the Etruscans and then by the Romans, before being converted into a building dating from the Early Christian era (6th century AD).

San Pietro is strikingly original, particularly in its wonderfully sumptuous decoration, which is more reminiscent of the Venetian than the local tradition. There are also numerous works of art by several notable artists, including Perugino, Guercino, Guido Reni and Sassoferrato.

An impressive amount of the original Romanesque church survives, including the partially frescoed façade. The exuberant decoration inside is late Renaissance, and includes cycles of large paintings reminiscent of those done by Tintoretto. There is also a painted coffered ceiling and wonderful wooden choir stalls, the work of various artists in the 16th century. The vault is frescoed with *Stories from the Old Testament*. In the sacristy are five small canvases by Perugino depicting the saints. Visitors should ask the sacristan for permission to view the artworks.

The 16th-century entrance to the church of San Pietro

---

④ *Palazzo dei Priori pp90–91*
⑤ *Galleria Nazionale dell'Umbria pp92–3*
⑥ Duomo
⑦ Etruscan Well
⑧ Palazzo del Capitano del Popolo

⑨ San Severo
⑩ Arch of Augustus
⑪ Oratorio di San Bernardino
⑫ San Michele Arcangelo (Sant'Angelo)

For keys to symbols *see back flap*

Perugia: Palazzo dei Priori

Piazza IV Novembre is home to two of the most important monuments in Perugia, the Palazzo dei Priori and the Fontana Maggiore. The imposing palazzo, topped by crenellations, was built to hold the town council's administrative offices, and was constructed in stages between 1293 and 1443, during an era of great splendour in the city. Though sombre outside, this is one of the most impressive medieval buildings in Italy, with truly gorgeous interiors. The palazzo is, in fact, composed of several buildings which face onto either Corso Vannucci or the piazza. These house four separate visitors' attractions, including the splendid Galleria Nazionale dell'Umbria *(see pp92–3)*.

★ Collegio del Cambio
In the Sala dell'Udienza of the Collegio del Cambio (1452–7), where money changers operated, there is a cycle of frescoes by Perugino, painted from 1496 to 1500. The iconography brings together religious themes and figures with secular ones, a hallmark of Renaissance Humanism.

KEY

① **The Arco dei Priori**, marks the start of Via dei Priori, which, it is said, flowed with rivers of blood as a result of civil strife during the Middle Ages.

② **Il Collegio della Mercanzia**, is a room on the ground floor of the palazzo which was placed at the disposal of the Merchants' Guild in 1390, for meetings. The ceiling and walls are lined with inlaid wood and date from the middle of the 15th century.

③ **The Guild of Money Changers**, acquired the right to establish its headquarters in the Palazzo dei Priori between 1452 and 1457.

④ **Belfry**

⑤ **A stone griffin**, (a copy of the 1274 original), high above the entrance, is the symbol of Perugia.

⑥ **The fan-shaped flight of steps**, in Piazza IV Novembre leads up to the Sala dei Notari.

★ Portale delle Arti
Framed by rounded arches, the doorway dates from 1346 and is adorned with sculptures and reliefs representing vices and virtues, as well as symbolic animals.

★ Sala dei Notari
The lawyers' meeting hall, with its magnificent vaulting, is one of the oldest parts of the palazzo, dating from the late 1290s. The rich decoration includes frescoes by local artists, dating from the same period.

VISITORS' CHECKLIST

Practical Information
Piazza IV Novembre. Sala dei
Notari: **Tel** 075 577 2339.
Open 9am–1pm, 3–7pm Tue–
Sun. Collegio della Mercanzia:
Tel 075 573 0366. **Open** Mar–Oct:
9am–1pm, 2:30–5:30pm Tue–Sat,
9am–1pm Sun & pub hols; Nov–
Feb: 8am–2pm Tue, Thu & Fri,
8am–4:30pm Wed & Sat,
9am–1pm Sun & pub hols.
🚏 combined ticket with Collegio
del Cambio. ♿ Collegio del
Cambio: **Tel** 075 572 8599.
Open 9am–12:30pm, 2:30–
5:30pm Mon–Sat, 9am–1pm Sun
& pub hols. 🚏 combined ticket
with Collegio della Mercanzia.
♿ **Closed** all sites: 1 Jan, 25 Dec
(Collegio del Cambio also Mon
pm Nov–31 Mar).

The Fontana Maggiore

Built from 1275 to 1278, and
recently restored, this fountain
was designed by a monk called
Fra Bevignate, and decorated
by Nicola Pisano and his son,
Giovanni. It is both a magnificent
architectural creation (one
of Italy's top Romanesque
monuments) and a complex
feat of hydraulic engineering.
It was thanks to the engineer
Boninsegna da Venezia that
waters from a new aqueduct
from Monte Pacciano
converged here.

The fountain is built on three
levels: two polygonal basins in
marble, one above the other, with
25 and 24 sides respectively, and a
third basin in bronze. The series of
bas-reliefs is exceptional: on the
lower basin are three consecutive
cycles depicting episodes from
the Old Testament, the Liberal
Arts and the Labours of the
Months. On the upper basin are
24 sculptures representing biblical
figures (David, Moses, Solomon,
Salome), saints, mythological
figures or allegories from the
history of the city, as well as
the Perugian *condottiere* Ermanno
di Sassoferrato, Capitano del
Popolo in 1278.

Stylistically, all kinds of
influences converge in the reliefs
(including classical, Byzantine
and medieval), making it difficult
to attribute individual panels
to one or other of the two artists.

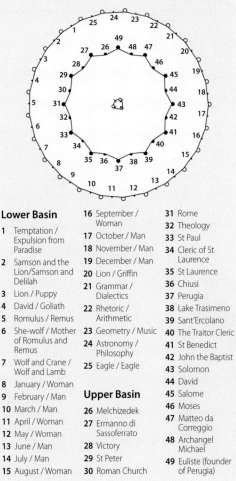

Lower Basin

1 Temptation /
  Expulsion from
  Paradise
2 Samson and the
  Lion/Samson and
  Delilah
3 Lion / Puppy
4 David / Goliath
5 Romulus / Remus
6 She-wolf / Mother
  of Romulus and
  Remus
7 Wolf and Crane /
  Wolf and Lamb
8 January / Woman
9 February / Man
10 March / Man
11 April / Woman
12 May / Woman
13 June / Man
14 July / Man
15 August / Woman

16 September /
  Woman
17 October / Man
18 November / Man
19 December / Man
20 Lion / Griffin
21 Grammar /
  Dialectics
22 Rhetoric /
  Arithmetic
23 Geometry / Music
24 Astronomy /
  Philosophy
25 Eagle / Eagle

Upper Basin

26 Melchizedek
27 Ermanno di
  Sassoferrato
28 Victory
29 St Peter
30 Roman Church

31 Rome
32 Theology
33 St Paul
34 Cleric of St
  Laurence
35 St Laurence
36 Chiusi
37 Perugia
38 Lake Trasimeno
39 Sant'Ercolano
40 The Traitor Cleric
41 St Benedict
42 John the Baptist
43 Solomon
44 David
45 Salome
46 Moses
47 Matteo da
  Correggio
48 Archangel
  Michael
49 Euliste (founder
  of Perugia)

Fontana Maggiore
This is a suberb piece of work,
featuring many exquisite
bas-reliefs and sculptures by
Nicola and Giovanni Pisano.

Perugia: Galleria Nazionale dell'Umbria

This is the most important museum, not only in Perugia but in Umbria as a whole, featuring works of art dating from the 13th to 19th centuries. Created partly out of Napoleon's seizure of works of art held by religious orders, the gallery was established in 1863. It was moved to the Palazzo dei Priori in 1879 and has been state-owned since 1918. A major renovation project has increased the number of rooms to 40, spread over two floors, mostly grouped to cover various eras, including the 15th-century Cappella dei Priori, which features some splendid Perugian scenes. While the emphasis is clearly on Umbrian art, Sienese masters are nevertheless dominant in the early rooms. Artsiders, a new project, will see new talent placed alongside old masters.

Donna alla Fonte (1278–81)
In Room 1 there are five statues which were originally part of a fountain, including the *Donna alla Fonte*, by Tuscan Arnolfo di Cambio (1240–1302). There are also two bronzes of a griffin and a lion.

★ **St Anthony Polyptych** (1459–68)
In this work by Piero della Francesca, on show in Room 11, innovative use of perspective blends with a structure and colours that are still medieval.

Room 6 is dedicated to the International Gothic style, of which Gentile da Fabriano (1370–1427) was one of the major Italian exponents. His *Madonna col Bambino e Angeli* is displayed here.

3rd Floor

16
17
18   19
20
21   1a
5
4
2
15   8
3
14   9
6
13   11   10   7
12
25   24   23
26
22
27   33
32   36
34
28
31
29   30

2nd Floor

★ **San Domenico of Fiesole Altarpiece** (1437)
This work by Fra Angelico (1395–1455) is one of the major Renaissance masterpieces in the museum. Also known as the *Guidalotti Polyptych*, it is displayed in Room 8.

Key

- 6th and 7th centuries
- 8th century
- 13th and 14th centuries
- Late Gothic period
- Early Renaissance
- 15th century
- Treasury and decorative arts
- Cappella dei Priori
- Renaissance masterpieces
- Perugian and Umbrian art
- Luigi Caratolli collection

To Rooms 22–40

Entrance and ticket office

39   40

38

Room 15 displays this *Adoration of the Magi* by Perugino (1450–1523). There are also splendid paintings from the Umbrian school. More works by Perugino can be found in Rooms 22–24, including the *Madonna della Consolazione*.

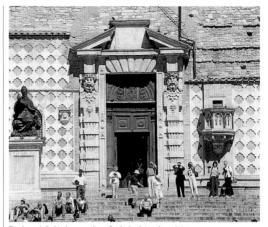

The duomo's Gothic doorway, the unfinished pulpit and papal statue

🏛 Duomo

Piazza Danti. **Tel** 075 572 3832.
Open 7:30am–noon, 3:30–6:45pm
Mon–Sat; 8am–1pm, 4–7pm Sun. 👤

The duomo, dedicated to San Lorenzo, was built on the site of a 10th-century basilica. The first stone of the new building was laid in 1345, but the Black Death (1348) delayed progress for many years, with work starting again properly only in 1437. Even then, the façade was left unfinished.

The façade, which gives onto Piazza Danti, is undoubtedly of much less interest than the left-hand side of the duomo, which overlooks Piazza IV Novembre. This is covered in distinctive pink and white marble, and features an impressive monumental Gothic doorway, designed by Galeazzo Alessi in 1568. In a niche above the doorway is a cross, beneath which the Perugians symbolically laid down the keys to the city following their defeat by Pope Paul III Farnese in the Salt War of 1540. In contrast, a statue of Pope Julius III, sculpted by Vincenzo Danti in 1555, to the left of the doorway, was commissioned by the people of Perugia to celebrate the pope who had restored some communal liberty to the city. On the right is an unfinished,

Detail from the cathedral

15th-century pulpit, from which St Bernardino of Siena preached to vast crowds of Perugians in the 1420s. The saint was so popular with Perugians that they built a church in his honour *(see pp94–5)*.

Also on the side of the duomo that overlooks the piazza is a loggia with an arched portico, built for Braccio Fortebraccio, the celebrated *condottiere* from Montone, in 1423.

The interior is bare and solemn, unusual in Italy, being more reminiscent of the great churches of northern Europe. Inside is the Virgin's "wedding ring", housed in the Cappella del Sant'Anello and said to change colour according to who wears it. On the left, just past the entrance, is the Cappella di San Bernardino da Siena, home to one of the two major works of art in the building, a *Descent from the Cross* by Federico Barocci, dated 1567–9. The other is a masterpiece by Luca Signorelli, *Enthroned Madonna with Saints*, which was painted in 1484 and has been beautifully restored to show off its original brilliance.

Another restored feature worth seeing is the choir, featuring inlaid wooden stalls: the work of Domenico del Tasso and Giuliano da Maiano.

Post-Modern Perugia

The quarter of Fontivegge is in the new part of Perugia, southwest of the historic centre, near the railway station. It stands out from the other quarters of the modern city because it was designed as a completely new district between 1982 and 1989 by the architect Aldo Rossi and his colleagues. It is one of the most successful examples of post-modern architecture in Italy, featuring buildings that are both futuristic and full of classical references (see in particular the Palazzo della Regione, in Piazza Nuova), and also include: elements from the past; a 17th-century fountain and a chimney from the old Perugina factory have both been incorporated into the new architectural context.

View of the Fontivegge quarter

Etruscan Well

Piazza Danti 18. **Tel** 075 573 3669. **Open** 10am–1:30pm, 2:30–6pm (Nov–Mar: 11am–1:30pm, 2:30–5pm). **Closed** Mon (except in Apr & Aug), 1 Jan, 25 Dec.

The Etruscan Well (Pozzo Etrusco) in the basement of Palazzo Bourbon-Sorbello, next to the cathedral façade in Piazza Danti, is an astonishing feat of engineering: it was capable of providing a constant supply of water to the entire city. The well (the bottom of which is accessible) is partially covered in vast blocks of travertine, from which the original cover was also made. You can still see the furrows left by the ropes that the Etruscans used to pull the buckets of water to the surface.

Behind Piazza Danti is the district of Rione di Porta Sole, where the Rocca del Sole fortress was built in 1372. It was the largest fortification of its time, but was destroyed shortly after its completion.

Piazza Matteotti

This long square, which runs parallel to Corso Vannucci, is home to two notable 15th-century buildings. The first is **Palazzo del Capitano del Popolo** (1472–82), designed by the Lombard architects Gasparino di Antonio and Leone di Matteo, and the seat of the judiciary in the era of the communes. Its traditional medieval town-hall design has been embellished with Renaissance elements. The palazzo was originally built on three floors, but the third was demolished following the earthquake of 1741. Behind the porticoes alongside the palazzo is a 1930s covered market, from where you can see the piazza foundations.

The other building of note is **Palazzo dell'Università Vecchia**, mostly from the same era as the Palazzo del Capitano del Popolo (the same Gasparino di Antonio collaborated in its construction); the building was made the seat of the university by Pope Sixtus IV in 1483.

Justice, detail

San Severo

Piazza Raffaello. **Tel** 075 573 3864. **Open** 10am–1:30pm, 2:30–6pm (Nov– Mar: 11am–1:30pm, 2:30–5pm). **Closed** Mon (except in Apr & Aug), 1 Jan, 25 Dec.

Following the narrow streets up through the Porta Sole quarter, you reach the church of San Severo, famous as the home of one of Raphael's earliest frescoes (1507–8), of the *Holy Trinity and Saints*. Perugino finished the work in 1521, adding the saints lower down on the same wall. Also look out for the 16th-century terracotta group of a Madonna and Child by an unknown Tuscan sculptor. The church is of ancient origin: it certainly existed in the 11th century, and the site was probably used for sacred buildings before that. Its current appearance dates from the mid-18th century.

Arch of Augustus

Piazza Fortebraccio.

A scenic descent signals the end of the Porta Sole quarter, marked by the splendid 3rd-century BC Arch of Augustus (Arco di Augusto). This civic gate is also known as the Etruscan Arch, since it was, in fact, of Etruscan origin, and was later modified by the Romans. The still-legible inscription, "Augusta Perusia", was placed here by Octavius Caesar (later Emperor Augustus); having destroyed and then rebuilt the city, he renamed it after himself.

Façade of the Oratorio di San Bernardino

Oratorio di San Bernardino

Piazza San Francesco al Prato. **Tel** 075 573 3957. **Open** 8:30am–12:30pm, 3:30–5:30pm daily.

Passing under the Arco dei Priori, part of the palazzo of the same name *(see pp90–91)*, and heading down Via dei Priori, you cross what was once a main road through medieval Perugia. Beyond the city walls, the street widens into a piazza with the church of **San Francesco al Prato**, built in the mid-13th century on a particularly subsidence-prone piece of ground; it is now partially ruined. To the left of the church is the small and elegant **Oratorio di San Bernardino** (1452), whose fine multicoloured bas-reliefs on the façade make it a masterpiece of the Umbrian Renaissance. The sculptures, by Agostino di Duccio, are remarkable for the realism of the undulating lines and of the drapery.

Inside, in the first chapel on the left, are a 15th-century gonfalon (banner) showing the Madonna sheltering Perugia from the plague, by Benedetto Bonfigli, and the tomb of Braccio Fortebraccio da Montone. The altar was made from an ancient Early Christian sarcophagus.

🚋 Borgo Sant'Angelo

Corso Garibaldi, running north from Piazza Fortebraccio, is the principal medieval street, along which the area of Borgo Sant'Angelo developed. Now the seat of Perugia's university, this district grew up around an Augustinian monastery and has the city's most important monastic buildings, including

The Early Christian church of Sant'Angelo

the monastery of San Benedetto, the former hospital of the Collegio della Mercanzia, the convent of Santa Caterina and the monastery of Beata Colomba. It is in this last monastery that, according to popular tradition, St Francis met St Dominic in 1220.

At the end of the road, in the shelter of the walls and in a pretty setting, is the circular church of **San Michele Arcangelo (Sant'Angelo)**, whose origins date back to the late 5th century. Thanks to excellent restoration work, which included the removal of Baroque additions, major parts of the original church are now visible, along with a 14th-century Gothic doorway. The interior is rich with frescoes, and also 14th century. This is one of the oldest proto-Christian churches in Italy.

🏛 San Michele Arcangelo
Via Sant'Angelo, Corso Garibaldi. **Tel** 075 572 2624. **Open** 9am–5pm daily.

Environs
Around 7 km (4 miles) southeast of the city, along road 75bis, is one of the most interesting burial sites among many in the area: the **Ipogeo dei Volumni**. Built into the side of a hill, it consists of a great tomb chamber where, in the 2nd century BC, the nobles of the Etruscan Velimna family were buried. Their Latin name of Volumni gives its name to their mausoleum.

Umbria Jazz

A festival stage just before a concert

First held in 1973, Umbria Jazz is – the experts say – Europe's top jazz festival. After the first concerts, held in different towns throughout the region, the event went into crisis and was suspended. The festival was then transferred to Perugia, where it now takes place every July, and enjoys a fame and success second only to the famous Montreal festival. Concerts take place in different venues: from fields and open-air sites (where events are generally free) to the Morlacchi and Pavone theatres, for which audiences buy tickets. Every evening, stretched out on the grass, thousands of young people listen to music for free: a flashback to a time when Umbria Jazz was briefly the setting for mass youth gatherings. Historic open-air venues include the Giardini del Frontone, used since 1984 for the jazz festival's most important evening concerts. The gardens have hosted some of the most historic events, from Stan Getz to the get-together between John Scofield and Pat Metheny, from Bobby McFerrin to Phil Woods and Dizzy Gillespie hugging each other in the rain. As well as the main festival there are other events, including a jazz festival at Orvieto (Umbria Jazz Winter), and a gospel and soul festival (at Terni, at Easter) (www.umbriajazz.it).

Since 1937, another annual event has been staged in Perugia: the Sagra Musicale Umbra, a festival of sacred music, draws artists from all over the world in September.

Inside the burial chamber of the Ipogeo dei Volumni

⑮ Lake Trasimeno

The fourth-largest lake in Italy, Lake Trasimeno covers an area of 126 sq km (48 sq miles). The perimeter is almost 60 km (37 miles) long, and the lake lies at the fortified heart of medieval Umbria. No matter where you gaze among the low hills that surround the lake, you will inevitably catch sight of a castle, a tower or a fortified village. In fact, Lake Trasimeno has been the scene of battles since antiquity, and it was on these shores that Hannibal defeated the Romans on 21 June 217 BC. Although the water levels rise and fall, and the lake periodically floods the surrounding land, the area has always been inhabited. Over the centuries villages grew up on the shores of the lake, and the islands became home to monasteries and convents, later active fishing communities.

★ Isola Maggiore
Briefly a refuge for St Francis, this island is inhabited by fishermen who still stretch out their nets to dry between the churches of Sant'Angelo and San Salvatore.

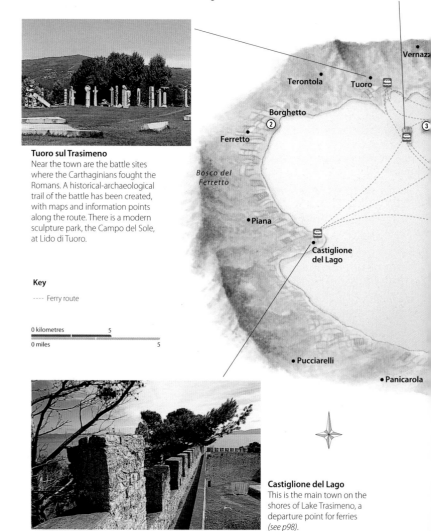

Tuoro sul Trasimeno
Near the town are the battle sites where the Carthaginians fought the Romans. A historical-archaeological trail of the battle has been created, with maps and information points along the route. There is a modern sculpture park, the Campo del Sole, at Lido di Tuoro.

Key

---- Ferry route

0 kilometres ———— 5
0 miles ———— 5

Vernazz

Terontola   Tuoro

Borghetto
②

Ferretto

*Bosco del
Ferretto*

③

• Piana

**Castiglione
del Lago**

• Pucciarelli

• Panicarola

Castiglione del Lago
This is the main town on the shores of Lake Trasimeno, a departure point for ferries *(see p98).*

Passignano sul Trasimeno
This town of Etruscan origin is built on a chalk promontory. The most important monument in the town is the church of San Cristoforo, with 15th-century frescoes.

★ **Isola Polvese**
This is the largest island on the lake. The Province of Perugia has created an oasis for wildlife here, among gardens and parks. The ruins of the monastery of San Secondo and a 15th-century castle can also be seen.

Passignano sul Trasimeno

Torricella

Magione ④

Monte del Lago

San Feliciano ⑤

San Savino

Sant'Arcangelo
⑥

Monte Buono

⑦

KEY

① **The southern shores**, are characterized, more so than the others, by marshy terrain, fringed with reedbeds.

② **Borghetto** is a small village among olive groves, with a 16th-century parish church, San Martino.

③ **Isola Minore** is private and the smallest of the three islands.

④ **Magione** is a town in the hills behind the most populated stretch of shore, and moderately developed in terms of tourism. There is a castle here, the Castello dei Cavalieri di Malta, and, at nearby San Feliciano, a Museo della Pesca (Museum of Fishing).

⑤ **La Valle** is the name given to this stretch of lake, where there are vast reedbeds and an area of protected fish-breeding grounds.

⑥ **The Badia di Sant'Arcangelo**, in a lovely setting by the lake, is a castle of medieval origin with a Romanesque church.

⑦ **The Castello di Montalera** is one of many fortified sites along the lakeshore. It was at one time the property of the Baglioni family.

The Battle of Lake Trasimeno

After defeating the Romans at the battles of Ticino and Trebbia, Hannibal was informed that his adversaries, led by Caius Flaminius, were directing part of the Roman army towards Lake Trasimeno. The Carthaginian leader distributed his men around the surrounding hills and then, on 21 June 217 BC, aided by foggy weather, he gave the order to attack the enemy forces. Trapped between the lake and the hills, the Roman soldiers suffered a crushing defeat: Hannibal lost 1,500 men, compared with the Romans' 15,000.

Portrait of Hannibal

View across Lake Trasimeno from Castiglione

⓰ Castiglione del Lago

Perugia. **Road Map** B3. 🚶 15,000.
🚆 Florence–Rome line. 🚌
ℹ️ Piazza Mazzini 10, 075 965 2484.
🎭 Festa degli Aquiloni, Apr.

The town of Castiglione del Lago occupies a promontory which dominates the western shore of Lake Trasimeno, and which, during floods, used to be cut off from the surrounding area, in effect becoming an island.

The area was fortified by both the Etruscans and the Romans because of its strategic position. Fought over by Perugia and by the Tuscans, the site was often destroyed and rebuilt. It was following the reconstruction ordered by Frederick II Hohenstaufen in the 13th century that the place acquired the name Castello del Leone, from which its current name derives.

In the 16th century, the village was given by the papacy to the della Corgna family, who built the town's most important building, the **Palazzo della Corgna**. It may have been designed by Galeazzo Alessi and the frescoes were done by Pomarancio.

Linked to the palazzo by a covered walkway, backing onto the lake and with a fine view, is the **Rocca del Leone**, an interesting example of medieval military architecture. In the 16th century it was considered to be one of the most impregnable fortresses in Italy. From the palazzo, the street leads towards the real heart of the town, which is centred around Piazza Mazzini. Here, the church of **Santa Maria Maddalena** is worth a visit: the building is Neo-Classical, built by Giovanni Caproni from 1836, but houses a 16th-century altarpiece (*Madonna and Child, St Anthony Abbot and St Mary Magdalene*). This was formerly identified as a youthful work by Raphael, but is now known to be by Eusebio da San Giorgio, one of Perugino's circle.

🏛️ Palazzo della Corgna and Rocca del Leone
Piazza Gramsci. **Tel** 075 951 099. **Open** Mar–Sep: 9:30am–7pm; Oct: 9:30am–6:30pm; Nov–Mar: 9:30am–5:30pm Fri–Mon & hols (Christmas period daily). **Closed** 1 Jan, 25 Dec. ♿

⛪ Santa Maria Maddalena
Via Vittorio Emanuele. **Tel** 075 951 159.

⓱ Città della Pieve

Perugia. **Road Map** A4. 🚶 7,000.
🚆 Chiusi–Chianciano, 10 km (6 miles), Florence–Rome line. 🚌 ℹ️ Piazza Matteotti, 0578 299 375. 🎭 Palio dei Terzieri, Aug. 🌐 **cittadellapieve.org**

The fame of Città della Pieve, on the Tuscan border, is due primarily to the fact that it was the birthplace of the great Renaissance painter Pietro Vannucci. Known as Perugino (1450–1523) and famous in his own right, he also taught the young Raphael. Città della Pieve is worth a visit above all because it houses several major works by this artist.

Adoration of the Magi, Perugino, detail

An Etruscan colony of Chiusi (in nearby Tuscany), and later Roman, Città della Pieve suffered frequently from barbarian invasions. It finally developed as a fortified town in about 1000, around the church of Santi Gervasio e Protasio. The distinctive red coloration is due to the use of bricks – there was no stone available locally.

Città della Pieve is known for its very narrow streets, including what some claim to be the narrowest in Italy, Vicolo Baciadonne, which is just 80 cm (31 in) wide. The central Piazza del Plebiscito is home to **Palazzo della Corgna** (with 16th-century frescoes by

Fresco by Pomarancio, Palazzo della Corgna

Pomarancio), the Biblioteca Comunale (library) and, most importantly, the cathedral of **Santi Gervasio e Protasio**. This was rebuilt on the site of the original parish church, perhaps in the 8th century, and then remodelled and restored at intervals between the 12th and 17th centuries. Inside, among various precious works of art (by Domenico Alfani, Giannicola di Paolo and Pomarancio), there are two paintings by Perugino – a *Baptism of Christ* and a *Madonna and Child and Saints Peter, Paul, Gervasio and Protasio*.

In the church of **Santa Maria dei Servi** (included in the ticket for Palazzo della Corgna), just south of the centre, there were once some spendid frescoes by Perugino; only a *Deposition* survives, dating from 1517. Visitors will find a far more beautiful fresco by Perugino in the church of **Santa Maria dei Bianchi**, in Corso Vannucci, just off Piazza del Plebiscito. This depicts the *Adoration of the Magi* (1504), and is perhaps the best of all the works by Perugino found in his native city; the scene includes the view from Città della Pieve towards Lake Trasimeno, as well as a party of elegant Renaissance figures.

⓲ Southern Lake Trasimeno

In the mountains that rise to the south of Lake Trasimeno lies a series of villages where art and history have always played an important role. The painter Pietro Vannucci, better known as Perugino, was born and worked here. This tour partly retraces the steps of the great artist and partly seeks out small medieval hill towns, among the great treasures of Umbria.

Tips for Drivers

🛈 Piazza Mazzini 10, Castiglione del Lago, 075 965 2484. Length of tour: 55 km (34 miles). Time needed: 1 day. Stopping-off points: in villages along the route.

② Panicale
This fortified town is perched on a rocky spur. Perugino's *Martyrdom of St Sebastian* (1505) can be seen in the church of San Sebastiano.

③ Tavernelle
Just north of this village is the Santuario della Madonna di Mongiovino, a 16th-century church with frescoes from the same period.

① Paciano
Encircled by walls and in a lovely hilly setting of woods and olive groves, this is one of the best-preserved of the medieval villages in the area.

Magione

S75b

Lake Trasimeno

Perugia

S599

S220

S71

S220

Città della Pieve

S220

Nestore

S71

↓ Orvieto

⑤ Corciano
Almost intact 13th-century walls, protected by tall towers and a castle, extend for a kilometre around this pretty village. Corciano has both Etruscan and Roman origins, as do other villages on this tour.

④ Fontignano
This medieval village, built on a hillside, was where Perugino died in 1523. He left his last work of art here: a *Madonna and Child* in the church of the Annunziata.

Key

▦ Tour route

╍╍ Other roads

0 kilometres 5

0 miles 5

SOUTHERN UMBRIA

The countryside of Southern Umbria is very hilly, rising to the peaks of the Monti Sibillini towards the eastern fringes. Rocks and water are constant features of the landscape, as at the spectacular Cascata delle Marmore and the springs of Clitunno. Most of the towns are medieval in appearance, but were once part of the Etruscan world. Even the language spoken has affinities with Tuscan.

In the past, this part of the region was dominated by the Duchy of Spoleto, whose lands were regarded by geographers as the real heart of Umbria until the 16th century. Also part of this territory, culturally and politically, were Todi, of ancient Italic and Etruscan origin, and the Roman town of Narni, while Orvieto was viewed as an independent commune.

Despite the vicissitudes of history, here, as in the rest of Umbria, the sense of local identity derived from a long-standing communal spirit is strong and heartfelt. Every town has its own artistic and historical treasures, and each cherishes and takes pride in its own ancient past, manifested in numerous feast days and secular festivals. Southern Umbria's cultural calendar, which includes the Festival di Spoleto and events in Orvieto and Terni, is varied and popular, and draws people from all over the world.

Hills, and especially water, feature large in the natural landscape of southern Umbria. The River Tiber forms the Lago di Corbara, while the River Nera flows along the edge of the splendid valley known as the Valnerina. In the west, pale tufa soil and the high ridges of Orvieto signal the land of the Etruscans. The wilder peaks of the Apennines, on the other hand, occupy the southeastern corner of the region. Here, Cascia, Piediluco and Norcia are the last towns before the steep rise towards the windswept plateaux of Castelluccio, just a stone's throw from Le Marche and Lazio.

The cultural and gastronomic traditions of this corner of Italy, although similar in many ways to those of the neighbouring regions, are still quite individual, successfully uniting flavours and ideas from different areas. Norcia, in the Valnerina, is a byword for good food all over Italy.

Detail of the *Coronation of the Virgin*, by Filippo Lippi (1467), apse of Spoleto cathedral

◀ Charming alleys in the hillside town of Spello

Exploring Southern Umbria

Orvieto, Todi, Terni, Spoleto: a string of historical towns
unravels from east to west in Southern Umbria. In between
is fertile countryside, with farmhouses and cultivated fields,
and important stretches of river, including the lower course
of the River Tiber and the River Nera. There are also thermal
springs and archaeological areas, as well as nature reserves,
chief of which is the spectacular national park of the Monti
Sibillini, superb territory for walking, mountain-biking and
hang-gliding.

Entrance to the duomo at Piazza del
Popolo, Todi

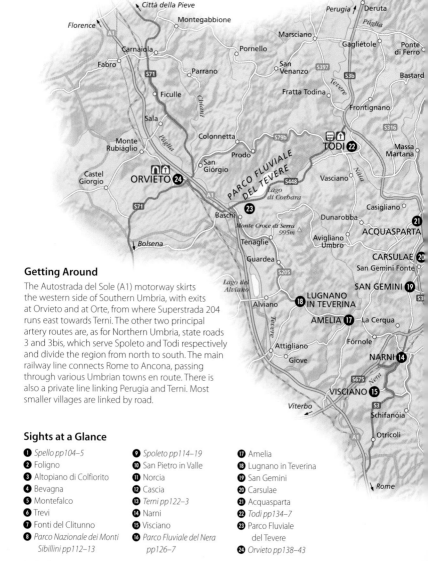

Getting Around

The Autostrada del Sole (A1) motorway skirts
the western side of Southern Umbria, with exits
at Orvieto and at Orte, from where Superstrada 204
runs east towards Terni. The other two principal
artery routes are, as for Northern Umbria, state roads
3 and 3bis, which serve Spoleto and Todi respectively
and divide the region from north to south. The
main railway line connects Rome to Ancona, passing
through various Umbrian towns en route. There is
also a private line linking Perugia and Terni. Most
smaller villages are linked by road.

Sights at a Glance

For hotels and restaurants see pp150–51 and pp162–7

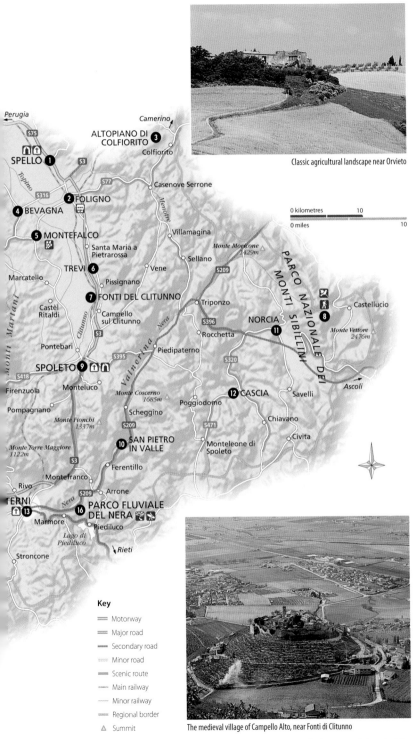

Classic agricultural landscape near Orvieto

Perugia

ALTOPIANO DI COLFIORITO ③

Camerino

Colfiorito

SPELLO ①

Casenove Serrone

② **FOLIGNO**

④ **BEVAGNA**

Villamagina

⑤ **MONTEFALCO**

Santa Maria a Pietrarossa

Monte Moricone 1429m

PARCO NAZIONALE DEI MONTI SIBILLINI

Marcatello

Vene

Sellano

TREVI ⑥

Castèl Ritaldi

Pissignano

⑦ **FONTI DEL CLITUNNO**

Triponzo

Castellucio

⑧

Monte Vettore 2476m

Campello sul Clitunno

NORCIA ⑪

Pontebari

Piedipaterno

Rocchetta

Ascoli

SPOLETO ⑨

Firenzuola

Monteluco

Monte Coscerno 1685m

Poggiodomo

⑫ **CASCIA**

Savelli

Pompagnano

Scheggino

Chiavano

Monte Fionchi 1337m

Monte Torre Maggiore 1122m

⑩ **SAN PIETRO IN VALLE**

Monteleone di Spoleto

Civita

Ferentillo

Montefranco

Rivo

Arrone

TERNI

⑬

⑯ **PARCO FLUVIALE DEL NERA**

Marmore

Piediluco

Stroncone

Lago di Piediluco

Rieti

Key

— Motorway

— Major road

— Secondary road

— Minor road

— Scenic route

— Main railway

— Minor railway

— Regional border

△ Summit

0 kilometres 10
0 miles 10

The medieval village of Campello Alto, near Fonti di Clitunno

For keys to symbols *see back flap*

❶ Spello

Spello lies on a hillside in the shadow of Monte Subasio and is built, like nearby Assisi, out of the same pink stone. A settlement founded here by the Umbri grew in size under the Romans, when it was known as *Hispellum*. The town walls, pierced by six gates, were built in the Augustan era. Later, the town was sacked by the Lombards, who made it part of the Duchy of Spoleto, and then, in 1238, crushed again by Frederick II. In 1389, by now a papal possession, Spello was given to the Baglioni family as a feudal estate. They ruled until the mid-16th century, after which Spello followed the fortunes of the rest of the region. The evident reminders of the town's past make it a fascinating place today.

Dispute in the Temple,
detail

🏛 Pinacoteca Civica
Piazza Matteotti 10. **Tel** 0742 301 497. **Open** Oct–Mar: 10:30am–12:30pm, 3–5pm Fri–Sun.

Since 1994 the civic art gallery has been housed in the Palazzo dei Canonici (15th century), to the right of Santa Maria Maggiore. Among the varied works in the collection, one highlight is a splendid *Wooden Madonna* dating from around 1240, brightly coloured and yet serene and stately. Also of note are several polyptychs of the 14th and 15th centuries and other significant works of the local school.

🏛 Sant'Andrea
Via Cavour.

Near the Pinacoteca, the church of Sant'Andrea (13th century) has a rather gloomy interior; and yet in the right transept is a superb fresco by Pinturicchio of the *Madonna and Child with Saints*. In the left transept, look out for the mummified body of Andrea Caccioli, one of the first followers of St Francis.

🏛 Piazza della Repubblica
In this not particularly notable square at the end of Via Cavour is the 13th-century **Palazzo Comunale** (now restored), which contains the Library and the Town Archive.

Heading north along Via Garibaldi, you pass **Palazzo Cruciani**, seat of the town council, and then the 12th-century church of **San Lorenzo**, an architectural hotchpotch. Of interest inside is the carved wooden pulpit, the work of Francesco Costantini (1600).

🏛 Porta Venere
Via Torri di Properzio.

A short detour west from Piazza della Repubblica takes you to Porta Venere, a Roman gateway flanked by two imposing 12-sided towers dating from the Middle Ages. The gate, heavily restored over the centuries, dates from the

Porta Consolare, one of the Roman gateways to the town

Exploring Spello
From Piazza Kennedy, access to the walled town is through Porta Consolare, a well-preserved Roman gateway. Heading north into the centre, Piazza della Repubblica marks the real centre of Spello.

🏛 Santa Maria Maggiore
Piazza Matteotti.

Completed in 1285, this fine church is the most important

monument in Spello. Its façade was reconstructed, using the original materials, in the 17th century.

The single-nave church owes its fame to the presence of the Cappella Baglioni, where there is a series of frescoes by Pinturicchio, perhaps the finest ever done by the artist. Painted from 1500–1501, the frescoes depict the *Four Sibyls* (on the vault) and *Scenes from the Life of Christ* (on the walls). The most important frescoes are an *Annunciation* (under which hangs a self-portrait of Pinturicchio), an *Adoration of the Magi* and a *Dispute in the Temple*. The floor of the chapel was made of majolica tiles from Deruta. More Pinturicchio frescoes can be found in the Cappella del Sacramento, reached from the left transept. In the right transept is the Cappella del Sepolcro, which at one time housed the town art gallery. Also of interest are a pulpit in sandstone and a tabernacle on the high altar.

View of the town of Spello, on a hillside above the Valle Umbra

Roman Porta Venere, with its two characteristic 12-sided towers

Augustan era: the structure that you see today originally had a double curtain giving way to an internal courtyard. The gate offers good views over the surrounding countryside.

Porta dell'Arce
Via Arco Romano.
One of the oldest entrances to the town, this gate is an example of how Roman buildings were integrated into the medieval fortifications. Nearby is the terrace of the Belvedere, from which the Topino valley, as well as the outline of Assisi's Santa Maria degli Angeli, can be admired.

San Claudio
Via Fontevecchia.
From the Belvedere, you can descend to the plain via the narrow Via dei Cappuccini and then the long Via Fontevecchia. Here, you'll find the delightful church of San Claudio, dating from the 12th century. Perhaps Spello's most interesting church architecturally, it has retained intact its Romanesque decoration and layout. The simple façade is topped by the original belfry.

The Romanesque façade of San Claudio

Roman Ruins
Via Centrale Umbra.
The Roman city was built at a lower level than the medieval town, which was constructed more defensively on the hill. The amphitheatre, near the church of San Claudio on the main road to Foligno, dates from the 1st century AD, but little survives.

A kilometre from Spello towards Perugia is **Villa Fidelia**, once at the centre of the Roman city, and where an epigraph, known as the "Rescritto di Costantino" (rescript of Constantine), was found in 1733. According to this ordinance, the great emperor, in the years between 324 and 337 AD, authorized the Umbrians to hold their celebrations at Spello and not in Orvieto.

Spello Town Centre
1. Santa Maria Maggiore
2. Pinacoteca Civica
3. Sant'Andrea
4. Piazza della Repubblica
5. Porta Venere
6. Porta dell'Arce
7. San Claudio
8. Roman Ruins

Foligno's Piazza della Repubblica with the cathedral's south façade

❷ Foligno

Perugia. **Road Map** D4. 🏛 56,000. 📖 Rome–Ancona line. 🚌 ℹ️ Corso Cavour 126, 0742 354 459. 🎪 Giostra della Quintana, 2nd Sun in Sep.

The town of Foligno, of Roman origin, lies in the plain of the River Topino, which skirts its northern edge. One of the few Umbrian towns to be built on flat land, Foligno was sited at the crossroads of two commercial roads of great importance: the Via Flaminia and the road from Perugia to Assisi.

A 15th-century fresco in Foligno's Palazzo Trinci

The principal manufacturing and commercial centre in the region, with the exception perhaps of Perugia, Foligno is a lively, dynamic city. Because of its location, the city has been able to sprawl out onto the plain, helped by the destruction of the 14th-century walls after the unification of Italy. While the original oval layout can still be discerned, the historic centre features a mix of old and modern architecture.

The railway station, east of the centre, is both a good point of reference and a good place from which to start a tour. From here, passing by streets where walls once stood, you rapidly reach the historic centre along Via Ottaviani and Via Umberto I. Halfway along Via Umberto I is Via Piermarini, named after the famous Foligno architect who

designed La Scala opera house in Milan. Opposite is the entrance to Via dei Monasteri, where you'll find the **monastery of Sant'Anna**. While still in possession of several precious works of art, the monastery is most famous as the former home (until 1798) of Raphael's celebrated *Madonna di Foligno*, removed by Napoleon's men and now on display in the Vatican museum in Rome.

Back on Via Umberto I, at the corner with Via Garibaldi, is the little brick church of the **Nunziatella** (late 15th century), of interest to visitors because of two works by Perugino. Above the right-hand altar is a *Baptism of Jesus* and, in the lunette, a *God the Father*. Both works date from 1507.

From here it is just a short distance to the central **Piazza della Repubblica**, the heart of the city and home to the main centres of religious and civic power, as was traditional in the Middle Ages. These include the **duomo**, built and modified between 1133 and 1512 and restored to its original Romanesque form in the early 20th century. The cathedral is unusual for having two façades. The main façade faces the small Piazza del Duomo. The building's better side, however, is the south front, with its richly decorated lateral façade

adorned with a splendid doorway (1201), which looks onto Piazza della Repubblica.

Opposite is the **Palazzo Comunale**, with a Neo-Classical façade. Originally built in the 13th century, the palace was rebuilt several times and altered completely following the earthquake of 1832. The only historic element to be kept was the battlemented tower, which, however, succumbed to the earthquake of 1997.

The palace is linked to Palazzo Orfini, which is famous because it was probably the home of the printing house of Orfini. This was among the earliest of all Italian printing houses (1470), and the first to publish a work in Italian, Dante's *Divine Comedy* (1472).

On the northwestern side of Piazza della Repubblica is another important building, **Palazzo Trinci**, home of the Pinacoteca Comunale and the Museo Archeologico. Among many works of art in the gallery are pictures by three notable painters born in Foligno: Ottaviano Nelli, Niccolò Alunno and Pier Antonio Mezzastris.

Via Gramsci, which leads west off the piazza, contains several palaces dating from the 16th to 18th centuries, some constructed over older medieval buildings. Of these, the Renaissance **Palazzo Deli** (Via Gramsci 6) is the most beautiful. It features a medieval

Nativity, Niccolò Alunno, church of San Niccolò

Well from 1340 in the Romanesque cloister of the abbey of Sassovivo

tower that was once part of Palazzo Trinci.

In Piazza San Domenico, at the end of Via Gramsci, is the Romanesque church of **Santa Maria Infraportas**, whose exterior portico dates from the 11th or 12th century. Inside is the Cappella dell'Assunta (12th century), which has Byzantine-like frescoes that are of interest even though they are in a rather bad state. Another fine work in the church is a *St Jerome and Two Angels* by Mezzastris.

The church of **San Niccolò**, nearby on Via della Scuola di Arti e Mestieri, was rebuilt in the 14th century by Olivetan monks, remodelled in the following century and then completely rebuilt again in the 18th century. Inside are several works by Niccolò Alunno, among them the *Polyptych of the Nativity*, one of his best-known works. The School of Arts and Crafts, after which the street is named, was based in the monastery alongside.

In Piazza XX Settembre, reached from San Niccolò along Via Mezzalancia, is one of the most beautiful private palazzi built in the 17th century, **Palazzo Monaldi-Bernabò**, now a school.

🏛 **Museo di Palazzo Trinci**
Piazza della Repubblica. **Tel** 0742 357 989. **Open** 10am–1pm, 3–7pm Tue–Sun. **Closed** 1 Jan, 25 Dec. 🖼 ⚕

Environs
Heading east out of Foligno along the main road no. 77, then taking a fork to the right after about 2 km (1 mile), drivers will come to a scenic road that leads up to the **Abbazia di Sassovivo** surrounded by a dense forest of holm oaks. Founded in around 1000, the Benedictine abbey was an important political and cultural centre at least until the 15th century. The abbey church is of much less interest than the 13th-century Romanesque cloister, which is the finest of its kind in the region. It features 128 variegated double or spiral columns supporting 58 round arches, decorated with coloured marbles and two bands of mosaics. There is a 13th-century fresco, too. Also of note is the Loggia del Paradiso in the monastery.

The façade of Santa Maria Infraportas

❾ Altopiano di Colfiorito

Perugia. **Road Map** E4. 🚆 Foligno, 24 km (15 miles), Rome–Ancona line. 🚌 ℹ Corso Cavour 126, Foligno, 0742 354 459.

Heading east from Foligno along main road no. 77, shortly before the border of Le Marche you reach the Altopiano of Colfiorito. This upland plain, which reaches over 700 m (2,300 ft) above sea level, consists of seven broad basins, once part of a lake which was drained in the 15th century. Of the original natural formation, a marsh called the Palude di Colfiorito remains. The 100-ha (250-acre) wetland is of great interest for its aquatic vegetation and associated wildlife.

Various calcareous plains alternate with steep slopes, in a fascinating undulating landscape. Silhouetted around the fringes are the Apennine peaks of Monte Pennino, Monte Acuto, Monte Le Scalette, Monte Profoglio and Col Falcone.

This upland plain and the surrounding area now form part of the Parco Regionale di Colfiorito, a protected area that was set up to preserve this unique region. Now that the park is well established, visitors can explore the Altopiano using a series of signposted routes. There are also traces of ancient human habitation, the most obvious of which are the so-called *castellieri*, pre-Roman villages. The most visited is that of Monte Orve. The park also houses **Museo Naturalistico**, which was set up for the observation of main species of flora and fauna here.

The slopes of Monte Pennino and the marsh of Colfiorito

Piazza Silvestri, in the heart
of Bevagna

❹ Bevagna

Perugia. **Road Map** D4. 🚗 5,100.
🚆 Foligno, 9 km (6 miles), Rome–
Ancona line. 🚌 ℹ️ Pro Loco, Piazza
Filippo Silvestri, 1, 0742 361 667.
🎭 Mercato delle Gaite, Jun.

Situated at the western
margins of the Valle Umbra,
Bevagna has long been
at the centre of a busy
road network, Inhabited
probably since the
7th century BC, ancient
Mevania experienced its
most affluent period
under the Romans, thanks
largely to its position on
the Via Flaminia. Many
illustrious citizens of
ancient Rome built their
country houses here.
Following a period of
decline during the
Lombard era, when
this branch of the Via
Flaminia lost importance,
the town experienced a revival
in the 12th century, and this
was when Bevagna acquired
its current appearance. Town
walls, incorporating part of the
Roman walls, were built, with a

Artemis, Museo
Civico

main square at the centre. Not
only are the walls still a feature,
but remarkably little has been
built outside them since the
Middle Ages.
   Porta Foligno is the main
entrance into the town, from
where Corso Matteotti leads
to the heart of the city, Piazza
Silvestri. Around this clearly
medieval piazza stand the
Gothic **Palazzo dei Consoli** and
three churches: **San Silvestro,
San Michele Arcangelo** and
Santi Domenico e Giacomo.
   Corso Matteotti follows the
route of the *cardo* – one of
the main streets through the
Roman settlement. In the
northern part, where the Forum
stood, various traces of the
Roman era have been restored
and some still survive, among
them the ruins of a temple
(incorporated into the church of
the Madonna della Neve),
a theatre and baths. In
the same district, off
Piazza Garibaldi, is the
13th-century church of
San Francesco. Inside
are frescoes by an artist
known as Fantino. This
painter was born in
Bevagna at the end of
the 16th century and left
works of art in many local
towns. The church also
contains a stone which
is said to have been
mounted by St Francis
when he preached to
the birds (see pp28–9), an event
which happened nearby.
   Also worth a visit is the **Museo
Civico**, which has many Roman
and pre-Roman finds, as well as
the fine *Ciccoli Altarpiece* (1565–
70) by Dono Doni. There is also

a section devoted to the local
16th- and 17th-century artists.

🏛️ **Museo Civico**
Corso Matteotti 70. **Tel** 0742 360 031.
Open Apr, May, Sep: 10:30am–
1pm, 2:30–6pm daily; Jun & Jul:
10:30am–1pm, 3:30–7pm daily; Aug:
10.30am–1pm, 3–7:30pm daily; Oct–
Mar: 10:30am–1pm, 2:30–6pm Tue–
Sun (to 5pm Nov–Mar). **Closed** 1 Jan,
25 Dec. 🎫

Ciccoli Altarpiece, 1565–70, by Dono Doni,
Museo Civico

❺ Montefalco

Perugia. **Road Map** D4. 🚗 5,592.
🚆 Foligno, 12 km (7 miles), Rome–
Ancona line. 🚌 ℹ️ Pro Loco, Via
Ringhiera Umbra, Montefalco, 348 782
5210. 🎭 Agosto Montefalchese, Aug.

Perched high on a hill
dominating the valleys of
the rivers Topino and Clitunno,
Montefalco offers superb views
over central Umbria, and has
been nicknamed "the balcony
of Umbria". It is also famous for
its Sagrantino wine.
   The small medieval comune,
known as Coccorone, was badly
damaged in 1249 in the course
of bitter battles fought between
the pope and Emperor Frederick
II. When the latter rebuilt the
town, he decided to call it
Montefalco, in honour of his
imperial eagle insignia. The
town's artistic high point came
in the 14th century, followed
by decline once Montefalco
came under papal jurisdiction.
   Montefalco retains some
elements of Roman origin, but

Historic Bevagna, at the fringes of the Valle Umbra

For hotels and restaurants see pp150–51 and pp162–7

the atmosphere is, above all, medieval, focused on the circular Piazza del Comune. This feudal nucleus is enclosed within a circle of medieval walls with five gates, from which five main streets lead, in the shape of a star, to the central piazza.

The main access to the town is via the 14th-century Porta Sant'Agostino, which has a tower on top. From here, Via Umberto I and then Corso Mameli lead up to the main square. Along the way is the church of **Sant'Agostino** (late 13th century), whose façade is adorned with slender columns and a rose window. Inside the church are a number of interesting frescoes, among them one attributed to Ambrogio Lorenzetti. You also pass palazzos Tempestini, Langeli and Moriconi.

Laid out during the 14th century, the central Piazza del Comune is home to the **Palazzo Comunale**, heavily reworked in the 19th century, the former church of San Filippo Neri (now a theatre) and the **Oratorio di Santa Maria**, which was used as a public meeting place during the Renaissance.

Just north of Piazza del Comune, along Via Ringhiera Umbra, is the most important monument in the town, and indeed one of the most famous in the entire region – the former church of **San Francesco**. The attached monastery houses the **Museo Comunale**. The highlight of a visit to the deconsecrated

Scenes from the Life of St Clare, detail, church of Santa Chiara

14th-century church are the frescoes painted by Benozzo Gozzoli (1420–97), a pupil of Fra Angelico and famous above all for his exquisite frescoes in the Palazzo Medici in Florence. Gozzoli's frescoes in San Francesco are found in the Cappella di San Girolamo and, more importantly, in the central apse, where the magnificent and colourful *Life of St Francis* (1452) is the most important pictorial cycle dedicated to the saint after the one in the Basilica di San Francesco in Assisi.

The church-cum-museum also contains works of art salvaged from other local churches, as well as other objects: note, in particular, a *Crucifix* by the Maestro Espressionista di Santa Chiara (late 13th–early 14th centuries), a *Madonna and Child* from the workshop of Melozzo da Forlì (late 15th century), a *Nativity* painted by Perugino (1503) and, among the sculptures, a *Coronation of the Virgin* from the workshop of Andrea della Robbia (16th century).

From Piazza del Comune, a flight of steps leads southwards down to the medieval church of **San Bartolomeo**, and to the town gate of the same name. Beyond is Viale Federico II (named in honour of the emperor who stayed in the town in 1240 during his battles against the pope), which leads on to

Crucifix, Museo Comunale

the quarter called Borgo di San Leonardo. Walking westwards, outside the old walls, you reach the convent and church of **Santa Chiara**. These are dedicated not to the famous Clare of Assisi, but to Chiara di Damiano of Montefalco (1268–1308), who had the complex built here in the 13th and 14th centuries, on the site of the older Cappella di Santa Croce. The chapel (opened on request by the nuns who still live in the convent) is now the apse of the church. It is completely covered in 14th-century frescoes by Umbrian artists, narrating the lives of the saints Chiara, Caterina (Catherine) and Biagio (Blaise), and of the Virgin. On the wall of the altar a *Calvary* includes more than 45 figures.

A short distance south, along Via Giuseppe Verdi, is the Renaissance church of **Santa Illuminata**, which was built from 1491 on the site where Santa Chiara and her sister were locked up by their father.

The Franciscan convent of **San Fortunato**, about 1 km (half a mile) south of the town, has frescoes by Benozzo Gozzoli (1449) in the church.

⬆ **San Francesco and Museo Comunale**
Via Ringhiera Umbra. **Tel** 0742 379 598. **Open** Apr, May & Sep: 10:30am–1pm, 2–6pm daily; Jun–Aug: 10:30am–1pm, 3–7pm daily; Oct–Mar: 10:30am–1pm, 2:30–5pm Wed–Sun. **Closed** 1 Jan, 25 Dec. 🚫 ♿

Porta Sant'Agostino (or dello Stradone), gateway to Montefalco

❻ Trevi

Perugia. **Road Map** D5. 🏔 8,500.
🚉 Rome–Ancona line, FCU Perugia–
Terni line. 🚌 ℹ Piazza Mazzini 5,
0742 781 150.

The historic centre of Trevi "unwinds" in a stunning spiral fashion around a steep conical hill, Monte Serano, which dominates the plain of Spoleto. Flooding from the nearby River Clitunno used to be a constant threat and forced the inhabitants of Roman Trevi to move to higher ground. Once this threat was averted, however, the modern city – the so-called Borgo Trevi – was free to develop down on the plain, among the fields and olive groves.

Trevi converted early to Christianity; according to legend, this was because of the presence of the martyr Emiliano. In the 4th century, after a brief period of liberty, the town became part of the papal states and remained so until the unification of Italy.

The central Piazza Mazzini is home to the **Palazzo Comunale**, built in the 14th century but with important later additions, such as the 15th-century portico. From here, Via San Francesco passes the monumental **Palazzo Valenti** en route to the enormous church of **San Francesco**.

This church, together with the adjacent **Raccolta d'Arte di San Francesco**, is the principal artistic attraction in the town. The church itself, which dates

Coronation of the Virgin (1522), detail

from the 13th century, contains interesting works, including a fine organ from 1209. However, Trevi's most important works of art are on display in the Raccolta, which has been housed in the church monastery since 1997. The finest work is the *Coronation of the Virgin* (1522), by Giovanni di Pietro, known as Spagna, which was commissioned by the friars of the church of San Martino *(see below)*; the predella includes two scenes from the lives of the saints: *St Martin gives away his Cloak* and *The Stigmata of St Francis*. The art collection also includes paintings from the Umbrian school from the 14th century, among the most complete anywhere; in particular, do not miss the *Life of Christ* by Giovanni di Corraduccio (first half of the 14th century). The

Painted cross (15th century),
Raccolta di San Francesco

cathedral of **Sant'Emiliano** stands at the summit of the hill. It was extensively restored in the 20th century, but still has the three original apses (12th century), which are among the best examples of Romanesque in the region. Next door is the Palazzo Lucarini, which houses the **Palazzo Lucarini Contemporary**, with a small permanent collection of contemporary art by Italian and foreign artists, as well as changing exhibitions.

A ten-minute walk along pedestrian Viale Ciuffelli takes you to the 14th-century parish church of **San Martino**, built in a panoramic position on the northeastern edge of town. Inside the church are works by Tiberio d'Assisi and Fantino, among the most famous artists of the Umbrian school. It is also worth visiting the **Santuario della Madonna delle Lacrime**, just south of the centre (not far from the train station), where there is a lovely *Epiphany* by Perugino (1512), as well as an important cycle of frescoes by Lo Spagna, in the chapel of San Francesco.

🏛 **Palazzo Lucarini Contemporary**
Via Lucarini 1. **Tel** 0742 381 021.
Open 3:30–6:30pm Thu–Sun.
🌐 palazzolucarini.it

Environs
Around 5 km (3 miles) north of Trevi rises the 14th-century church of **Santa Maria a Pietrarossa**. Its name derives from the red stone (*pietra rossa*) in the presbytery, to which miraculous powers were attributed. The church has an extensive portico, beneath which is a vast cycle of votive frescoes dating from the 15th century. A few metres from the church is the San Giovanni spring, whose water is said to be therapeutic.

Interior of the church of San Martino

The pool formed by the Fonti del Clitunno springs, framed by weeping willows and poplars

❼ Fonti del Clitunno

Perugia. **Road Map** D5. **FS** Campello sul Clitunno, Rome–Ancona line, Trevi, 10 km (6 miles), FCU Perugia–Terni line.

These famous springs emerge alongside the Via Flaminia, at Vene, and have been known since antiquity. The cool, limpid waters of this series of karst springs create a large pool dotted with small islands, as well as a river of the same name.

On a literary level, the historic reputation of the springs derives from the oracular skills attributed to the god of the River Clitunno (Clitumnus, the messenger god). The oracle was often cited by poets through the ages, from Virgil to Byron. This does not mean that drinking the water makes you a good orator. The water's main effect, some

The Roman Tempietto

say, is to remove the urge to imbibe alcohol.

The site really owes its fortune to the fertility of the soil and the sheer abundance of water, which rises in such quantity that at one time the river was navigable. The Romans exploited the site and created a holiday area here, using the springs to create public baths. Numerous buildings were constructed, including several villas dotted along the river banks, although today they have almost totally disappeared. Votive buildings include the **Tempietto**, which many experts now believe was built in the 8th century, using the materials from an earlier Christian building. About 1 km (half a mile) north of the Fonti, the temple has a crypt and a room for worship. The latter is

decorated with 7th-century frescoes, thought to be the oldest paintings with sacred subjects in Umbria.

🏛 Fonti del Clitunno
Tel 0743 521 141. **Open** daily from 8:30am, 9am or 10am (check website for details); closed between 1–2pm Oct–Feb. **Closed** 25 Dec.
W fontidelclitunno.it

🏛 Tempietto
Tel 0743 275 085. **Open** 12:15– 5:45pm Tue–Sun **Closed** Mon.

Environs

Just south of the springs is **Campello sul Clitunno**, whose church of the Madonna della Bianca has fine 16th-century frescoes. Follow the steep road up from the village to **Castello di Pissignano**, where Barbarossa once stayed.

A trapezoid tower, part of the Castello di Pissignano

Umbrian Olive Oil

Olive oil made in Umbria can bear the label "denominazione di origine controllata" (denomination of controlled origin) if it conforms to the high quality standards set for the product. Umbria has been divided into five producing districts, each with differing quality criteria. The strictest rules are applied in the district centred around Trevi, one of the most important olive-growing areas.

❽ Parco Nazionale dei Monti Sibillini

Established as a national park in August 1993, the mountainous Sibillini park is exceptional. Extending over 70,000 ha (173,000 acres), the park is divided between Umbria and Le Marche and offers a bewitching combination of nature and history. There are numerous abbeys and medieval hill towns as well as rich natural diversity. Trails cover the entire park and are suitable for both walkers and mountain bikers. The windy upland plains are popular for hang-gliding, and in winter the mountains attract skiers. Among the refuges higher up are Rifugio Città di Ascoli (Passo di Forca Canapine), Capanna Ghezzi (above the plains of Castelluccio) and Rifugio San Severino Marche.

Abbazia di Sant'Eutizio
The buildings of this abbey date from the late 12th century, but the area drew hermits from the 6th century onwards, and was important politically and culturally during the early Middle Ages.

Key

≈≈ Park road

▬▬ Scenic route

≈≈ River

△ Peak

0 kilometres   3

0 miles   3

Spoleto

Collesanto

Cicconi

Lago di Fiastra

Fiastra

Fiastro

Acquacani

Sasso

Calcara

S209

①

Monte Moricone 1,429 m/4,687 ft

Nera

Castelsantangelo

Passo di Gualdo

Monte Patino 1,884 m/6,180 ft

Norcia

Monte Ventoso 1,719 m/5,638 ft

Marcite di Norcia
These irrigated meadows benefit from the water that flows from karstic springs.

Wildlife in the Monti Sibillini

The park is an ideal habitat for many species. In terms of mammals, the wolf and wildcat are present in small numbers, but there are healthy populations of roe deer, marten and especially wild boar (to the degree that they are becoming a problem). Lynx have been seen, but doubt has been cast on sightings of the Marsican bear. The birdlife in the mountains is very varied. Foremost is the golden eagle, an elegant predator which is easily spotted in the area. Some rarer species such as the peregrine falcon and the goshawk are also present. Alpine choughs and wall creepers are common.

Golden eagle

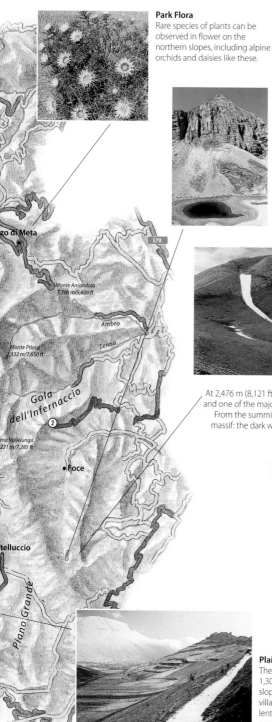

Park Flora
Rare species of plants can be observed in flower on the northern slopes, including alpine orchids and daisies like these.

Lago di Pilato
According to legend, Pontius Pilate was buried in this lake after the buffaloes pulling his hearse refused to go any further, though another story says that a remorseful Pilate drowned himself here. The lake turns blood-red owing to a rare red-coloured algae that grows here.

VISITORS' CHECKLIST

Practical Information
Road Map F5. **i** Ente Parco, Visso, 0737 972 711.
w sibillini.net

Transport

Monte Vettore
At 2,476 m (8,121 ft), this is the highest peak in the park and one of the major mountains in the Apennine chain. From the summit there are fine views over the entire massif: the dark waters of Lago di Pilato dominate the scene below.

KEY

① **Visso**, now the park headquarters, was said to have been founded 907 years before Rome. From the Middle Ages to the 18th century, its territory was divided into five districts called "*guaite*" (guards). Castles and look-out towers are visible.

② **Monte Sibilla** is the peak that gave its name to the park. There is a grotto here: according to legend this was the home of the mythical Sibyl (*sibilla*), capable of predicting the future.

Plains of Castelluccio
There are three high plains at over 1,300 m (4,264 ft) on the western slopes of the park above the isolated village of Castelluccio (famous for its lentils). In spring, the ground here is carpeted in a breathtaking abundance of flowers, known as the *fioritura*.

❾ Spoleto

Spoleto is one of the most important towns in Umbria. It occupies a striking hillside position, at the foot of Monteluco, is home to a host of fine monuments, and enjoys an international reputation. The last started with the travellers on the Grand Tour and continues today with the cosmopolitan crowd that has flocked to the famous Festival di Spoleto since 1958. The first settlement here was founded, probably by the Umbri, high up where the fortress was later built: traces of the massive 4th-century-BC walls are still visible. Spoletium, founded in 241 BC, became a major Roman colony, thanks partly to its proximity to the Via Flaminia, used by people travelling to Rome from the north. Spoleto later became the seat of a Lombard dukedom and then an important commune. Numerous monastic orders were established here and the town maintained its prosperity over the centuries. In 2011, Spoleto's Tempietto del Clitunno was listed as a UNESCO World Heritage site.

The entrance to San Nicolò, framed by Gothic arches

View of the city of Spoleto, dominating the Spoletine valley

Exploring Spoleto

The main approach into the city is from the northern side, over the Ponte Sanguinario, a Roman bridge. From here, the route of the tour climbs upwards, via several sites of importance, to the highest and oldest part of the city, where both the duomo and the Rocca d'Albornoziana, essential sights on a visit to Spoleto, are found.

🏠 San Gregorio Maggiore
Piazza Garibaldi.

Just over Ponte Sanguinario, the gateway to the town, is Piazza Garibaldi, home to the church of San Gregorio Maggiore. It was founded in the 4th century, in the early Christian era, outside the walls, as were all the oldest churches in the city. It was renovated in the 12th century, incorporating materials from various Roman remains. The façade is adorned with statues and a huge campanile (notice the Roman

blocks used in the lower half) and has a portico modelled on that of the duomo *(see p117)*. Despite frequent restoration and embellishment, the Romanesque interior still bears traces of interesting medieval frescoes.

The façade of San Gregorio with portico and bell tower

🏠 San Nicolò
Via Cecili.

From Piazza Garibaldi, Via dell'Anfiteatro heads towards the centre, past the meagre ruins of a 2nd-century-AD Roman amphitheatre. Continuing up Via Cecili you reach the deconsecrated church of San Nicolò.

What looks like a single church is, in fact, a complex of religious buildings placed one on top of the other over the course of the centuries. The imposing Gothic church, which played host to Martin Luther in 1512, is now used for plays and concerts.

🏠 San Domenico
Via Pierleoni.

Via Cecili leads to Piazza della Torre dell'Olio, with the 14th-century tower of the same name. Taking Via Pierleoni, which runs south, you reach the large monastic church of San Domenico (13th century), with its distinctive pink and white striped design.

Restored to its original Gothic form in the 1930s, the church has a single, unusually long nave. Here, you can admire interesting frescoes dating from the 14th and 15th centuries, some of which have come to light only in recent decades. In particular, linger over the Cappella di San Pietro Martire (the first on the left), the Cappella di Santa Maria Maddalena, on the right-hand side of the apse, and the Cappella Benedetti di Montevecchio, on the left of the presbytery.

The Roman theatre in Spoleto, dating from the 1st century AD

⬆ Santi Giovanni e Paolo

Via Filitteria.

Heading up Via Sant'Andrea from San Domenico, you pass the **Teatro Nuovo**, a grand theatre built over the ruins of a monastery and inaugurated in 1864. A little further on is the deconsecrated church dedicated to saints John and Paul in 1174. It is worth a visit for the frescoes inside: the oldest is the one depicting the *Martyrdom of Thomas Becket*, painted after his canonization in 1173.

🏛 Palazzo Collicola Arti Visive

Palazzo Collicola Arti Visive, Piazza Collicola 1. **Tel** 0743 464 34.

Open mid-Mar–mid-Oct: 10:30am–1pm, 3:30–7pm daily; mid-Oct–mid-Mar: 10:30am– 1pm, 3:30–5:30pm Wed–Mon. 🖼

The collection in this modern art gallery is divided into three sections. The most interesting is the first, which has works by contemporary Italian artists, participants in the "Premio Spoleto" (Spoleto Prize), among them Arnaldo Pomodoro and Giulio Turcato.

VISITORS' CHECKLIST

Practical Information
Perugia. **Road Map** D5. 🚗 38,000.
ℹ Piazza della Libertà 7, 0743 218 620. 🎭 Festival di Spoleto, Jun–Jul.

Transport
🚉 Rome–Ancona line, 892021.
🚌 075 963 7637
🌐 umbriamobilita.it

🏛 Teatro Romano

Piazza della Libertà.

Corso Mazzini eventually widens out into Piazza della Libertà. This is the site of a much-restored Roman theatre, built in the 1st century AD and with a capacity of 3,000. It was excavated only in the late 19th century. It is used for festival performances.

In the nearby monastery of Sant'Agata, one of the oldest religious buildings in the city, is the **Museo Archeologico Nazionale**, with important pre-Roman finds.

🏛 Museo Archeologico Nazionale

Via Sant'Agata 18. **Tel** 0743 223 277.
Open 8:30am–7:30pm Mon–Sat.
Closed 1 Jan, 1 May, 25 Dec. 🖼

Spoleto Town Centre

① San Gregorio Maggiore
② San Nicolò
③ San Domenico
④ Santi Giovanni e Paolo
⑤ Palazzo Collicola Arti Visive
⑥ Teatro Romano
⑦ Sant'Ansano and the Crypt of Sant'Isacco
⑧ Arco di Druso
⑨ Piazza del Mercato
⑩ Museo Diocesano and Sant'Eufemia
⑪ La Rocca d'Albornoziana
⑫ Duomo
⑬ San Ponziano
⑭ San Salvatore

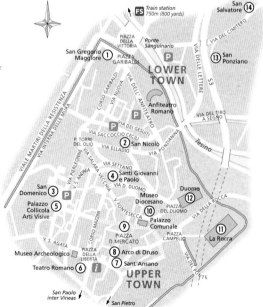

0 metres 250
0 yards 250

⬆ Sant'Ansano and the Crypt of Sant'Isacco

Via Brignone.

Climbing up towards the oldest part of Spoleto, you follow the route of the "cardo maximus", one of the main roads through the Roman settlement. The church of Sant'Ansano is, in fact, built on the ruins of a 1st-century temple. What you see today dates from the 18th century, but the church has a complex architectural history. The crypt of Sant'Isacco (St Isaac) provides evidence of a 12th-century church dedicated to both saints. It contains Roman columns and striking Byzantine-style frescoes. The church above contains a *Madonna* by Spagna (first half of the 16th century).

The Crypt of Sant'Isacco, beneath Sant'Ansano

🏛 Arco di Druso

Piazza del Mercato.

The Arch of Drusus, one of many arches scattered around the town, marked the point where the *cardo maximus* entered the forum (now Piazza del Mercato). It was erected in AD 23 in memory of the son of Emperor Tiberius.

🏛 Piazza del Mercato

This square lies at the heart of the oldest part of Spoleto. With an open market, shops and bars, it is always busy.

In terms of monuments, of particular note is a fountain built in the mid-18th century with material taken from other buildings, among them four coats of arms and a slab commemorating Pope Urban VIII. In the northwestern corner is one side of the **Palazzo Comunale**, originally medieval but rebuilt in the late 1700s, after earthquake damage. The **Museo del Tessuto e del Costume**

The fountain in Piazza del Mercato, built in 1746–8

contains over 2,500 pieces spanning the 14th to the 20th centuries, including liturgical vestments, clothing, fans, hats and folk textiles.

Nearby is a **Casa Romana** (Roman house), dating from the 1st century BC, which has some lovely mosaic floors.

🏛 Casa Romana

Via di Visiale. **Tel** 0743 234 250.
Open 11am–7pm daily. **Closed** Mon (Oct–Mar). 🖼

🏛 Museo del Tessuto e del Costume

Via delle Terme 5. **Tel** 0743 459 40.
Open 3:30–7pm Fri–Sun. 🖼

🏛 Museo Diocesano and Sant'Eufemia

Via Saffi 13. **Tel** 0743 231 022.
Open 11am–1pm, 3–6pm Wed–Sun.
Closed Mon & Tue. 🖼

The architectural history of this palace, in front of Palazzo Comunale, constitutes a virtual narrative in stone of the history of Spoleto. It began

with the construction of a Roman building (still partially visible), above which it is thought that the Palazzo dei Longobardi was built when Spoleto was a duchy. In the 12th century the building was incorporated into a monastery, and became the bishop's palace in the 16th–17th centuries.

Inside is a good collection of works of art and, in the courtyard, the 12th-century church of **Sant'Eufemia**. This church is Romanesque but more Lombard than Umbrian in style. It is famed for its rare women's galleries above the nave.

🏛 La Rocca d'Albornoziana

Piazza Campello 1. **Tel** 0743 224 952.
Open La Rocca and Camera Pinta 9:30am–7:30pm daily; Museo Nazionale del Ducato di Spoleto 9am–1:30pm Tue–Sun.

In 1359, when the city was an outpost of a Church intent on reconquering Umbria, Cardinal Albornoz, papal legate for Innocent VI, ordered the construction of a military fortress (*rocca*) at the highest point of the city. It was linked to the hill behind, Monteluco, by the impressive Ponte delle Torri, which still straddles the Valle del Tessino (*see p113*). **La Rocca** can be visited by bus (buses run hourly from Piazza Campello) or the escalators can help cover the climb.

The fortress is built on a rectangular plan around two courtyards, the Corte d'Armi and the Cortile d'Onore, both surrounded by towers. Over the centuries, La Rocca has

The Rocca, seen from the far side of the Ponte delle Torri

been home to various notable figures, among them Lucrezia Borgia, whose caprices were perhaps responsible for the naming of the tower called "della Spiritata" (the spirited one). Converted into a prison for over a century, in 1984 the Rocca underwent restoration.

The highlights inside are the frescoes in the **Camera Pinta** (in one of the main towers). These chivalric scenes were painted by artists from the school of Terni in the 14th–15th centuries. Also inside is the **Museo Nazionale del Ducato di Spoleto**.

Behind La Rocca is the masterly, ten-arch **Ponte delle Torri**, crossing the River Tessino. It is 230 m (755 ft) long and over 70 m (230 ft) high: the date of construction is uncertain and it is probable that today's bridge evolved from a Roman bridge-cum-aqueduct. In the middle of the bridge is an opening offering lovely views.

Mosaic by Solsternus on the façade of the duomo

↑ Duomo

Piazza del Duomo. **Open** 8:30am–12:30pm, 3:30–7pm (Nov–Mar: 5:30pm) daily.

A short climb from Piazza del Mercato leads to the sloping Piazza del Duomo, home of Spoleto's cathedral. As a backdrop to the Festival di Spoleto, this church's image is now world-famous.

The cathedral, built and consecrated at the end of the 12th century, is dedicated to Santa Maria Assunta, and rises on a site where there were at least two earlier religious buildings. The façade, one of

The duomo's façade, backdrop to the annual Festival di Spoleto

the most superb examples of Umbrian Romanesque, is divided into three orders and is the result of at least three successive phases of construction.

The original project resulted in the basilica layout, and the bell tower probably dates from the same era (12th century). A second phase of construction (early 13th century) saw the building of the façade, with the mosaic of Solsternus (1207) and the three upper rose windows, which frame the original Cosmatesque one underneath, one of the most beautiful in central Italy. The portico, with its magnificent central door, was added at the end of the 15th century. The bronze bust of Urban VIII above the central door was sculpted by Gian Lorenzo Bernini in 1640.

The interior of the church, rebuilt in Baroque style in 1648, is built on a Latin cross plan, divided into three aisles separated by a colonnade. There are various important works of art here. Just past the entrance, on the right, is the Cappella del Vescovo Costantino Eroli, built in 1497 and entirely decorated with frescoes by Pinturicchio. Don't miss those in the chapel altar niche, depicting *God the Father*

Transition of the Virgin, Filippo Lippi, detail

and Angels, *The Madonna and Child* and *John the Baptist and St Stephen*. There is also a fine series of figures from the Old Testament on the vault. The other important cycle of frescoes (1467–9), by the artist Filippo Lippi, is found on the walls of the apse. The subject is the life of Mary. Among the scenes are an *Annunciation*, a *Transition of the Virgin*, a *Nativity* and a *Coronation of the Virgin*. The sarcophagus of the Tuscan artist is also kept in the church, although his remains are no longer here.

On the two sides of the apse, extending outwards from the main body of the church, are two chapels, the Cappella della Santissima Icona and the Cappella del Sacramento. In the first is an image of the Virgin in the form of an icon, much venerated because it is attributed to St Luke. On the left, to the side of the transept is the lovely Cappella delle Reliquie. Besides some fine frescoes and painted panels, this chapel contains a 14th-century wooden statue of a *Madonna and Child* and a letter written by St Francis to his disciple Fra Leone. On the first altar on the left, in the nave, hangs a *Crucifix* by Alberto Sotii, painted on parchment applied to board, dated 1187. Other similar treasures are kept in the Archivio Capitolare.

Detail of a Pinturicchio fresco in the duomo's Cappella Eroli

Detail of a bas-relief on the façade of the church of San Pietro Fuori le Mura

🏛 San Paolo inter Vineas

Via San Paolo.

The first of four important churches, which form a curve around the eastern side of the historic centre of Spoleto, lies south of the city, beyond the Giardino Pubblico (public gardens) and the stadium.

San Paolo inter Vineas was built on the site of an early Christian religious building, mentioned by St Gregory the Great in the 6th century. The present Romanesque church, flanked by a cloister, dates from the 12th and 13th centuries, and was skilfully restored in the latter half of the 20th century. The most important feature inside is the fresco cycle, which was painted in the early 13th century and is considered to be among the oldest in the region. It depicts the *Prophets* and *Scenes from the Creation of the World*.

The Romanesque church of San Paolo inter Vineas

🏛 San Pietro Fuori le Mura

Via Matteotti, then Via Roma, beyond main road Strada Statale Flaminia.

Whereas at San Paolo inter Vineas it is the interior frescoes which are the most important feature, here it is the decorations on the façade.

San Pietro Fuori le Mura ("outside the walls"), which lies south of the town centre, stands

at the top of a flight of steps on a plateau from where there are fine views.

The building has ancient origins, probably dating back to the 5th century, when the relics of the chain of St Peter were moved here. The current church dates mainly from the 12th century. The carved stone reliefs on the façade are regarded as one of the most prized examples of Umbrian Romanesque. The reliefs on the lower, older part of the structure, produced in the 12th and 13th centuries, tell complex stories rich in symbolism. They relate lay episodes, taken from medieval encyclopedias, and other religious stories linked to the life of Christ.

Façade of San Pietro Fuori le Mura

🏛 San Ponziano

Strada Statale Flaminia, road to the cemetery.

This church lies northeast of the centre, alongside Via Flaminia, and at the foot of the Cinciano hill. It occupies the site of the tomb of the martyr Ponziano, patron saint of Spoleto, who is commemorated on 14 January. This is a convent church, first the home of Poor Clares and later Augustinian nuns, with a Romanesque exterior and an interior which was completely restructured in 1788 by Giuseppe Valadier. (He also designed the doors and altars of the cathedral.)

The main feature of interest is the crypt, which is original. Divided into three aisles, like the church above, and with five apses, this contains Roman

The Festival di Spoleto

The most important event in Spoleto's recent history occurred when it was chosen by the Italian-American composer Gian Carlo Menotti as the venue for the Festival dei Due Mondi, which was to become a major international arts event. The choice fell on Spoleto because of its central location within Italy, its historic appeal and its plentiful theatres and cinemas. In 1958 a performance of Verdi's *Macbeth*, directed by Luchino Visconti, inaugurated the first festival. Since then, despite the controversy with which the festival has always been associated and the change of name (today it is called the "Festival di Spoleto"), every summer the event attracts an enthusiastic audience, as well as artists from all over the world, to this splendid city.

A closing concert at the Festival

fragments and some pretty votive frescoes, which include one showing the *Archangel Michael* with a globe and staff, in the right-hand apse. On the left is an *Enthroned Madonna*.

The formal interior of the church of San Salvatore

🏛 San Salvatore
Via del Cimitero, off Strada Statale Flaminia.

From San Ponziano, the road goes up the Cinciano hill and brings visitors to the last, and perhaps the most historically interesting, of all the religious buildings close to Spoleto.

This UNESCO-protected site, the church of San Salvatore is an exceptional example, perhaps unique in Umbria, of a building constructed using mainly salvaged material, almost all dating from the Roman era. The columns, decorative elements, capitals, architraves – most of the architectural features in the three-aisled basilica church, in fact – date from the Roman period. For this reason, it has been difficult for art historians to date San Salvatore with any great precision, although it is undoubtedly one of the oldest churches in the country. Two theories circulate currently. According to the first, the church dates from the early Christian period, and bears witness to the heights of splendour achieved in late Roman art in this area (the Tempietto del Clitunno would be of the same era). According to the second theory, however, the building was probably designed in the 8th and 9th centuries.

❿ San Pietro in Valle
Perugia. **Road Map** E5. 🚆 Rome–Ancona line, Terni, 20 km (12 miles); FCU Perugia–Terni line. 🚌 Abbey: **Tel** 0744 780 129 (hotel). **Open** summer: 10am–1pm, 3–6pm daily; winter: 10am–noon daily (call ahead). 🌐 sanpietroinvalle.com

It is difficult to try to rank Umbrian abbeys in order of importance, but clearly no classification could omit the Benedictine abbey of San Pietro in Valle, situated in the lower part of the Valnerina, just north of the village of Ferentillo (see p127).

Set against a backdrop of wooded hills, San Pietro in Valle is of significant artistic and religious interest. The abbey's roots lie deep in legend. Its foundation, as one of the frescoes in the left-hand transept of the church testifies, traditionally dates from the 5th century AD, when the Lombard duke of Spoleto, Faroaldo II, met the Syrian hermit Lazarus. St Peter had suggested to the duke in a dream that he should transform the hermit's small chapel into a powerful abbey, and so San Pietro in Valle was built. Faroaldo later decided to stay here, becoming a monk, and he rests here still: his splendid sarcophagus can be seen in the right-hand transept. The abbey was severely

Capital, San Pietro in Valle

damaged by the Saracens in the 9th century, but was restored in around 1000 by Ottone III and then by his successor, Enrico II. In the 1930s, extensive renovation revealed the medieval linear forms which the building had managed to retain, despite all the alterations. Today, the abbey is privately owned, and has been converted into an appealing, sought-after hotel and restaurant, part of the Relais & Châteaux chain, though parts are open to the general public.

The abbey church is owned by the state and is well worth a visit. Long and formal, with a single nave ending in a short transept and three apses, the church contains some superb works of art. On the walls is a cycle of frescoes, which ranks among the finest examples of Romanesque painting in Italy in its complexity and in the precision of its execution. On the left-hand wall and on the upper right-hand side are *Stories from the Old Testament*, while in the remaining space on the right-hand side are *Scenes from the Life of Christ*. The inner façade and the transept are decorated with works from later eras.

Look out for the beautifully preserved Lombard altar (8th century), which bears the self-portrait and signature of the sculptor: "Ursus".

The medieval Benedictine abbey of San Pietro in Valle

The broad Piazza San Benedetto, in the centre of Norcia

⓫ Norcia

Perugia. **Road Map** 5F. 🚍 5,000. 🚌
ℹ️ Piazza San Benedetto, Via Solferino
22, 0743 828 173. 🎪 Mostra Mercato
del Tartufo Nero, Feb. 🌐 **norcia.net**

At the foot of the Monti Sibillini,
on the edge of the plain of
Santa Scolastica, and on the
borders of the ancient duchies
of Spoleto and Benevento,
Norcia was a trading city and
a staging post for centuries.
Today, the town is known above
all for its local produce, in
particular for its black truffles
and for the production of
high-quality meat,
sausages and salami.
(The word "norcino" –
from Norcia – is now
synonymous with
superior meat
products.) Browsing
around the
wonderful *salumerie* and other
food shops is a highlight of any
visit to the town.

Lunette from the door of San
Benedetto, detail

The walls built by the Romans
(who conquered the city in 290
BC) were replaced by another,
heart-shaped set in the 13th
century. These walls, and the
city itself, have been damaged
by disastrous earthquakes over
the years. Along the perimeter,
however, the ancient gates
(eight in all) can still be seen.

One of these gates, Porta
Romana, marks the start of
Corso Sertorio, which leads to
Piazza San Benedetto, the heart
of the town since the Middle
Ages. At its centre is a statue of
St Benedict (1880). Facing onto
the square is **Palazzo**

Comunale, of 14th-century
origin but partly rebuilt after
the earthquake in 1859. The
portico is original, while the
soaring bell tower dates from
the 18th century.

Alongside the palazzo is
the church of **San Benedetto**,
which was founded in the
Middle Ages and extensively
rebuilt in 1389 and at various
later dates. The 14th-century
façade is dominated by a
monumental
doorway (1578),
with two statues
representing
St Benedict and Santa
Scolastica on either
side. On the right
side of the church
is a 16th-century
portico, the Portale
delle Misure, which
has a stone step
bearing the commercial
measures used for the sale
of grain. The interior, which
was reconstructed in the 18th
century, contains a crypt built
on the site where, according
to tradition, St Benedict and
Sta Scolastica were both born.
Traces of the oldest church and
fragments of frescoes are visible
in the crypt.

The cathedral of **Santa
Maria Argentea**, built in the
16th century and remodelled
in the 18th, also stands on the
piazza but is of little interest.
Much more impressive is the
Castellina, a fortress built for
Pope Julius III in 1554. Its square
layout, centred on a courtyard
with a loggia, was the work of

the prestigious architect
Jacopo Barozzi, also
known as Vignola. The
fort houses the **Museo
Civico Diocesano**,
where the highlights
include two crucifixes
and a five-figured
sculptural group of the
Deposition (13th century).
The latter is perfectly
preserved and provides
important evidence of
the popular art being
done at that time (such
groups would have been
carried in processions).

For a taste of Norcia of
old, follow Via Roma as far
as Porta Ascolana, past several
churches, or take Via Anicia
from the main square up to
the highest part of the city.
The palazzi here date from
the 17th and 18th centuries, when
Norcia was a major trading
centre on the borders with the
Adriatic regions. Here, too, is
Sant'Agostino, with some fine
16th-century frescoes by local
artists. Also of note are the
Gothic church of **San Francesco**
on Piazza Garibaldi, and the
14th-century **Tempietto** on
Via Umberto, which has some
pretty bas-reliefs.

🏛 **Museo Civico Diocesano**
Piazza San Benedetto. **Tel** 0743 817
030. **Open** Jan–Jun, Oct–Dec:
10am–1pm, 3–5pm (5:30pm Sat &
Sun); Jul–Sep: 10am–1pm, 4–7:30pm
daily. 🐾 📷 ♿ 🏠

The courtyard of the Castellina with its
loggia and gallery

A Land Renowned for Saints

Two of the most important saints in Umbrian history (St Francis apart) were born in this area, just a few kilometres from each other but separated by nearly 1,000 years.

St Benedict, founder of the oldest monastic order in the West, was born (with his twin sister Santa Scolastica) in Norcia, in 480. After studying in Rome he settled at Montecassino, where he wrote his famous *Rule*. This became a major influence on medieval monastic life. The patron saint of Norcia (as well as of Europe), St Benedict's saint's day is celebrated on 21 March.

Santa Rita (born Rita Lotti, commemorated on 21 May) was born at Roccaporena, near Cascia, in around 1380, and died in the mid-15th century. The factional struggles between the Guelfs (pro the papacy) and the Ghibellines (pro the German

Monument to St Benedict by Giuseppe Prinzi, 1880

emperors) caused her much suffering. Her parents were part of the so-called "peacemakers of Christ", or mediators between the two factions, and Rita carried on their work, even after the assassination of her husband and the subsequent murder of her two sons, killed while trying to avenge their father.

Rita entered the Augustine convent of Santa Maria Maddalena at Cascia, where she remained for 40 years, until her death in 1457. She developed a sore on her forehead, which was said to have been caused by a thorn falling from a crown of thorns as she knelt in prayer beneath a statue of Christ; it was viewed by fellow nuns as a stigmata. The miraculous story of Rita gave rise to a popular cult that has lasted for centuries. Indeed, it was thanks only to a popular campaign that Rita was eventually made a saint, on 24 May 1900.

View of Roccaporena, with the cliff of Santa Rita behind

⑫ Cascia

Perugia. **Road Map** 5E. 🚉 3,300. 🚌
ℹ Piazza Garibaldi 1, 0743 711 47.
🎭 Celebrazioni per Santa Rita, 21–22 May.

Inhabited since late antiquity, because of its strategic position, high on a hill, Cascia has had a turbulent past: Umbrian, then Roman and Byzantine, then part of the Duchy of Spoleto, but independent from the 10th century. In the early Middle Ages, it was a Ghibelline city, locked in bitter struggle with Norcia and Spoleto, cities owing

allegiance to the pope. Taken by Rome in 1517, Cascia immediately acquired great importance because of its position on the border with the Kingdom of Naples. This brought great prosperity.

With the unification of Italy, Cascia lost its political relevance and fell into a long period of decline, halted in the 20th century only thanks to religious tourism, which brought large numbers of pilgrims dedicated to the memory of Santa Rita.

The cult is still a significant feature of life in Cascia today, so the focus is no longer the now-destroyed hilltop fortress, but a modern **Sanctuary** dedicated to the saint. It was built in 1947, replacing a church dating from 1577. To the left of the sanctuary

is the convent of Santa Rita, where the saint lived for much of her life.

Other sites to visit in the town include the **Museo Civico** (divided between Palazzo Santi and the church of Sant'Antonio Abate), in particular for the fine wooden sculptures, and the churches of **San Francesco** and Santa Maria. In the outskirts of the town is **Roccaporena**, Rita's birthplace, dominated by a hill known as the "scoglio" (cliff) of Santa Rita. The area's many castles and towers, which formed an effective system of fortification, are evidence of the historical importance of the region.

Not far from Cascia is the Parco Nazionale dei Monti Sibillini *(see pp112–13)*.

Fresco in the lunette above the door to the church of San Francesco

⑱ Terni

The only Umbrian provincial capital apart from Perugia, Terni has always been the most developed centre for industry in the region – the result of its position: at the centre of a plain and at the confluence of the River Nera and the Serra and Tescino streams. The availability of water was crucial for the development of heavy industry during the 19th century (the famous Italian steelworks Acciaierie Breda is based here). Terni is also crossed by the Via Flaminia, an extremely important route since Roman times, linking Rome with the north and the Adriatic coast. Terni's industrial importance made it a target for heavy bombardment during World War II and today, despite its Bronze Age origins, it looks modern compared with most other Umbrian towns. With the ruined Roman town of Carsulae and man-made Marmore falls, Terni is a delight. It is the unlikely birthplace of St Valentine, the patron of lovers and one of the world's most popular saints.

Madonna and Saints, Benozzo Gozzoli

Exploring Terni

Although it is a fairly large city, Terni – or at least the most important sights – can be visited in a relatively short time and on foot: the historic centre, located on the western side of the River Nera, is reasonably compact.

Visitors should leave their cars near the railway station (to the north of the centre), and then follow Viale della Stazione to Piazza Tacito, from where Corso Cornelio Tacito leads directly to the heart of Terni. This is focused around the squares of Piazza della Repubblica, where the main public buildings are located, and Piazza Europa. The latter is home to Palazzo Spada, which was designed, according to local tradition, by Antonio da Sangallo the Younger.

🏛 San Francesco

Piazza San Francesco. **Open** 8am–12:30pm, 3:30–7:30pm daily.

It is worth making a detour to the right halfway along Corso Tacuto to look at this 13th-century church, which was originally designed in typical Franciscan style with a single nave and transept. In the course of the 15th century, the lateral aisles and the bell tower were added.

Industrial Terni

A huge ladle in action in a steelworks

The industrial importance of Terni goes back to the dawn of the industrial revolution in Italy (beginning of the 19th century), when the Vatican ironworks were based here. During the 19th century the industries multiplied: foundries, saw-mills, wool mills, as well as the hugely successful Acciaierie Breda steelworks. All found an ideal environment on this plain, which is well supplied with water and in a strategic position for trade. Industry has altered both the countryside and the town itself. Today the factories are, for the most part, dismantled or converted for other use, but the industrial archaeology of Terni is still a reason to visit the area. There are other reasons, of course: this "outdoor museum" extends to cover Terni itself, the waterfalls of Marmore and the town of Narni.

Inside, the Cappella Paradisi contains a cycle of frescoes *(The Last Judgment)*, painted by Bartolomeo di Tommaso, of the Giotto school. The cycle dates from the middle of the 15th century.

🏛 Museum of Modern and Contemporary Art

Viale Campofregoso 98. **Tel** 0744 258 946. **Open** 10am–1pm, 4–8pm daily (winter: 7pm).

This former chemical plant houses the Aurelio de Felice collection of modern art, including lithographs by Chagall, Mirò, Picasso and Kandinsky. The museum's broad sweep also encompasses works representative of the medieval Umbrian school, such as by Benozzo Gozzoli *(The Marriage of St Catherine)*, Spagna and Nicolò Alunno. It also displays works of young, upcoming artists.

🏛 Sant'Alò

Via Sant'Alò. **Tel** 320 252 8895. **Open** by appt.

This Romanesque church, just off Via XI Febbraio, dates from the 11th century and is notable for the abundant re-use of Roman statuary on the exterior. It is thought that the church was built on the ruins of an earlier pagan temple.

🏛 Duomo (Santa Maria Assunta)

Piazza Duomo. **Open** 9am–noon, 3:30–7pm daily.

The Duomo, located south of the city centre, near the public gardens, was built on the site of

Detail of the decoration on the main door of the duomo

earlier religious buildings, the first of which existed at least by the 6th century; numerous churches were later built on the same site. The current basilica is the result of reconstruction in 1653, although there are still some traces of a Romanesque church. Look out for the bird and animal reliefs on the main door as you enter. There's also Museo Diocesano e Capitolare inside the duomo, displaying works of religious art.

🏛 Roman Amphitheatre

Piazza Duomo, Via dell'Anfiteatro. **Open** 10am–1pm, 4–8pm (winter: 7pm).

This amphitheatre (1st century AD), not far from the duomo, is very much a ruin but is still one of the best-preserved Roman sites in Terni. Used as a quarry and later covered by buildings, it was discovered in the mid-19th century and was finally excavated in the 1930s.

On the left is Palazzo Vescovile, whose curvilinear rear façade follows the line of the old bastions. There are lovely views from the adjacent public gardens.

🏛 San Salvatore

Via San Salvatore. **Open** 9am–noon, 4–6pm daily.

The town's most interesting church, just off Piazza Europa,

The round church of San Salvatore

was erected on the ruins of Roman buildings, but it has been impossible to establish exactly when. Also known as *Tempio del Sole* (Temple of the sun), the main body of this church was built on a circular plan and thought to have been a Roman temple to the sun. It is now believed to date from the 11th century; the rectangular avant-corps is more recent, built perhaps in the 12th century.

Inside the church are traces of frescoes; the ones in the Cappella Manassei date from the 14th century.

VISITORS' CHECKLIST

Practical Information

Road Map D6. 🏠 235,000. 🛈 Via Cassian Bon 1 (behind Piazza Tacito), 0744 423 047. 📅 Feste di San Valentino, 14 Feb; Cantamaggio, May. 🌐 regioneumbria.eu

Transport

🚉 Rome–Ancona line, 892 021. 🚌 075 963 7637.

🏛 San Pietro

Piazza San Pietro. **Open** 8am–noon, 3:30–7:30pm daily.

This 14th-century church, not far from Palazzo Comunale, was enlarged and restored several times. It contains many 14th- and 15th-century frescoes representative of the local school.

🏛 Mostra Permanente di Paleontologia

Ex-chiesa di San Tommaso, Largo Liberotti. **Tel** 0744 285 946. **Open** 10am–1pm Thu, 4–7pm Sat. 🎫 ♿

A vital tool for anyone studying the early history of Umbria, this permanent exhibition has a rich collection of fossils, the remains of several ancient mammals, and a diorama of Umbria when it was covered by the waters of the ancient Tiberine Lake.

Terni Town Centre

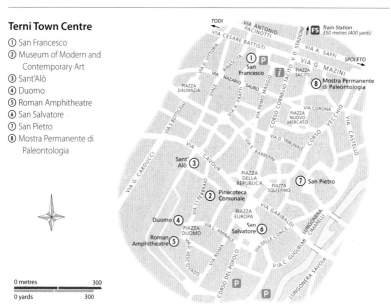

0 metres 300
0 yards 300

⑭ Narni

Terni. **Road Map** C6. 🚉 20,000.
🚆 Rome–Ancona line. 🚌 *i* Piazza
dei Priori 3, 0744 715 362. 🎭 Corsa
dell'Anello, mid-May for 2 weeks.
🌐 **comune.narni.tr.it**

This fine and unspoilt hill town,
located dramatically above a
bend in the River Nera, is the
geographical centre of Italy.
Its origins date back to the
Umbri people, who founded
Nequinum. This settlement was
conquered by Rome in 299 BC
and was renamed *Narnia*, after
the nearby river. Its importance
under the Romans derived
from the fact that it was the
birthplace of Emperor Nerva, in
AD 32, and also a major stopping
point on the Via Flaminia. Narni
grew until it occupied the entire
rocky spur above the Nera.

Medieval Narni knew tough
years during the wars between
the papacy and the empire, but
it continued to grow, even after
the establishment of papal rule
in the mid-14th century. The
building of a great fortress, on
the orders of Cardinal Albornoz,
emphasized papal authority.
In the 16th century, Narni
was devastated by the
Lanzichenecchi on their return
north after the Sack of Rome.
During the following centuries,
the slow rate of growth kept
the town centre in the form in
which it can still be seen today.
Porta Ternana, on the Via
Flaminia, is the main point of

Detail of the bas-reliefs to the right of the door of Palazzo del Podestà

entry to Narni. From here, Via
Roma leads straight to Piazza
Garibaldi, at one time known
as Piazza del Lago because of
a great subterranean cistern,
fed by the Roman aqueduct
of Formina; this now supplies
the water for a 14th-century
fountain with a bronze basin.

Most of the sights are close
to the main axis of the
town, formed by
Via Garibaldi and Via
Mazzini. At one end is
Piazza Garibaldi, home
of Narni's **duomo**,
an imposing and
beautiful building
dedicated to San
Giovenale, the town's
patron saint. It was
founded in 1047,
but reconstructed in
the 12th century. The
façade has a portico and a portal
decorated with carvings. Inside,
two low arcades separate the
three aisles. On the right is the
mausoleum of the bishops of
Narni, which is dominated by a
tombstone dating from 558.

From the duomo, it is a
short walk up Via Garibaldi to
the central Piazza dei Priori, the
attractive seat of civic power in
Narni. Facing the square are
the **Palazzo dei Priori**, with a
portico and an impressive loggia
designed by Gattapone –
responsible also for the Palazzo
dei Consoli in Gubbio *(see p64)* –
and the **Palazzo del Podestà**
(or Palazzo Comunale); both date
from the 14th century. In the
atrium of the Palazzo del Podestà
is a series of Roman and
medieval archaeological stones
and finds, while inside is a
superb *Coronation of the*

Detail of the fountain in
Piazza Garibaldi

Virgin by Ghirlandaio, and
frescoes by Benozzo Gozzoli
and others. **Casa Sacripanti**,
also in the square, features three
medieval bas-reliefs of griffins
and knights.

Beyond Piazza dei Priori, the
main street (now Via Mazzini)
continues north. Immediately
on the right is the façade of
the little Romanesque church
of **Santa Maria in
Pensole**, built in
around 1175. Of
particular interest is
the exterior, with its
attractive portico and
three doorways carved
with classical motifs. A
little further on, where
the road widens out
into Piazza XIII Giugno,
is the church of **San
Domenico** (12th
century). Now deconsecrated,
it houses the Public Library,
Historical Archive and the town
art gallery. The main reason to go
inside is to see some of the most
interesting medieval frescoes in
Narni: among the often faint
fragments, of particular note are
those by the Zuccari family, found
in the large chapel off the left-
hand aisle. San Domenico also
has many other works from other
churches in the town, among
them an *Annunciation* by
Benozzo Gozzoli, at the end of
the right-hand aisle. In the
underground areas of the church,
you can visit the Inquisition
cells, with graffiti made by the
prisoners of the ecclesiastical
court. To return to Piazza dei Priori
from San Domenico, make your
way along the narrow streets
which run parallel to Via Mazzini.
This area is home to the church

The duomo, facing onto
Piazza Garibaldi

of **San Francesco**, built in the 14th century on the site where it is said that St Francis stayed during his sojourn in Narni in 1213, and where he founded an oratory. The church is Romanesque, but with some Gothic elements. Among these, the most important feature of the exterior is the doorway, with a niche above. Inside, frescoes adorn every inch of wall: of special interest are the frescoes by Mezzastris, in the first chapel, depicting *Scenes from the Life of St Francis* and *Scenes from the Life of St Benedict*, as are those by Alessandro Torresani (16th century), in the sacristy.

On top of the hill that dominates Narni is a vast fortress known as the **Rocca**. It was built in the 1370s by Gattapone, at the behest of Cardinal Albornoz, one of the most important figures in the history of the early Middle Ages in Umbria *(see p44)*, and responsible for numerous fortresses which still bear his name. Narni's fortress was abandoned for years, but it has now been restored. It is open daily and visitors can enjoy fine views from the site.

The intriguing underground of the city can also be toured now; visit www.narnisotterranea. it for details.

Environs

Heading out of Narni, towards Terni, you reach, after a short detour to the left, a bridge over

The Romanesque abbey of San Cassiano, dating from the 12th century

the River Nera. Though easy to miss among the modern development of industrial Narni Scalo, this is the best possible observation point from which to admire a majestic Roman arch in the middle of the river, the only one surviving from the **Ponte d'Augusto**. At 160 m (525 ft) long and 30 m (98 ft) high, this must have been one of the most impressive bridges in the whole of Umbria when it was built. It is known as the Augustan bridge, because it dates from the era of the first emperor (27 BC). This bridge was one of the most popular sights on the Grand Tour.

Continuing along the same road, over the Nera, a climb leads to the **Abbazia di San Cassiano**, perhaps the most important of the many religious buildings that dot the Narni countryside. Set in a panoramic position, the Romanesque, 12th-century complex is enclosed by battlemented walls

and includes a pretty church with a bell tower.

To the southeast, 13 km (8 miles) from Narni, is the **Convento del Sacro Speco**, founded in 1213 by St Francis, who often prayed in a cave nearby. The place is imbued with a mystical atmosphere.

⓰ Visciano

Terni. **Road Map** C7. 🚆 Narni, 8 km (5 miles), Rome–Ancona line. 🚌 ℹ️ Piazza dei Priori 3, Narni, 0744 715 362.

Heading south from Narni, a tortuous but scenic road leads up to the hilltop hamlet of Visciano. The reason for coming here is to visit the small and simple church of **Santa Pudenziana** (check with the tourist office to book a visit). This is a typical example of Umbrian Romanesque, built in the 12th and 13th centuries, and making abundant use of Roman materials. It has a tall stone campanile and a sober façade with a small portico. The interior is divided into three aisles, with an inlaid floor of precious marble and fragments of Roman mosaics.

The church is famous for its frescoes. Behind the façade are *Christ, San Vittore* and *San Medico*, and other saints, as well as the *Madonna and Child*, all contemporary with the construction. The other figures, such as *Santa Pudenziana*, date from the 14th and 15th centuries.

The Rocca, one of many fortresses built by Cardinal Albornoz

⑯ Parco Fluviale del Nera

Known as the "water park", this natural park extends along the course of the River Nera from Terni to Ferentillo, leading to the heart of the National Park of the Monti Sibillini *(see pp112–13)*, and thereby forming what is virtually a single protected reserve of huge interest. Within the park is one of the most famous and much-loved sights in Italy, the Cascata delle Marmore, the highest waterfalls in the country, where the waters from the River Velino spill over from the upland of the Marmore down into the River Nera. Visitors should note that the water for the waterfall is switched on only for brief periods, which vary from month to month, so you should call ahead if you don't want to miss the spectacle. The park has much else of interest, however, and offers excellent opportunities for watersports.

Sweet violets, found in the pasture areas in the park

Cascata delle Marmore
The tremendous spectacle of the Falls, a popular destination with travellers throughout the ages, is created by the River Velino, which reaches this point via an artificial channel. Water then cascades down in three stages, over a total height of 165 m (541 ft), to reach the River Nera below. The Falls can be seen from both the lower road (SS209) and the upper road (S79).

Terni

S209

Nera

Nera

Marmore

Velino

Key

🚗 Park road

🚗 Scenic road

Constructing a Waterfall

In antiquity, the River Velino did not spill into the River Nera as it does today, but stagnated in the marshes of the Rieti plain. In 271 BC the Romans decided to link the two by digging a channel, the Cavo Curiano, which feeds today's main waterfall. Since then, the Cascata delle Marmore has been at the centre of the entire river system of central Italy, provoking bitter debate between those who wanted to close it down and others who wanted to extend it. The latter option was chosen in the 15th and 16th centuries, with the work entrusted by the popes to the great architects of the day (Antonio da Sangallo, Giovanni Fontana and Carlo Maderno), who were to transform the Falls. The latest alterations, to adapt the falls for hydroelectric power, took place in the 1920s.

The hydroelectric plant at the Marmore Falls, one of Italy's main sources of energy

Montefranco

This small village, perched in a splendid panoramic position, is a centre for mountain sports. There are numerous rock climbing schools and manageable cliff faces.

VISITORS' CHECKLIST

Practical Information
Terni. **Road Map** D6. *i* Via Cassion Bon, 0744 423 047. Park: **Tel** 0744 629 82. **Open** Jan: 11am–5pm Sat & Sun; Feb, Nov & Dec: 11am–5pm daily (Feb: to 6pm Sat & Sun); Mar: 10am–6pm daily (to 10pm Sat & Sun); Apr & May: 10am–7pm Mon–Fri, 9am–10pm Sat & Sun; Jun–Sep: 10am–10pm daily (from 9am Sat & Sun); Oct: 10am–6pm Mon–Fri, 10am–8pm Sat & Sun. **W** marmore.it

Transport
FS Terni, Rome–Ancona line. 🚌

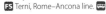

• **Monterivoso**

S209

Nera

• **Montefranco**

S209

• **Arrone**

• **Casteldilago**

• **Forca dell'Arrone**

Lago di Piediluco

② ⛺

↓ *Rieti*

0 kilometre 1

0 mile 1

Ferentillo

Guarded from above by twin 14th-century citadels, Ferentillo is a major climbing centre. It owes its fame also to the church of Santo Stefano, whose crypt contains several mummified bodies.

KEY

① **The Observatory** along the upper road, in the village of Marmore, is one of many points from which to admire the falls in all their glory. It dates from 1781.

② **Piediluco** is popular because of its pretty setting on the shores of Lake Piediluco, the second-largest lake in Umbria after Trasimeno, and just outside the park. The church of San Francesco is worth a visit, and boat rides on the lake are recommended.

Rafting

Water is the crucial element in the park and various watersports can be practised here, including rafting, canoeing and kayaking.

For keys to symbols *see back flap*

The 17th-century Porta Romana, inserted into the ancient walls

⑰ Amelia

Terni. **Road Map** C6. 🗺 12,200.
🚆 Narni, 11km (7 miles), Rome–
Ancona line. 🚌 ℹ Via Orvieto 1, 0744
981 453.

Perched on a hill between the
Tiber and Nera valleys, Amelia is
a city of ancient origin. In fact, it
was in antiquity that the town
knew its greatest importance,
when it was located on the Via
Amerina, one of several Roman
roads linking southern Etruria
with Umbria.

Still standing today are
parts of the impressive **Mura
Poligonali** (Polygonal Walls),
built by the Umbri and among
the oldest walls in Italy. Their
age is not certain, but they
date from no later than the
5th century BC. Some 8 m
(26 ft) high, and 3 m (10 ft)
wide, the bastions are, for the
most part, made up of
vast polygonal stone blocks,
fitted together without mortar.
The size of the walls can best
be seen at **Porta Romana**,
framed by a Classical-style
17th-century arch.

This same gate is also the
main entrance to the historic
centre. Close by, in Palazzo
Boccarini, is the **Museo
Archeologico**, home to
all manner of Roman finds
from tablets to sarcophagi. Of
huge interest is a magnificent
statue of the Roman general
Germanicus; discovered locally,
it was for years kept in Perugia;
Amelia has won it back, for
the time being at least.

A short way up Via
della Repubblica is the
13th-century church of
Santi Filippo e Giacomo.
It contains seven tombs
of the Geraldini family,
one of the most
important dynasties in
Amelia. Cardinal Alessandro
Geraldini is famous for
helping to persuade
the Spanish monarchy
to authorize the first
voyage of Christopher
Columbus to the Indies. The
church's funerary monuments
include the 15th-century tombs
of Elisabetta and Matteo
Geraldini, the work of Agostino
di Duccio.

Palazzo Farattini, just off
Via della Repubblica, is Amelia's
most impressive private
building. It was designed by
Antonio da Sangallo the
Younger in the 16th century

Detail from the tomb of
Matteo and Elisabetta
Geraldini

for the Farattini, the other family
to feature large in the history
of Amelia. Via della Repubblica
climbs further to Piazza
Marconi, the town's lovely main
square, and then continues up
Via Duomo to the highest point
of the city and the **duomo**.

The cathedral's appearance
today is the result of almost
total reconstruction in the 17th
century, which replaced the
original Romanesque church,
though the fine 11th-century
bell tower remains. Inside are
several works of importance
including a panel with a
Madonna and Child attributed
to Antoniazzo Romano,
and two paintings by
Nicolò Pomarancio in the
Orataorio del Sacramento.
Returning to the lowest
part of the town along
Via Geraldini, you
reach Piazza
Matteotti, whose
architectural highlight
is the charming
Palazzo Comunale.
Beyond Porta
Romana, you can
visit the country
church of **Santa Maria delle
Cinque Fonti**, built on the site
where St Francis is said to have
given a sermon in 1213. The
church is named after a
fountain with five spouts
that stands nearby.

🏛 Museo Archeologico
Piazza Augusto Vera.
Tel 0744 978 120. **Open** Apr–Jun &
Sep: 10:30am–2pm, 4–6pm Tue–
Sun; Jul & Aug: 10:30am–1:30pm,
4:30–7pm Tue–Sun; Oct–Mar:
10:30am–1pm, 3–5pm Fri–Sun.
Closed 1 Jan, 25 Dec. 🏛 🎫

View of Amelia, showing how the village expanded down the hillside

◀ The incredible Cascata delle Marmore or Marmore Falls, the tallest man-made waterfall in Europe

Environs

The area around Amelia is dotted with abbeys and sanctuaries that are easy to reach and a delight to visit. About 4 km (2 miles) southwest of Amelia, on the road to Attigliano, is the 13th-century **Monastery of the Santissima Annunziata**, which belongs to the Friars Minor. There is a *Last Supper* on the wall of the refectory. Heading eastwards, past the village of Capitone – which was the castle of nearby Narni in the Middle Ages – you reach the village of La Cerqua and the **Sanctuary of the Madonna della Quercia**. This was built in the 16th century to hold an image of the Virgin Mary, now on the apse altar.

The Roman **Via Amerina** is a historical object in itself, and has maintained its role as a communication route.

Interior of Santa Maria Assunta, in Lugnano

⓲ Lugnano in Teverina

Terni. **Road Map** C6. ⓜ 1,600.
🚆 Attigliano, 11km (7 miles), Milan–Rome line. 🚌 🛈 Pro Loco, Piazza S Maria 1, 0744 900 072.
🎄 Christmas concerts and Living Nativity, 24 Dec–6 Jan.

Following the main road S205 from Amelia towards Lago di Alviano, after around 10 km (6 miles) you come to the small town of Lugnano in Teverina. Set in a panoramic position along a ridge and enclosed by medieval walls, Lugnano began life as the feudal village of a Provençal count, in around 1000.

Lago di Alviano, along the border with neighbouring Lazio

Although some way from the usual tourist trails, Lugnano is well worth visiting simply to see one of the most interesting Romanesque churches in Umbria, the church of **Santa Maria Assunta**. The building dates from the 12th century, although it has undergone much restoration, especially in the 15th century. In common with various other Umbrian churches of the same era, such as the cathedral of Spoleto, the façade features a beautifully decorated portico, some of which is the work of the famous Roman marble workers, the Cosmati. There is more Cosmati work inside, both in the nave (which has a Cosmatesque pavement) and in the crypt, which also has a finely sculpted screen. Other works of art include a triptych of the *Annunciation* by Niccolò Alunno, in the apse, and a *Crucifixion* of the Giotto school.

Capital in Santa Maria Assunta

Environs

A short distance southwest of the town centre are traces of the Assisi saint in the church of **San Francesco**. It was erected in 1229 on the spot where a miracle occurred, as shown in the fresco above the right-hand altar.

After passing ancient Roman ruins, the road descends towards the Tiber and the hamlet of **Attigliano**. Proceeding north on the Via Amerina, along the banks of the

Tiber, after about 8 km (5 miles) you come to the **Lago di Alviano** (open Sundays and public holidays). This is part of an artificial basin created to generate hydroelectricity and today is an oasis run by the World Wide Fund for Nature and part of the Parco Fluviale del Tevere (*see p137*). From the nearby medieval town of Alviano, birthplace of *condottiere* Bartolomeo di Alviano, steps lead to **Santa Illuminata**, a pilgrimage site linked to an order of hermits called the Camaldolese.

A lovely 10-km (6-mile) stretch of the Via Amerina runs to **Montecchio**, with an interesting necropolis (6th–4th centuries BC) nearby.

One of the chambers in the necropolis near Montecchio

Gate at the entrance to the medieval town of San Gemini

❶ San Gemini

Terni. **Road Map** D6. 🅰 4,300.
🚉 Rome–Ancona line, Terni, 11 km (7 miles); FCU Perugia–Terni line. 🚌 ℹ Piazza San Francesco 4, 0744 630 130.

The medieval town of San Gemini was built over the ruins of an ancient Roman settlement, alongside Via Flaminia. The only traces of the Roman town are a tomb, the so-called Grotta degli Zingari and a ruined villa.

The heart of San Gemini is Piazza di Palazzo Vecchio, home to the medieval **Palazzo Pubblico**, whose tower was much altered in the 1700s. Under an exterior arcade is an image of St George, patron saint of the town. The 13th-century **Oratorio di San Carlo**, nearby, has striking frescoes.

On the edge of town are the churches of **San Francesco**, with a fine Gothic doorway, and **San Giovanni Battista**, with a 13th-century façade and a lovely Romanesque door decorated with mosaics. One of the façade inscriptions bears the date of its founding, 1199, with the names of the architects and sculptors, Nicola, Simone and Bernardo.

Just outside San Gemini's old gateway is the privately owned church of San Nicolò. The beautifully sculpted Romanesque portal is a copy, since the original is in the Metropolitan Museum in New York. There is more fine (and original) sculpture inside.

There's also an interactive science museum, Geolab, for children and those interested in geology.

Environs
Just to the north, on flatter ground, is the modern spa town of San Gemini Fonte, with facilities for spa water treatments. The famous mineral waters of Sangemini and Fabia are bottled here. Sangemini water, known in antiquity and exploited since the late 19th century, is rich in calcium but low in chlorine and sodium, so is particularly recommended for children. Fabia water has average levels of minerals and is today promoted as a light table water good for the digestion.

The ancient spring at the Terme di San Gemini

❷ Carsulae

Terni. **Road Map** D6. 🚉 Rome–Ancona line, Terni, 14 km (9 miles); FCU Perugia–Terni line. 🚌 ℹ Soprintendenza Archeologica dell'Umbria, 0744 630 420; Sito Archeologico di Carsulae, 0744 334 133. **Open** 8:30am–7:30pm daily (Oct–Mar: 5:30pm).

From San Gemini Fonte, a detour of 3 km (2 miles) along part of the old Via Flaminia brings you to the ruined Roman town of Carsulae, founded in the 3rd century BC on the slopes of the mound bearing the pretty name of Chiccirichì.

At first merely a staging and garrison post, then a village, Carsulae eventually became a town in Augustus' Region VI. It experienced its greatest period of splendour between 30 and 10 BC, when work was being done on the Via Flaminia. The town was abandoned following the decline in importance of the road. Carsulae was attacked and raided by barbarians and marauders on a number of occasions, and was also badly damaged by earthquakes.

From the 16th century onwards, the aristocratic families of the region, in particular the Cesi family of Acquasparta, began to carry out excavations in search of objects of interest for their own private collections. The modern archaeological excavations date back to the 1950s, when a number of sites were uncovered, including a basilica, the old forum, and temples. The great value of Carsulae as an archaeological site lies in the fact that the original layout has remained complete for the most part, despite the encroachment of the modern Via Flaminia, which crosses the site.

The small church of **San Damiano** was built in the 11th century, using the remains of a Roman temple. From here, you can follow a stretch of the original Via Flaminia to the **Forum**, with an adjacent

The little church of San Damiano, inside Carsulae's archaeological area

The ruins of the Roman theatre at Carsulae, showing clearly the supports for the stalls

basilica with three aisles and an apse. In front of the forum is a public square where numerous low walls – the ruins of religious and secular buildings – can be seen: among them are the bases of the **Tempietti Gemelli** (twin temples) and the remains of baths.

Continuing up the old Via Flaminia, visitors arrive at the **Arco di San Damiano**, a monumental gate which once had three arches: only the central one survives. A burial site is also nearby. Behind the basilica, beyond the modern Via Flaminia, is the **Amphitheatre**, used for circus games, and the **Theatre**; sadly only the foundations of the stage and the supports for the stalls (orchestra seats) remain of this building.

㉑ Acquasparta

Terni. **Road Map** D6. 🚗 4,500.
🚊 Rome–Ancona line, Terni, 20 km (12 miles); FCU Perugia–Terni line. 🚌
ℹ️ Via Tiberina 43, 0744 943 286.
🎭 Arte estate, Jul–Aug.

The first records of Acquasparta date from the 10th century. The name derives from the local spa waters, which were known to the Romans and, it is said, taken by St Francis. Acquasparta's appearance today recalls the influence of the Cesi family, who changed the face of the town during the 15th and 16th centuries. Among the features dating from this era are a palace named after the noble family, walls and towers.

Palazzo Cesi, commissioned by the Cesi family from the architect Giovanni Domenico Bianchi, was completed in 1565. The interior of this aristocratic residence is richly decorated: Giovan Battista Lombardelli produced the first paintings, while an artist from the north was responsible for the remainder. The rooms have splendid coffered wooden ceilings; the one in the Sala di Ercole (Room of Hercules) is particularly fine. Palazzo Cesi belongs to the University of Perugia and is used for seminars and conferences as well as a summer art exhibition.

Palazzo Cesi, now part of the University of Perugia

Along Corso Umberto I, the main street, are the church of **Santa Cecilia** and the **Oratorio del Sacramento**, where a mosaic floor from the ruins of Roman Carsulae has been put into new use.

The 200,000-year-old fossil forest at Dunarobba

Environs
A detour 15 km (9 miles) west of Acquasparta skirts Casteltodino and leads to the fossil forest of **Dunarobba**, close to the village of Avigliano Umbro. This ancient forest, which dates from the Pliocene age, is made up of around 40 petrified trunks of large trees similar to today's sequoia. The trees were preserved for centuries under a blanket of clay on the shores of Lago Tiberino (which once filled the Tiber Valley).

A few kilometres north is the medieval castle and village of **Casigliano**. Within is Palazzo Atti, a project of Antonio da Sangallo the Younger which was based on Roman designs. It was the inspiration for Palazzo Cesi.

㉒ Todi

The city of Todi occupies a stunning spot, on a hilltop halfway between Perugia and Terni. First built on land occupied by the Umbri, Todi was later appropriated by the Etruscans (its name derives from the Etruscan word *tutere*, meaning "border") and then, in 89 BC, by the Romans. Under the Romans, Todi's two hilltops were levelled out to make Piazza del Popolo and new walls were built around the Etruscan ones. Todi today would not have looked very different during the Middle Ages, a time of great splendour, when the town expanded southwards and was divided into four districts, surrounded by a third circle of walls. The city became a papal possession, along with all the other towns of Umbria, and there was only minor subsequent modification during the Renaissance.

Exploring Todi

The centre of the city is, as it was in Roman times, Piazza del Popolo. This truly magnificent square contains the duomo, as well as three fine monuments to temporal power: Palazzo del Popolo, Palazzo del Capitano and Palazzo dei Priori. Following years of research, this largely medieval square was chosen as the starting point for excavations which have provided the information necessary to reconstruct the layout of the ancient city.

The eagle of Todi, Palazzo dei Priori

in bronze, the symbol of the city and the work of Giovanni di Gigliaccio in 1339. (According to tradition, the original Umbrian town was built where an eagle had dropped a tablecloth taken from a local family.) Over the centuries the palazzo has housed the city's various and varied rulers, including the leaders of the medieval commune and the papal governors.

🏛 Palazzo dei Priori

Piazza del Popolo. **Tel** 075 894 4148.
Closed to the public.

This palace, situated on the southern side of Piazza del Popolo, is the least attractive of the three palazzi. It was built between 1293 and 1385. At the top left of the façade is an eagle

🏛 Palazzo del Popolo

Piazza del Popolo. **Tel** 075 894 41 48.
Open see Palazzo del Capitano.

This is one of the oldest buildings of its type in Italy: construction began in 1213, though the palace has been considerably restored. Built in Lombard-Gothic form, the palace's left-hand side faces Piazza del Popolo, while the

front can be admired from nearby Piazza Garibaldi. In particular, look out for the swallowtail crenellations (a Guelf motif) and the external staircase, which gave access to the hall on the first floor, above the porticoed space of the ground floor. Public assemblies were held here.

The palace shares an entrance with Palazzo del Capitano and houses part of the Museo Pinacoteca.

Three-mullioned window, Palazzo del Capitano

🏛 Palazzo del Capitano

Piazza del Popolo. Museo Pinacoteca: **Tel** 075 894 4148. **Open** Apr–Oct: 10am–1:30pm, 3–6pm; Nov–Mar: 10:30am–1pm, 2:30–5pm. **Closed** Mon (except hols), 25 Dec. 🕿 📷 📱

This palace dates from the late 13th century and faces the eastern side of the square. The façade has mullioned Gothic windows and a monumental arched staircase which serves both the Palazzo del Capitano and the adjacent Palazzo del

Piazza del Popolo, an excellent example of a well-preserved medieval square

Popolo. In particular, it gives access to the Sala del Capitano, with remains of frescoes, medieval coats of arms and a 14th-century *Crucifixion*.

Sculptural detail from the door of the duomo

The **Museo Pinacoteca**, which spans the adjacent palazzi, includes a decent archaeological collection, the **Museo Etrusco-Romano**, as well as paintings, of which the most significant is a *Coronation of the Virgin* (1507–11) by Giovanni di Pietro, known as Spagna. The palazzo also houses the Museo della Città (Civic Museum).

🏛 Duomo

Piazza del Popolo. **Tel** 075 894 30 41. **Open** 8am–1pm, 3–6pm Mon–Fri; 8:30am–1pm, 3–6pm Sun & hols.

Dedicated to Maria Santissima Annunziata, the duomo was founded in the 12th century, probably on the site of a Roman temple, but wasn't completed for another 200 years, with further additions being made after that. The simple façade, which is divided horizontally by cornices, is lovely. An 18th-century flight of steps leads up to a carved 16th-century door set into a decorative framework, above which, as befits the façade's Romanesque simplicity, is a beautiful rose window (1515). Pilaster strips, small loggias and mullioned windows decorate the right-hand side and the tall apse.

Inside, the church has a decorative beamed roof and splendid Gothic capitals, as well as a superb 16th-century choir. The entire central space as well as the chapels contain various works of art, the most interesting of which are near the altar: two paintings by Spagna, to the sides, and, above, a painted wooden Crucifix dating from the 13th and 14th centuries. There is also a crypt, which contains

VISITORS' CHECKLIST

Practical Information
Perugia. **Road Map** C5.
🏛 17,000. 🛈 Piazza Umberto I, 075 894 3395. 🎭 Todifestival Sep.

Transport
🚆 FCU Perugia–Terni line
🚌 Umbria Mobilità 075 963 7637.

three figures originally on the façade, as well as a handful of Roman remains.

The magnificent rose window on the façade of the cathedral

Todi Town Centre

① Palazzo dei Priori
② Palazzo del Popolo
③ Palazzo del Capitano
④ Duomo
⑤ San Fortunato
⑥ Corso Cavour
⑦ Nicchioni
⑧ Santa Maria della Consolazione

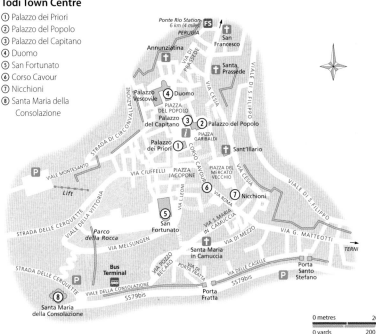

0 metres 200
0 yards 200

For keys to symbols *see back flap*

Detail from the main door of the church of San Fortunato

🏛 San Fortunato

Piazza Umberto I. **Open** Nov–Mar: 10:30am–1pm, 2:30–5pm Tue–Sun; Apr–Oct: 10:30am–1pm, 3–6:30pm Tue–Sun. **Closed** 25 Dec.

Heading south along Via Mazzini, which skirts around the medieval heart of Todi, is the enormous hilltop church of San Fortunato, a sight which is not to be missed.

This is a Franciscan church, but with many anomalies: the dedication, for example, is not to the Assisi saint but to Fortunato, patron of Todi. (The reason for this was that the church replaced a building used by Benedictine monks.) The construction took place in two phases: the first from 1292–1328, the second in the 1400s. It was commissioned by the bishop of Todi, Matteo d'Acquasparta.

The unfinished façade, a mixture of Romanesque and Gothic

The unfinished façade of the church of San Fortunato

styles, stands out at the top of an imposing flight of steps. Through the fine Gothic central doorway lies a wonderfully airy Gothic interior, which does not follow the traditional Franciscan model. It is a rare example in Italy of a Gothic hall church; that is, in which the two side aisles are as high as (though much narrower than) the nave. Note the lovely and unusual ribbed cross vaults, the fine late 16th-century choir stalls, the raised chapels along the sides, and the Gothic baptismal font.

Frescoes decorate many of the chapels and include, in the fifth chapel on the left, some scenes from the *Life of St John the Baptist* by the Giotto school, and, in the fourth chapel on the right, a *Madonna and Child* (1432) by Masolino di Panicale.

The church is also famous for the tomb of Jacopone da Todi, in the crypt beneath the altar. Jacopone was a rich merchant who, following the death of his devout wife, Vanna, became a mystic and a poet. His devotion was reputedly so extreme that he was rejected even by the Franciscans. He was accused of heresy on a number of occasions and is mainly remembered for his *Laudi*, one of the fundamental texts in the birth of Italian literature *(see p34)*. The great man, a native of Todi, died in 1306 and gradually became the symbol of the medieval city. He is still the best-known figure in the cultural history of Todi. Extending westwards from

San Fortunato is a large public park, where a fortress commissioned by Cardinal Albornoz stood until 1503.

🏛 Corso Cavour

Descending the steps of Via San Fortunato brings you to the steep Corso Cavour, the "Rua degli Speziali" (spice sellers' street) of medieval Todi. Halfway along is a fountain known as the **Fonte Rua** (1606), or Fonte Cesia (after the bishop who had it built), and, at the end, **Porta Marzia**, a medieval arch made out of material salvaged from other buildings.

The 17th-century Fonte Rua, in Corso Cavour

🏛 Nicchioni

Piazza del Mercato Vecchio. Walk through Porta Marzia, and turn left into Via Mercato Vecchio, which leads to Piazza Garibaldi (a car park). The level part of this street, the old medieval market square, is dominated by four Roman arches, the so-called Nicchioni (niches). These most probably date from the Augustan era, and either supported a raised street or formed part of the wall of a Roman basilica.

🏛 Santa Maria della Consolazione

Viale della Consolazione. **Open** Apr–Jun, Sep & Oct : 9am–12:30pm, 3–6:30pm; Jul & Aug: 9:30am–12:30pm, 3:30–6:30pm; Nov–Mar: 9:30am–12:30pm, 2:30–5pm. **Closed** Tue (except during Christmas hols).

This church, located outside the city walls, is one of the

The church of Santa Maria della Consolazione, outside Todi

masterpieces of the Umbrian Renaissance. Begun in 1508 and finished in 1607, it has been attributed by some to Bramante, one of the architects of St Peter's in Rome. In fact, there is no documentary evidence of any such project by the great architect, though it is just possible that Cola di Caprarola, who started the project, may have used drawings by Bramante.

The distinctive silhouette of the church – familiar from the covers of dozens of publications devoted to Todi – is built on a square plan and rises to a great dome. Encircling the main structure are four apses, of which one, to the north, is semicircular and three are polygonal; they have two orders of pilasters, with a mixture of capitals, and are pierced by elegant windows. The drum which supports the great dome is narrower than the main body of the church, leaving space for a raised terrace, guarded by four eagles sculpted by Antonio Rosignoli in the 17th century. There are great views from here. The Baroque doorways date from the 18th and 19th centuries.

The airy and light interior, in the form of a Greek cross, is also Baroque and contains statues of the apostles. In the apse is the venerated fresco of the *Madonna della Consolazione* (15th century). The church was built to protect the fresco.

Eagle on the terrace, Santa Maria della Consolazione

❷ Parco Fluviale del Tevere

Terni. **Road Map** B5. FS Orvieto, Milan–Rome line; Todi, FCU Perugia–Terni line. 🚌 ℹ️ Piazza Umberto I, 16, Civitella del Lago, Baschi, 0744 950 732. W parks.it

This river park extends for some 295 ha (18,025 acres) from the bridge of Montemolino, at the gates of Todi, south as far as Lago di Alviano, and has great wildlife and lovely scenery. It includes around 50 km (31 miles) of land along the banks of the Tiber, the largest river in central Italy, and two artificial lakes (Alviano and Corbara). The main access to the park is at the medieval hill town of Baschi, about 24 km (15 miles) from Todi, close to the junction of road S448 and the motorway. The Tiber River,

one moment placid and the next turbulent, is home to a variety of birds, among them blue heron and kingfishers, as well as freshwater fish. Poplars, alders and willows, typical riverside vegetation, cloak the sides.

Steep valleys sweep away from the river and extend as far as the Apennines: the wildest is the **Gole del Forello**, considered one of the most interesting biotopes in the region. On the northern banks of Lago di Corbara, not far from the fortified village of Prodo, winds the **Gole di Prodo**, a deep gorge best suited to hikers or experienced and well-equipped mountain climbers. Diverse birds of prey, including buzzards, sparrowhawks and kites, can be seen in these inaccessible areas, where the vegetation consists mainly of trees such as holm oaks and hornbeams and shrubs such as broom and heather. The marshes in the Lago di Alviano basin (*see p131*), with its own particular birdlife and plants, are also of great interest.

Besides the natural beauty and the opportunities for outdoor sports, the park also incorporates sites of historical and archaeological interest. Digs are under way in various spots, including in the Vallone di San Lorenzo (site of several necropolises) and in the area of the ancient river port of **Pagliano**, at the confluence of the Paglia and Tiber rivers; the port's existence confirms the importance of the Tiber as a communication route of the central Italic peoples.

The wild Gole del Forello, a fascinating wildlife habitat

❷❹ Orvieto

A sheer tufa outcrop, the remains of ancient volcanoes fractured by millennia of ice, sun and rain, rises abruptly from the plain and supports the spectacular medieval city of Orvieto. In the Etruscan era a city called *Velzna* stood here and became rich through commerce with traders from the Tyrrhenian Sea (part of the Mediterranean) and the north. The Romans took over in 264 BC and virtually destroyed the town. Revival came only in the Middle Ages, when Orvieto developed into a free and powerful commune, albeit one troubled by civic strife. The Black Death of 1348 was devastating, however, and Orvieto eventually came under papal control. The old city, with its superb duomo (which is reached by bus from the train station or by funicular and shuttle bus), has changed little in the last 500 years, and attracts thousands of tourists every year.

The imposing tufa platform supporting Orvieto

🏛 Duomo
See pp140–41.

🏛 Museo Archeologico Nazionale
Piazza del Duomo. **Tel** 0763 341 039.
Open 8:30am–7:30pm daily.
Closed 1 Jan, 1 May, 25 Dec. 🅿 ♿

On the scenic Piazza del Duomo, next to the imposing mass of the cathedral, stands the **Palazzo Papale**, which includes three 14th-century buildings, commissioned by popes Urban IV, Gregory X and Martin IV and later combined into one complex.

The Museo Archeologico Nazionale, housed in the Palazzo del Martino IV, has a particularly fine Etruscan collection, including bronzes and mirrors. Several tombs and funerary objects are among the exhibits, including frescoes from 2nd-century-BC tombs and two painted 4th-century tombs from Settecamini.

🏛 Museo dell'Opera del Duomo
Piazza del Duomo. **Tel** 0763 343 592.
Open Apr–Sep: 9:30am–7pm daily; Oct & Mar: 10am–5pm daily; Nov–Feb: 10am–1pm, 2–5pm daily.
Closed Tue.

Orvieto Town Centre

① *Duomo pp140–41*
② Museo Archeologico Nazionale
③ Museo dell'Opera del Duomo
④ Palazzo Soliano
⑤ Palazzo Faina
⑥ San Francesco
⑦ Torre del Moro
⑧ Sant'Andrea
⑨ Palazzo del Popolo
⑩ San Domenico
⑪ Pozzo di San Patrizio
⑫ Rocca dell'Albornoz

Underground Orvieto

🏛 Parco della Grotte

Società Speleotecnica. **Tel** 0763 344 891, 339 733 2764. **Open** tours depart from Piazza del Duomo; call ahead to book. 🅿
W orvietounderground.it

🏛 Pozzo di Via della Cava

Trattoria Sciarra, Via della Cava 28. **Tel** 0763 342 373. **Open** 8am–8pm Tue–Sun. **Closed** Sun after Epiphany–2 Feb. 🅿
W pozzodellacava.it

Passages below the town

The people of Orvieto are used to living with cellars: every house or shop has its own cave, and every family has its own story to tell of the underground. Marco Marino, for example, an antiques dealer in Via della Cava, found the remains of the oldest ceramics kiln known in the world by digging in his cellar. He uses it to display his collection of 15th-century ceramics.

A group of enthusiasts developed a project to open up some of Orvieto's caves to visitors, and the Società Speleotecnica is one of the groups to run tours. The caves underneath the embankment that separates the hospital from the walls of the cliff are examples of underground Orvieto: caves which were re-used over the centuries, as workshops, and storerooms for cereals, oil and wine. In addition to the intriguing Pozzo di San Patrizio *(see p142)*, it is well worth visiting the Pozzo di Via della Cava, an Etruscan well. Used in the 16th century and then covered up, the well now forms part of the basement of a restaurant.

VISITORS' CHECKLIST

Practical Information
Perugia. **Road Map** B5. 🔼 22,000.
ℹ Piazza del Duomo 24, 0763 341 772. 🎪 Corpus Domini procession; Palombella Pentecoste, 30 May. **W** orvietoviva.com

Transport
FS Milan–Rome line, 892021. 🚌

🏛 Palazzo Faina (Museo Civico and Museo Claudio Faina)

Piazza del Duomo 29. **Tel** 0763 341 511. **Open** Apr–Sep: 9:30am–6pm daily; Oct–Mar: 10am–5pm Tue–Sun. 🅿 ♿ **W** museofaina.it

This 19th-century palazzo opposite the duomo houses two museums. The Museo Civico, on the ground floor, is of much less interest than the Museo Claudio Faina, an extraordinarily rich private collection gathered by the Faina counts in the 19th century. Among the exhibits are beautiful Etruscan vases, superb jewellery from the 5th century BC onwards, and a series of exquisite Attic vases. There is a wonderful view of the duomo from the top floor.

Cinerary urn kept in the Museo Civico, Palazzo Faina

🏛 San Francesco

Piazza dei Febei.
The Romanesque church of San Francesco was founded in 1240, but it has been much altered over the centuries.

The large church has a tufa façade with three arched doorways and mullioned windows. Inside, the vault is supported by wooden trusses of huge dimensions given the era in which they were made.

Look out for the 14th-century wooden *Crucifixion*, attributed to Maitani (a key person involved in the construction of the duomo) or his school.

The Palazzo Papale also houses a museum dedicated to the cathedral. Exhibits include paintings, statues and other works of art that once filled the cathedral, dating from the Middle Ages up to the 18th century. Among them are paintings by Simone Martini, a series of large statues formerly

Detail from an Etruscan fresco, Museo dell'Opera del Duomo

in the cathedral and also a collection of church ornaments.

🏛 Palazzo Soliano and Museo Emilio Greco

Piazza del Duomo. **Tel** 0763 344 605. **Open** 10:30am–1pm, 2:30–6pm daily. 🅿 ♿
Commissioned in 1297 by Pope Boniface VIII, this austere building was not completed until 1359. In the early days, it was used as a storehouse by the Fabbrica del Duomo (cathedral works). Later, from the mid-16th century onwards, the hall on the ground floor was used by Orvieto's stonemasons. The structure is very simple, consisting of two large rooms one on top of the other. The lower room has a line of pilasters and arches and opens out into a grand, monumental staircase.

Palazzo Soliano houses a substantial collection of 20th-century sculptures, drawings and lithographs given to the city by Emilio Greco, a contemporary Sicilian artist.

Orvieto: Duomo

Orvieto's magnificent Duomo, which dominates the skyline, was founded by Pope Nicholas IV in 1290. Things got off to a bad start and, in 1308, the Sienese architect and sculptor, Lorenzo Maitani, was brought in to save the building. It wasn't finished for another 300 years. Maitani himself was largely responsible for the 52-m (170-ft) façade, with his own magnificently detailed bas-reliefs of scenes from the Old and New Testaments, a superb rose window, 16th-century statues and multicoloured mosaics (not original). The striped design outside is carried through into the Romanesque nave, which has alabaster windows and is divided by columns with elaborate capitals. Inside, the masterpiece is the chapel of the Madonna di San Brizio, with frescoes by Fra Angelico and Luca Signorelli and portraits of famous poets such as Dante.

Stained Glass
Among the stained glass in the apse is this *Nativity* by Giovanni Bonino di Assisi.

Sanctuary
The sanctuary walls feature 14th-century frescoes by Ugolino di Prete Ilario, a local artist. Above is a detail from the *Adoration of the Magi*.

KEY

① **The exterior** is characterized by horizontal bands of white travertine and blue-grey basalt.

②**The Reliquario del Corporale**, the design of which copies the duomo's façade, contains the altar cloth associated with the Miracle of Bolsena.

③ **The rose window**, with Christ at the centre, is the work of Florentine artist Andrea Orcagna (1360). The window is encircled by sculptures.

Cappella del Corporale
This chapel contains the superb 14th-century *Madonna dei Raccomandati* (left) by the Sienese artist Lippo Memmi, and frescoes (1357–64) of the *Miracle of Bolsena and Miracles of the Sacrament* by Ugolino di Prete Ilario.

Frescoes by Luca Signorelli

A fascinating cycle of frescoes narrating events related to the Apocalypse unfolds on the walls of the Cappella della Madonna di San Brizio. Signorelli tackles the themes of the Last Judgment – *The Day of Judgment, The Preaching of the Antichrist, The Resurrection of the Dead, The Damned Consigned to Hell, The Blessed Entering Heaven* and *Angels Guide the Elect to Paradise* – blending spatial harmony and dynamism in a synthesis of the art of central Italy of the time. The three-dimensionality and energy emanating from the figures heighten the drama and anticipate the painting of Michelangelo in the Sistine Chapel.

Detail from the fresco of The Day of Judgment by Signorelli

VISITORS' CHECKLIST

Practical Information
Piazza Duomo. **Tel** 0763 341 167, 0763 343 592 (tickets). Duomo and Chapel: **Open** Apr–Sep: 9:30am–7pm daily; Oct & Mar: 9:30am–6pm daily (1–5:30pm Sun & hols); Nov–Feb: 9:30am–1pm, 2:30–5pm daily (2:30–5pm Sun).

★ **Cappella della Madonna di San Brizio**
The fresco cycle in this Gothic chapel, begun by Fra Angelico (1447) with the assistance of Benozzo Gozzoli, and later completed by Luca Signorelli (1499–1504), is one of the finest of the Renaissance.

★ **Façade**
Bas-reliefs and statues (the originals of some are in the Museo dell'Opera), mosaics, pilasters and arches characterize this perfect synthesis between architecture and the decorative arts. It is a stunning example of Italian Gothic.

Main Door
The decorated bronze panels of the main door were the work of Emilio Greco in the 1960s.

🏛 Torre del Moro

Corso Cavour 87. **Tel** 0763 344 567.
Open Mar, Apr, Sep, Oct: 10am–7pm;
May–Aug: 10am–8pm; Nov–Feb:
10:30am–1pm daily. 🅿

The 12th-century "Tower of the Moor" towers 42 m (137 ft) above Corso Cavour, Orvieto's main street, where it meets Via del Duomo. It owes its name to the figure on the coat of arms of the Pucci, a local family. Its 14th-century bell is still in working order.

Alongside the tower is the **Palazzo dei Sette** (1300), built as the seat of the seven (sette) magistrates in charge of the commune, and later the seat of the papal governor.

The Torre del Moro rising above the roofs of old Orvieto

🏛 Sant'Andrea

Piazza della Repubblica.
This church is one of the oldest buildings in Orvieto. Founded in the 7th century, Sant'Andrea was built upon walls of probable Etruscan origin, over which a Roman temple was later built. It was then rebuilt in stages during the 12th–14th centuries. Sant'Andrea was once the most important

church in Orvieto. It was here that Pope Innocent III proclaimed the Fourth Crusade in 1201 and that Martin IV was crowned pope in 1281, in the presence of Charles of Anjou.

Important elements include the Gothic door, by Marco da Siena, designed by Maestro Vetrino (1487), and the imposing 12-sided bell tower, with three orders of two-mullioned windows and a series of coats of arms, placed here when restoration was undertaken in 1920–30. The interior is supported by great granite columns, probably Roman, and is decorated with fragments of frescoes and a 10th-century pulpit.

🏛 Palazzo del Popolo

Piazza del Popolo. **Closed** to the public.
The heart of the city in ancient times, Piazza del Popolo is home to the Palazzo del Popolo, first described in the town records at the end of the 13th century. Built from the local tufa stone and topped by a bell tower, it is an important example of Orvieto civic architecture from the late 13th century. Ornamentations include an external staircase, an open loggia, crenellations, and mullioned windows linked by a cornice. It is now a conference centre.

Detail from the Palazzo del Popolo

The façade of San Domenico with the original striped pilasters

🏛 San Domenico

Piazza XXIX Marzo.
It was here that the unusual striped stonework, in dark-coloured basalt and pale travertine, appeared for the first time in Orvieto, in the late 13th century. The style was then extensively used in the duomo and became a signature motif for the city. Despite substantial restoration in the Baroque era, the façade maintains its simple Romanesque-Gothic austerity, with a beautiful doorway, a tall two-mullioned window and a rose window which repeats the two-coloured motif.

Half the church was taken down in the 20th century to make room for the nearby barracks; the interior space today consists merely of the original transept and the tribune. The main work of art is the splendid tomb of Cardinal Guglielmo de Braye by Arnolfo di Cambio (1282), but there are also frescoes and other examples of sculpture.

🏛 Pozzo di San Patrizio

Viale Sangallo. **Tel** 0763 343 768.
Open daily. Apr–Sep: 10am–6:45pm; Oct–Mar: 10am–5:45pm. 🅿

Located at the eastern end of Corso Cavour is one of Orvieto's best-known monuments. Commissioned in 1527 by Pope Clement VII and designed by Antonio da Sangallo the Younger, the 62-m

The church of Sant'Andrea with its unusual 12-sided tower

The impressive depths forming the Pozzo di San Patrizio

(203-ft) well is a superb piece of engineering. Crucial to the design are two 248-step spiral staircases: one was used for the descent and one for the ascent, so that donkeys carrying pitchers of water would not meet on the way. The stairways are lit by 72 windows.

Looking over the plain from the bastions of the Rocca

🏛 Rocca dell'Albornoz
Viale Sangallo. **Open** always open. 🏛

Dominating the eastern end of Orvieto, near the terminus of the funicular that connects the old city with the railway station down on the plain, is the **Rocca**, built by Cardinal Albornoz in 1364 to bolster the power of the papacy. The locals destroyed it soon afterwards, and not much remains today.

The Rocca is an excellent vantage point from which to enjoy superb views over the city and the plain, as well as being a tranquil spot, surrounded as it is by several pretty gardens.

Environs
Around 1.5 km (1 mile) north of Orvieto, at the foot of the tufa cliff, is the **Necropoli del Crocifisso del Tufo**. This Etruscan cemetery complex dates from the 6th–3rd centuries BC and consists of small chambered tombs built of tufa blocks and containing a stone bench for laying out the corpse. On the lintel over the entrance to each tomb is the name of the person or family buried there. The site seems to have an essentially "urban" layout, following what would be defined today as a town plan.

The site was discovered only in the 19th century, by foreign archaeologists who passed on some of the finds to the Louvre and the British Museum. It wasn't until 1880 that the site was first explored in a scientific, non-intrusive way and finally began to arouse the interest of the Italian authorities. Over 100 tombs have now been found. The majority of the important

funerary objects discovered in the tombs are now distributed among Orvieto's museums.

On the south side of the cliff is the **Necropoli della Cannicella**, another burial site used by the Etruscans from the 7th–3rd centuries BC. It follows a similar layout to the necropolis at Crocifisso del Tufo.

Around 3 km (2 miles) south of Orvieto, just off SS71, is the **Abbazia di Santi Severo e Martino**, a great medieval monastery complex. Now partly converted into a hotel (La Badia, see p151), the monastery belonged to the Benedictines until 1221 and then the Premonstratensians (a French Order founded in 1120 by St Norbert).

Apart from the rooms used by the hotel, several areas of the monastery can still be visited. There is much that dates from the original construction (12th–13th-centuries). The splendid 12-sided Romanesque tower dates from the 12th century. The church, reached through a great 13th-century arch, features a single nave with a ribbed vault, an inlaid marble floor in the Cosmatesque style and several fragments of medieval frescoes. The barrel-vaulted Oratorio del Crocifisso, once the monks' refectory, is adorned with a 13th-century fresco depicting the *Crucifixion with Saints*. Also of interest is the 13th-century Abbot's House.

🏛 Necropoli del Crocifisso del Tufo
Tel 0763 343 611. **Open** 8:30am–7pm (winter: 5pm) daily. 🏛 ♿

Etruscan necropolis of the Crocifisso del Tufo, 6th century BC

TRAVELLERS' NEEDS

WHERE TO STAY

The range of accommodation in Umbria is impressively varied and caters to all tastes and pockets. While the traditional hotel is still an option in the main tourist centres, a large number of *agriturismo*, or working-farm, establishments have sprung up out of town, as have more luxurious country-house hotels, some with spas or wellness centres. Compared to similar complexes in Italian cities, these upscale rural hotels often offer excellent value for money. Bed-and-breakfast accommodation has also become more popular, and there is now a substantial network of B&Bs, both in the countryside and in the region's towns. More basic accommodation is offered by religious institutions to groups and individuals alike, while camping is another popular option in this region, often referred to as the green heart of Italy.

Grading and Prices

Hotels in Umbria are classified according to the standards followed in the rest of Italy. The categories run from one to five stars, plus a top luxury hotel category (L). Services offered are generally good. Prices vary according to the season and are higher during festivals and major cultural events. Most hotels accept credit cards.

Booking

Umbria does not really have much of a low season, although visitor numbers drop between November and February. Booking ahead is strongly advised; an email to confirm the booking is often requested when checking-in.

Hotels

Many of the hotels in Umbria's major towns are grouped into local consortiums – this is done in order to promote standards and to protect the interest of both the hotel and the guests. Lists with prices and other information are published annually by the Perugia tourist office (APT).

Historic Residences

A strong sense of the past is palpable in Umbria. For an unforgettable holiday, you might want to stay in a place that is steeped in history. The region features a wealth of centuries-old buildings, a number of which have been adapted to accommodate visitors. Standards are strictly regulated, so that the carefully refurbished interiors lose none of their character and charm; period furniture and artistic treasures abound in these establishments.

For a night or two in the peaceful environment of a monastery, try the tranquil La Badia (see p151), just outside Orvieto, or the equally lovely Eremo delle Grazie (see p151), near Spoleto.

A luxury hotel complex created out of 17th-century farm buildings

Those with aspirations of grandeur, could opt for an actual castle. Try the opulent Relais Il Canalichio (see p149), in Deruta, or, in Acquasparta, the Castello di Castigliano (see p150), with 16th-century cottages and rooms set inside a fortification.

Agriturismo and Country Houses

Holidaying at a working farm, or *agriturismo*, has become a tremendously popular option throughout Umbria. Also – either in rooms on B&B terms, or in independent self-catering apartments – many places offer a wide variety of facilities, including swimming pools and bikes. Horse-riding and other activities, such as cookery, pottery or yoga classes, are sometimes available, and guests are often encouraged to take an active part in farm life. Meals prepared with traditional local ingredients, some of which must be produced by the farm itself, are usually served to external diners as well as guests. The self-catering option generally

The welcoming reception area at Le Silve hotel in Assisi

◀ Lovely alfresco café lining Piazza IV Novembre in Perugia

requires a longer stay, paid for in advance, especially in high season.

Country-house hotels are a more upmarket option to stay in rural surroundings. A country house is usually more luxurious than an *agriturismo*, often with more sports and wellness facilities and a more refined restaurant, without the home-grown produce aspect.

Local tourist offices can provide visitors with full listings containing information on costs and facilities.

Hilltop hamlet converted into *agriturismo* accommodation

Campsites

There are campsites all over the region: all the historic Umbrian towns have at least one, and the area around Lake Trasimeno has a range of sites suited to tents, camper vans or caravans.

All Umbrian campsites are registered with the authorities and listed in regional tourist guides issued by the Perugia and Terni tourist offices.

Sites are usually clean and well run, and often located in attractive settings. Overnight stops by camper vans are strictly regulated; overnight stays are prohibited in historic centres, while in the modern or less touristy centres there are often designated parking places.

Bed & Breakfast

Bed-and-breakfast establishments can be found throughout Umbria, both in the region's towns and in the countryside. Expect to find homely, simple accommodation and a friendly welcome. Rooms are usually limited, so if you wish to stay at a particular place, it is wise to book well in advance.

Self-Catering Apartments

One option for a longer stay in the area is to rent an apartment. Whether you want to be based in the countryside, by a lake, in the mountains or in a town, you will find there is a good choice of properties available for short-term lets. Many of them are attached to an *agriturismo* or grouped together in a holiday village, with the benefit of shared facilities.

Religious Institutions

Many religious institutions offer simple accommodation to visitors. This may be in the form of a no-frills hotel, but some convents or monasteries provide special lodgings for pilgrims. There is a wide choice in Assisi, a major pilgrimage destination, but it is also worth looking in much smaller places, such as Bevagna or Spello. Meals are not normally provided, with the exception of the busy hostels in Assisi. The accommodation lists supplied by the tourist office are the best source of information.

Youth Hostels and Student Accommodation

Perugia, a university town, has youth hostels and student accommodation of various types; for sources of information, *see p175*.

Recommended Hotels

The hotels in this section have been chosen to reflect their quality and amenities within the themes of Luxury, Historic, Rural, Boutique and Value for Money, although it is fair to say that some establishments will fall into more than one category. Umbria has luxury and an especially large number of historic hotels and we have selected the best from the lot. The Rural category covers hotels in villages and those standing in acres of countryside, while the Boutique theme is given to the hotels that have been given a chic, contemporary makeover in recent years. Umbria has a wide selection of hotels we consider Value for Money and will stretch the budget that little bit further. The DK Choice hotels are extra special. They may have above average standards and amenities or a breathtaking location, or simply have a charm that sets them apart.

DIRECTORY

Agriturist Umbria
W agrituristumbria.com
Perugia
Via Savanarola 38. **Tel** 075 32028.

Perugia IAT
Piazza Matteotti 18.
Tel 075 573 6458.
W turismo.comune.perugia.it

Terni IAT
Via Cassian Bon 1.
Tel 0744 423 047.
W marmore.it

Umbria Bed and Breakfast
W bed-and-breakfast-in-umbria.it

Umbria Information
Umbrian region tourist information.
W regioneumbria.eu
W bellaumbria.net
W lamiaumbria.it

Where to Stay

Northern Umbria

ASSISI: Tre Esse Country House
Rural   €   **Map** D4
Via di Valecchie 41, 06081
Tel *075 81 63 63*
W countryhousetreesse.com
Old-fashioned hotel in a centuries-old stone building reached by a steep uphill climb. Classic décor, antique furnishings and lovely gardens.

ASSISI: Fontebella
Historic   €€   **Map** D4
Via Fontebella 25, 06081
Tel *075 81 28 83*
W fontebella.com
Restored 17th-century building with elegant rooms and suites, many with sweeping views of the Umbrian valley. Limited parking.

ASSISI: Hotel Giotto
Luxury   €€   **Map** D4
Via Fontebella 41, 06081
Tel *075 81 22 09*   **Closed** *Jan–Feb*
W hotelgiottoassisi.it
Located at one of the highest points in Assisi, the Giotto offers panoramic views from its rooms, terraces and restaurants. Offers fine dining as well as an informal dining option and an on-site day spa facility.

ASSISI: Romantik Hotel Le Silve
Rural   €€   **Map** D4
Località Armenzano 82, Parco Regionale del Monte Subasio, 06081
Tel *075 801 90 05*
W lesilve.it
Set in a 10th-century stone farmhouse east of Assisi, this upmarket hotel, with pretty rooms and apartments, offers spa, pool, fine dining facilities and even horse riding.

BETTONA: Relais La Corte di Bettona
Rural   €€   **Map** C4
Via Santa Caterina 2, 06084
Tel *075 98 71 14*
W relaisbettona.com
Plush rooms, vaulted ceilings and lavish décor; this rural hotel also has a wellness suite and a gourmet restaurant.

CALZOLARO: La Preghiera
Rural   €€   **Map** B2
Via del Refari, Calzolaro, 06019
Tel *075 930 24 28*
W lapreghiera.com
Complete with its own chapel in a secluded 800-year-old monastery, La Preghiera has

attractive rooms, landscaped gardens, sun terraces, a swimming pool and a wellness centre. It also runs a cookery school.

CIGLIANO: Agriturismo Cigliano
Value for Money   €   **Map** D3
Frazione Colpalombo 22, 06020
Tel *333 603 3998*
W agriturismo-cigliano.it
Escape modern-day trappings at this intimate *agriturismo* that has no electric lighting and uses only candle light. Meals on request.

DK Choice

CITTÀ DELLA PIEVE: Hotel Vannucci
Boutique   €€   **Map** A4
Via Icilio Vanni 1, 06062
Tel *0578 29 80 63*
W hotel-vannucci.com
Chic hotel in a 19th-century palazzo built by King Vittorio Emanuele II. Antique furniture, modern art, a walled garden with a pool, a wellness suite, a fine dining restaurant and superb rooms combine to make this place really special.

CITTÀ DELLA PIEVE: Hotel Relais dei Magi
Country House   €€€   **Map** A4
Via Santa Lucia 53, 06062
Tel *0578 298133*
W hotelpiccoloeden.it
Ideally suited for exploring both Umbria and Tuscany, this stylish 18th-century villa, high in the hills outside the town, is surrounded by woodlands as well as formal gardens. The hotel has only 14 rooms and a couple of apartments. Excellent panoramic restaurant and caring service.

Price Guide

Prices are based on one night's stay in high season for a standard double room, inclusive of service charges and taxes.

€	up to €100
€€	€100 to 200
€€€	over €200

CITTÀ DI CASTELLO: Hotel Garden
Value for Money   €   **Map** B2
Via Aldo Bologni, 06012
Tel *075 855 05 93*
W hotelgarden.com
Understated elegance is the draw at this spacious hotel that has a wellness suite, à la carte restaurant and gardens.

CITTÀ DI CASTELLO: Hotel Tiferno
Historic   €€   **Map** B2
Piazza R Sanzio 13, 06012
Tel *075 855 03 31*
W hoteltiferno.it
Once a monastery, centrally located Tiferno is today a hotel with elegant rooms and lounges. The owner's Alberto Burri paintings line the walls.

CORCIANO: La Contea
B&B   €   **Map** C3
Via Cattaneo 25, San Mariano di Corciano, 06073
Tel *320 662 5469*
W bblacontea.it
Located next to a golf course, this cosy B&B with vaulted ceilings occupies a family house that dates back almost 500 years.

DERUTA: Antica Fattoria del Colle
Boutique   €   **Map** C4
Strada Colle delle Forche 6, 06053
Tel *075 97 22 01*
W anticafattoriadelcolle.it
This *agriturismo* with a sun terrace and pool has tastefully done rooms and lounge. Meals use products from the farm.

Relaxed setting at the poolside in Hotel Vannucci, Città Della Pieve

DK Choice

DERUTA: Relais Il Canalicchio €€
Luxury   Map C4
Via della Piazza 13, Collazzone, 06053
Tel *075 870 73 25*   **Closed** *Nov–Mar*
Ⓦ relaisilcanalicchio.it
The 1,000-year-old castle-like structure together with original features like stone arches and ceiling beams, an old press and millstone, evoke a real sense of history. The luxurious accommodation is backed by a gym, a relaxation suite and a wood-panelled dining hall.

GUBBIO: La Rocca €
Boutique   Map D2
Via Monte Ingino 15, 06024
Tel *075 922 12 22*
Ⓦ laroccahotel.net
Stylish hotel built against a rock face high on Mount Ingino two minutes from the medieval town of Gubbio by cable car.

GUBBIO: Park Hotel ai Cappuccini
Spa hotel   €€   Map D2
Via Tifernate, 06024
Tel *075 92 34*
Ⓦ parkhotelaicappuccini.it
Just a short walk from the town centre, this attractive hotel in a restored 17th-century monastery has tasteful rooms, an à la carte restaurant, fine wine shop, art gallery, spa and sports amenities, including a neon-lit indoor pool and water park with a hydro-massage room.

GUBBIO: Relais Ducale €€
Luxury   Map D2
Via Galeotti 19, 06024
Tel *075 922 01 57*
Ⓦ relaisducale.com
This annexe of the Ducal Palace located just off Gubbio's main square, offers luxurious accomodation and includes a lovely terrace garden. Both child- and pet-friendly.

LAKE TRASIMENO – CASTIGLIONE DEL LAGO: Bandita
Value for Money   €   Map B3
Localita Vitellino
Tel *075 965 3082*
Ⓦ casedelmelograno.it
A restored stone house divided into comfortable apartments, each with views over the lake. It also has a pool and tennis courts.

A well-decorated room at the luxurious Relais Il in Deruta

LAKE TRASIMENO – CASTIGLIONE DEL LAGO: Miralago
Value for Money   €   Map B3
Piazza Mazzini 6, 06061
Tel *075 95 11 57*
Ⓦ hotelmiralago.com
The 19th-century home of the Miralago dominates a square in this walled town. Terrace garden dining overlooking the lake,

LAKE TRASIMENO – ISOLA MAGGIORE: Da Sauro €
Rural   Map B3
Via Guglielmi 1, 06060
Tel *075 82 61 68*
Ⓦ dasauro.it
Family-run hotel at an idyllic location in a fishing village on Isola Maggiore. Lovely rooms and an excellent fish restaurant.

LAKE TRASIMENO – PASSIGNANO: Hotel Kursaal €
Value for Money   Map B3
Via Europa 24, 06065
Tel *075 82 80 85*   **Closed** *Dec–Mar*
Ⓦ kursaalhotel.net
Elegant 1930s villa with contemporary rooms, popular restaurant and terrace pool, nestled among trees, on the shores of Lake Trasimeno.

MIGLIANO DI MARSCIANO: Il Casale Di Buccole €€
Luxury   Map B4
Vocabolo Buccole 25, 06050
Tel *075 870 81 26*
Ⓦ ilcasaledibuccole.it
A 19th-century farmhouse with rooms that have Italian-style décor, some with four-poster beds. Lovely views from the pool.

PANICALE: Villa di Monte Solare €€
Luxury   Map C4
Tavernelle di Panicale, 06068
Tel *075 83 23 76*
Ⓦ villamontesolare.com
Ivy-covered villa and farmhouse amid olive groves; offers

luxurious rooms, spa centre and a celebrated restaurant.

PERUGIA: Hotel Rosalba €
Value for Money   Map C3
Via del Circo 7, 06121
Tel *075 572 82 85*
Ⓦ hotelrosalba.com
Centrally located and with its own parking, this simple yet charming hotel is set in a 18th-century townhouse.

DK Choice

PERUGIA: Etruscan Chocohotel €€
Boutique   Map C3
Via Campo di Marte 134, 06124
Tel *075 583 73 14*
Ⓦ chocohotel.it
From the decor and room furnishings, including desks and headboards resembling chocolate bars, to the crockery and a breakfast menu featuring chocolate pastries, this fun hotel is all about chocolates. Has an outdoor pool and a restaurant that serves Umbrian classics.

PERUGIA: Brufani Palace €€€
Luxury   Map C3
Piazza Italia 12, 06100
Tel *075 573 25 41*
Ⓦ brufanipalace.com
Five-star elegance in every detail – from the restaurant and boudoir-style rooms to the spectacular pool built over glass-covered Etruscan ruins.

PETRIGNANO DI ASSISI: Parco dei Cavalieri €€
Historic   Map D3
Via Matteotti 47, 06081
Tel *075 809 80 12*
Ⓦ parcodeicavalieri.it
Medieval building, with richly decorated rooms and an elegant à la carte restaurant, surrounded by acres of neat gardens.

For more information on types of hotels *see pp 146–7*

Idyllic views from Le Tre Vaselle in Torgiano

DK Choice

PIEGARO: Ca' de' Principi   €€
Luxury   Map B4
Via Roma 43, 06066
Tel *075 835 80 40*
w dimorastorica.it
Outstanding frescoes adorn
the halls of this lavish hotel
housed in an 18th-century
royal palace. Highlights include
a vaulted restaurant that uses
produce from the estate's
farms and orchards, luxurious
boudoir-style rooms furnished
with period pieces, a swimming
pool and terrace.

TORGIANO: Le Tre Vaselle   €€
Boutique   Map C4
Via Garibaldi 48, 06089
Tel *075 988 04 47*
w 3vaselle.it
A 17th-century villa forms
the setting for this stylish
hotel that also has a spa and
wellness centre.

Southern Umbria

**ACQUASPARTA: Agriturismo
Santomanno**   €
Value for Money   Map D6
Strada delle Molinelle 142, 05021
Tel *338 297 5216*
w santomanno.com
Five apartments have been
created within a farmhouse at
this *agriturismo* farm that also
has a play area for children and
on-site barbeque facilities.

**ACQUASPARTA: Castello di
Casigliano**   €
Historic   Map D6
Piazza Corsini 1, 05021
Tel *0744 94 34 28*
w castellodicasigliano.com

The hotel, a tastefully converted
set of 16th-century cottages
and rooms inside a fort, is
furnished to complement the
rustic features that have been
retained. It also has a gourmet
restaurant and a beautiful garden
offering panoramic views.

**BASCHI: La Penisola Villa
Bellago**   €
Value for Money   Map B6
*Località Pian delle Monache 138
(Todi-Baschi road), 05023*
Tel *0744 95 05 21*
w lapenisola.com
Centuries-old hotel with a
tranquil feel, located on the banks
of the Lago di Corbara. Tennis
courts and fish restaurant too.

**BEVAGNA: L'Orto degli
Angeli**   €€
Luxury   Map D4
Via Dante Alighieri 1, Bevagna 06031
Tel *0742 36 01 30*
w ortoangeli.it
Antiques and contemporary
furnishings work together at this
elegant hotel created from two
period buildings. Excellent
restaurant and spa. Choose
rooms carefully since they vary.

**BRUFA DI TORGIANO:
Borgo Brufa**   €€
Luxury   Map C4
Via del Colle 38, 06089
Tel *075 98 52 67*
w borgobrufa.it
Get pampered at this tranquil
rural spa resort. Its well-equipped
wellness centre features a swim-
through indoor and outdoor pool,
a Finnish sauna and a host of
treatments. Lavish rooms, a
gourmet restaurant and several
leisure activities including
horse riding and tennis complete
the package.

DK Choice

**CASCIA: Casale Sant'Antonio
Agriturismo**   €
Rural   Map E5
Casale Sant'Antonio 59, 06043
Tel *333 321 2344*
w casalesantantonio.it
Working organic farm rearing
cattle and producing grains
and pulses for its restaurant.
It is located in a protected area
on the slopes of Monte
Meraviglia with numerous
paths for wandering the
countryside. Rooms and
apartments are elegant in a
country-house style.

FOLIGNO: Le Mura   €
Value for Money   Map D4
Via Bolletta 27, 06034
Tel *0742 35 73 44*
w lemura.net
Beside Foligno's medieval
walls near San Giacomo; an old-
fashioned hotel with tastefully
done rooms and a restaurant
serving Umbrian fare.

**NARNI: Colle Abramo delle
Vigne Agriturismo**   €
Rural   Map C6
*Strada di Colle Abramo 34, Vigne,
05035*
Tel *0744 79 64 28*
w colleabramo.com
Cosy rooms and apartments
in a group of traditional stone
farm buildings in the unspoilt
countryside. Amenities
include alfresco dining area,
lush gardens, sun terraces, a
swimming pool and children's
playground. Riding stables
are nearby.

NARNI: Terra Umbra   €€
Modern   Map C6
*Strada Provinciale, Maratta Bassa 6,
05036*
Tel *0744 75 03 04*
w terraumbra.it
Smart hotel with a gym and
sauna and a restaurant serving
excellent Umbrian fare.

**NORCIA: Il Casale nel Parco
dei Monti Sibillini**   €
Rural   Map F5
Località Fontevena 8, 06046
Tel *0743 81 64 81*
w casalenelparco.com
Housed in a group of farm
buildings that have been
transformed into spectacular
spaces showcasing exposed
beams and stone walls, this
agriturismo offers great rooms
and amenities including a shop
for organic produce, restaurant,
pool, stables and a farm.

ORVIETO: Agriturismo Titignano €
Rural   Map B5
Località Titignano, 05010
Tel *0763 30 80 00*
W titignano.com
Overlooking Lake Corbara, this wine-producing *agriturismo* is set in a medieval castle. Rooms have classic Umbrian styling.

ORVIETO: Hotel Duomo €€
Value for Money   Map B5
Vicolo di Maurizio 7, 05018 Orvieto
Tel *0763 34 18 87*
W orvietohotelduomo.com
This centrally located, popular hotel takes its name from the Duomo, which many of its rooms overlook. Décor tastefully combines antiques with artwork.

DK Choice

ORVIETO: La Badia €€
Luxury   Map B5
Località Badia 8, 05019
Tel *0763 30 19 59*
W labadiahotel.it
This 6th century abbey with its 12-sided tower added in AD 1103, has been creatively converted into a beautiful honey-coloured landmark hotel. The romantic rooms as well as the fine dining restaurant have period features. It also offers a state-of-the-art spa.

PARRANO: Il Poggiolo di Parrano €€
Rural   Map B6
Contrada Bagno 43, 05010
Tel *0763 83 84 71*
W ilpoggiolo.com
Rooms and restaurant are in stylishly renovated farm buildings. The surrounding olive groves are known for their oil products.

PRECI: Hotel Agli Scacchi €
Value for Money   Map E5
Quartiere Scacchi 12, Preci, 06047
Tel *074 39 92 21*
W hotelagliscacchi.com
Simple but elegant rooms and an organic restaurant within a centuries-old palace inside the Monti Sibillini National Park.

SAN GEMINI: Albergo Duomo €€
Historic   Map D6
Piazza Duomo 4, 05029 San Gemini
Tel *0744 63 00 15*
W albergoduomosangemini.it
Once home to Italian nobility, the hotel has tasteful décor with 18th-century frescoes. Neat rooms, including one with its own spa.

SPELLO: Hotel del Teatro €
Historic   Map D4
Via Giulia 24, 06038
Tel *0742 30 11 40*
W hoteldelteatro.it
Del Teatro, with well-equipped rooms and tasteful interior, is located in an 18th-century building, with some parts dating back to medieval times.

SPELLO: Terme Francescane €€
Luxury   Map D4
Via delle Acque, 06038
Tel *0742 30 11 86*
W termefrancescane.com
This refined spa resort uses natural sulphur springs for a host of health treatments. Smart rooms and restaurants.

SPOLETO: Clitunno €€
Boutique   Map D5
Piazza Sordini 6, 06049
Tel *0743 22 33 40*
W hotelclitunno.com
A restored town house near the Duomo, this family-run hotel offers contemporary rooms and a popular fine-dining restaurant.

DK Choice

SPOLETO: Eremo delle Grazie €€
Historic   Map D5
Strada per Monteluco 13, Monteluco, 06049
Tel *074 34 96 24*
W eremodellegrazie.com
Staying at this luxurious hotel in a restored 5th-century monastery is an experience. Wooden beams, wall paintings and antique furnishings add to the original architectural details visible throughout. Cosy rooms, library, restaurant and wine cellar lend charm to the atmosphere.

A bright room in one of the two period buildings of L'Orto degli Angeli, Bevagna

SPOLETO: Palazzo Leti €€
Luxury   Map D5
Via degli Eremiti 8–10, 06049
Tel *0743 22 49 30*
W palazzoleti.com
Dating from medieval and Neo-Classical times, this palazzo, standing in beautiful gardens, is one of Spoleto's finest. Lavish rooms.

TODI: Hotel Bramante €€
Historic   Map C5
Via Orvietana 48, 06059
Tel *075 894 83 81*
W hotelbramante.it
Upscale hotel, restaurant and spa in a restored 800 years old convent outside Todi's city walls.

TODI: San Lorenzo Tre €€
Historic   Map C5
Via San Lorenzo 3, 06059
Tel *075 894 45 55*
W sanlorenzo3.it
This countryside hotel, with fabulous views, is a Todi landmark. The 19th-century building displays beautiful antique furnishings and old photographs tracing the story of the Gagliardi-Pellegrini family that once lived here. Smart en-suite rooms with Wi-Fi.

TODI: Relais Todini €€
Luxury   Map C5
Vocabolo Cervara 24, Collevalenza, 06059
Tel *075 88 75 21*
W relaistodini.com
Todini is a charming hotel in a 14th-century manor house. Period features abound complemented by lavish furnishings. Superb spa.

TREVI: Antica Dimora Alla Rocca €
Value for Money   Map D5
Piazza della Rocca 1, 06039
Tel *074 23 85 41*
W hotelallarocca.it
With furnishings matching the style of the 17th-century palazzo it occupies, this hotel is one of Trevi's best. Convenient central location.

TREVI: Casa Giulia €€
Rural   Map D5
Località Corciano, Bovara, 06039
Tel *0742 782 57*
W casagiulia.com
Housed in a 17th-century manor house near the Clitunno Springs, Casa Giulia offers bright rooms, restaurant and even a swimming pool with a panoramic view of the Umbrian valley.

For more information on types of hotels *see pp146–7*

WHERE TO EAT AND DRINK

One of the main reasons to visit Umbria is the excellent food. A land of robust flavours, ancient culinary traditions and fabulous fresh produce, Umbria is brimming with cosy, family-run trattorias and traditional restaurants where you can try the local cuisine, often in atmospheric, historical surroundings. Many restaurants now offer international, fish and seafood, and vegetarian cuisine, especially in the major towns, in addition to true Umbrian.

The region's many food-based festivals and fairs, known as sagre, offer an ideal opportunity to find out more about and taste some authentic local produce. These lively events are often devoted to a particular crop, such as mushrooms, chestnuts, truffles or olives. Most agriturismo structures (farm lodgings) provide meals for their guests, and some are open to external diners, too, the hosts often eating together with the guests.

Opening Hours and Prices

Restaurant and trattoria opening hours in Umbria are similar to those found all over central Italy. Generally, lunch is served from noon to 2:30pm, and evening meals from 7pm onwards. Closing times depend on the season and on the type of place: earlier for small trattorias and in winter; later in summer and during the holiday season, and in busy historic centres. Many restaurants close for a week or two during August for holidays.

Prices vary enormously depending on the type of establishment. In some of the most famous restaurants, the bill can easily exceed 50 euros per person, excluding wine, while in a village trattoria you can usually eat for around 20 to 30 euros per person. Most establishments charge a *coperto* (cover charge), which is usually 1–3 euros per customer; some places also add a 10 per cent service charge to the bill.

The Produce of Umbria

Umbrian cuisine consists of dishes deriving from an ancient tradition, sometimes re-interpreted

The dining room at Le Mura restaurant in the historic centre of Foligno

by enterprising chefs. The region yields excellent produce of all kinds, and crops cultivated using organic methods are becoming increasingly widespread.

Umbria produces high-quality red and white wine, which are highly respected all over the country; the region also produces some of Italy's best olive oil. Mushrooms are another delicacy, and some of the finest black and white truffles in the world are found here. Cured meats are another specialty, particularly in Norcia, while good freshwater fish can be found in Lake Trasimeno and other lakes around the region. The tiny village of Castelluccio, in the

Monti Sibillini, gives its name to a renowned and tasty variety of lentil.

Top Restaurants

In response to the growing interest in the region's gastronomic traditions, some prestigious restaurants have been established in Umbria. Such places alone can make a trip to the region worthwhile.

One of the most famous is the restaurant of chef Gianfranco Vissani (see p162), in Baschi, on the shores of Lago di Corbara, but there are other restaurants worthy of note, including Il Postale (see p161) of Marco Bistarelli, in Perugia. Tables at these and other top-class restaurants are in high demand, so booking ahead as far as possible is a necessity.

Trattorias

A traditional trattoria is a good choice for an authentic taste of the local specialities. Often family-run, and sometimes incorporating an all-day bar or general store, down-to-earth trattorias can be found in every town and village around Umbria. Unpretentious and affordable, they are often the first choice among the locals when eating out with family or friends, so they make an ideal spot for people-watching, too.

Specialities of the Lake Trasimeno area, including local wine and oil

Relaxing outside the San Francesco restaurant in Assisi

Agriturismo

Agriturismo farms are obliged to use locally grown ingredients, some of which are usually produced on the farm itself. The sometimes limited choice of dishes is made up for by the genuine farmhouse flavours and the welcoming atmosphere. Furthermore, these properties often have lots of space, as well as play areas – perfect for small children.

Cookery Courses

Umbria has numerous cookery schools, where both professionals and amateurs can learn the secrets of the region's traditional cuisine. There are also plenty of *agriturismo* farms that run cookery courses.

Bars and Cafés

Bars are an important part of everyday life all over Italy, and no less so in Umbria. Although the locals will often just pop in for a quick espresso or an apéritif standing at the bar, many places also have plenty of seating – both inside and out– for you to linger and take in the view. Table service generally costs a little extra. Hot and cold snacks are usually available, and if it's a *bar-pasticceria*, the cakes will be made on the premises.

Local Festivals

The traditional fairs and festivals held all over Umbria attract visitors and locals alike, and they provide a great opportunity to try local food and wine specialities at reasonable prices. People flock to Norcia (in February) and Città di Castello (in November) to taste the precious truffle, while wine is the attraction at Todi and Torgiano, and particularly at the Sagrantino festival in Montefalco, held in September.

One event of great interest is the Mercato delle Gaite, an event usually held in two parts, one in April and the other May in Bevagna (*see p108*). The town adopts the dress and ways of the 14th and 15th centuries, and local restaurants offer tasty menus that feature ancient dishes.

A more modern event of international importance is Perugia's Eurochocolate.

Disabled People

More and more places in Umbria, including restaurants and hotels, are upgrading their buildings by installing slopes and bathrooms in order to facilitate access for the disabled. Even so, the streets can be steep in Umbria's medieval hill towns, and steps are common.

Smoking

All restaurants and bars throughout Italy are obliged to adhere to a strict no-smoking policy. Some places do have a properly ventilated room for smokers, and the no-smoking restrictions do not apply at outside tables.

Recommended Restaurants

The restaurants in this section have been chosen to reflect their quality, amenities and variety of cuisine. Umbria has a large number of traditional restaurants and we have selected those that offer the most authentic dining experience. Similarly, Umbria has restaurants serving international cuisine, although it is fair to say that many of these may also include classic local dishes on their menu. Umbria has fish restaurants, and others that offer good vegetarian menus, and we have selected the best. The DK Choice restaurants are extra special. We consider them to have historical charm, especially high standards or an above average location.

The Festa di San Benedetto in Norcia, held in March

The Flavours of Umbria

Umbria has an earthy cuisine based on what ingredients are in season. Like their Etruscan ancestors, Umbrians have an affinity with the land and enjoy hunting for edible bounty from their beautiful countryside. In spring there is wild asparagus, and in summer there are fruit and herbs to be picked and preserved. Autumn and winter have their fair share of culinary delights; as the weather turns colder, market stalls and restaurants display the hunters' catch – hare, pheasant, pigeon, woodcock and quail, as well as chestnuts, porcini mushrooms and truffles sniffed out by the hunters' dogs. Winter vegetables like *cavolo nero* are also popular.

Black truffles

Local olives mixed with tiny chillies on a market stall

Northern Umbria

Landlocked Umbria has always depended on its rivers and lakes for fish, including Lake Trasimeno. In waterside villages, the daily catch of carp, trout, perch, pike, tench and eel are made into soups and stews, or baked with herbs. Eel is simmered with fresh tomatoes, while trout is cooked with wild fennel.

The largest carp are roasted whole in a the same way as a suckling pig *(regina in porchetta)*. There is fine lamb from the hillside herds of prime beef-cattle. The regional capital, Perugia, is noted for its Chianina beef, as well as for its chocolate.

A wide variety of vegetables and cereals, like barley and spelt, are cultivated on the fertile land. Olive trees are everywhere: their oil is some of Italy's finest – light but scented, and full of flavour. Special sweets and pastries are made to mark historical and religious celebrations. Perugia's patron saint, San Costanzo, is honoured with the *torcolo*, a ring-shaped cake studded with aniseed, pine nuts and dried fruit. From Assisi, *ossa di morta* are bone-shaped marzipan sweets prepared for All Souls' day in November.

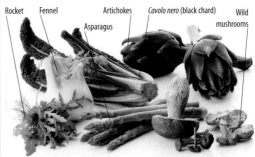

Rocket   Fennel   Artichokes   *Cavolo nero* (black chard)   Wild mushrooms
                 Asparagus

Typical selection of fresh Umbrian vegetables

Umbrian Dishes and Specialities

Cured meats, salami and black olives marinated with orange peel, are typical *antipasti*. Asparagus is used in tomato or cheese sauces with pasta, or fried with beaten eggs to make a *frittata*. Pastas include *ciriole* (like tagliatelle), often served with fried onions and garlic. *Porchetta* is a whole young pig, stuffed with offal and herbs, and roasted on a spit until the skin is deliciously crisp; it is sometimes served sliced, in bread rolls. Game is roasted or cooked with wine to make rich stews such as *piccione in salmi* (pigeon). *Torta al testo* is a flattish bread made with olive oil and stuffed with herbs, sausage or ham. *Pan pepato* is sweetened with sugar, candied fruit and nuts. Coffee may be accompanied by Baci (meaning "kisses") from Perugia *(see p171)*.

Baci chocolates

Teggacmaccio is a stew from Lake Trasimeno, made with perch, trout, tench and eel, in a tomato and wine broth.

Chefs prearing to serve freshly roasted *porchetta*

Southern Umbria

The south of the region has prime agricultural areas, like the Castelluccio plains, where tiny, distinctively flavoured lentils are grown and used in many local dishes, such as rustic hearty soups made with seasonal vegetables. Among these are cardoons (*cardone*), which look like giant celery and have a rather bitter taste.

Traditionally, meat is often grilled or spit-roasted with herbs, especially sage and rosemary. Norcia is an important gastronomic centre, famous for black truffles and as the home of marvellous hams (*prosciutti*), salami and sausages. Throughout Italy, *norcino* means "pork butchery". Dozens of recipes hail from the town, including *mazzafegati* (pig's liver sausages with raisins, pine nuts and orange peel) and *beccacce alla norcina* (woodcock stuffed with sausage, herbs and truffles). Orvieto is wine country, as reflected in *gallina umbriaca* ("drunken chicken", cooked in wine). Orvieto is also known for quails (*quaglie*) baked in bread,

while Todi's speciality is ox tongue (*lingua di bue*) in a sweet-and-sour (*agrodolce*) sauce.

Umbrian Truffles

Truffles are part of Umbrian life and are used liberally in its cuisine, elevating even basic salads or scrambled eggs to gourmet fare. They appear in classic recipes, grated over risottos or sliced thinly onto *crostini* (bread fried in olive oil). Black truffles are added to cheese (*pecorino tartufato*) and can be frozen or preserved. Rarer white truffles are always eaten fresh.

REGIONAL WINES

Orvieto Famous for crisp, dry white wines, but there are also some lesser-known reds and dessert wines.

Torgiano Rosso Riserva Possibly Umbria's finest red, it is made from Sangiovese grapes and ages well.

Sagrantino di Montefalco This full, rich red wine has been produced for centuries in vineyards around Montefalco.

Colli Perugini Red and white wines from a number of grape varieties, including Pinot Grigio, Grechetto and Montepulciano.

Vin Santo A lusciously sweet wine, pressed from semi-dried Grechetto or Malvasia grapes.

Black grapes, ripe and ready to be pressed to make wine

Cinghiale alla cacciatore is wild boar cooked with red wine, herbs and vegetables until tender.

Lenticche di Castelluccio (lentils) are often served as an accompaniment to fennel-flavoured pork sausages.

Strangozzi pasta with sugar, walnuts, cinnamon, cocoa and lemon is a Christmas Eve treat in Umbria.

Where to Eat and Drink

Northern Umbria

ASSISI: Enoteca San Pietro €
Classic Umbrian   Map D4
Via Borgo San Pietro 18, 06081
Tel *075 81 33 03*   **Closed** *Mon*
Surrounded by convents in a quiet hillside location, this cosy restaurant with stone walls and rattan chairs has an à la carte menu with truffles among the Umbrian classics and local artisan beer and wines. Specializes in using Km0 or local ingredients.

ASSISI: La Fortezza €
Classic Umbrian   Map D4
Vicolo della Fortezza/Piazza del Comune, 06081
Tel *075 81 29 93*   **Closed** *Thu*
The combination of simple Umbrian dishes and elaborate gourmet-style cuisine sets the tone here. *Cannelloni all'assisiana* (pasta and veal) is the speciality.

ASSISI: Pasticceria Pizzeria Bagnoli €
Pizza & Pasta   Map D4
Via Patrono d'Italia 3, Santa Maria degli Angeli, 06081
Tel *075 80 40 611*
Friendly little pizzeria with the distinct aroma of pizza fresh from the oven. Pizza Napoletana and Pizza Salmino Piccante are the crowd favourites.

ASSISI: Pizzeria Il Duomo €
Pizza & Pasta   Map D4
Via Porta Perlici 11, 06081
Tel *075 81 63 26*
Housed in a stone building with arches and gallery seating, this welcoming pizzeria is always

busy. Well-known for their imaginative toppings.

ASSISI: Armentum €€
Gourmet   Map D4
Località Armenzano, 06081
Tel *075 80 19 000*
Located in Hotel Le Silve, with lovely views from outside terrace, this eatery has an eclectic menu and wine list, as well as a wide selection of olive oils to compliment its cuisine.

ASSISI: Brilli Bistrot €€
Café & Patisserie   Map D4
Via Los Angeles 83, 06081
Tel *075 80 43 433*   **Closed** *Lunch except Sun; Sun eve for gourmet*
Artfully presented dishes define this trendy bistro-style restaurant just outside Assisi. Creative *antipasti* and pizzas, fish dishes, pastries and mouth-watering desserts. Serves a range of liqueurs.

DK Choice

ASSISI: Buca Di San Francesco €€
Classic Umbrian   Map D4
Via Eugenio Brizi 1, 06081
Tel *075 81 22 04*   **Closed** *Mon*
Umbrian fare such as succulent filet steak flavoured with local truffle followed by *claramicola* (a meringue-topped cake drenched in the ruby red spirit, Alchermes) make this elegant restaurant delightful. Located in renovated medieval cellars beneath a townhouse in central Assisi, this restaurant has a good cellar and a terrace for alfresco dining in summers.

ASSISI: Castel San Gregorio €€
Classic Umbrian   Map D4
Via San Gregorio 16, 06081
Tel *075 80 38 009*
Atmospheric hotel restaurant in a 13th-century castle just off Assisi. Serves hearty meat dishes like wild boar and game, often flavoured with local truffle. Rounded off with tempting home-made desserts.

ASSISI: Da Erminio €€
Classic Umbrian   Map D4
Via Montecavallo 19, 06081
Tel *075 81 25 06*   **Closed** *Thu*
Fashionable trattoria with menus that typically feature wild boar and rabbit with herbs, and pasta dishes like the house speciality *strangozzi alla boscaiola* with walnuts. Good wine list.

ASSISI: Il Frantoio €€
Classic Umbrian   Map D4
Vicolo Illuminati 10, 06081
Tel *075 81 29 77*
Elegant restaurant laid-out within a renovated 17th-century olive press on the grounds of the Fontebella Hotel. A superb wine list complements the Umbrian menu. The house speciality is *strangozzi paesani* (hand-rolled spaghetti tossed with tomatoes, artichokes and chilli flakes).

ASSISI: La Bella Stazione €€
Pizza & Pasta   Map D4
Piazza Dante Alighieri 5, Santa Maria degli Angeli, 06081
Tel *075 80 41 647*
Traditional pizza and pasta dishes are given a modern twist with creative toppings and sauces at this intimate restaurant with panoramic views of the city. Located on the first floor of Assisi railway station.

ASSISI: Medio Evo €€
International   Map D4
Via Arco dei Priori 4, 06081
Tel *075 81 30 68*   **Closed** *Mon*
Subtly lit to enhance its 13th-century vaulted interiors, this cosy trattoria is a memorable place to enjoy authentic local dishes. Try the house special truffle risotto.

ASSISI: Ristorante Carfagna €€
Classic Umbrian   Map D4
Ponte San Vittorino, 06081
Tel *075 81 30 63*
A large restaurant situated at the foot of the hill topped by the Basilica of Assisi. It is part of a *agriturismo* farm complex that uses home produce. Open from breakfast until late.

ASSISI: Ristorante da Cecco €€
Classic Umbrian   Map D4
Piazza San Pietro 8, 06081
Tel *075 81 24 37*   **Closed** *Thu*
This hotel restaurant celebrates the art of gastronomy with specials like *agnello al tartufo* (lamb with truffles) and *tagliata di chianina* (steak and tagliatelle with truffle). Excellent wine list.

L'Antico Forziere is set in a Casalina country house

ASSISI: Ristorante da Elide €€
Pizza & Pasta   Map D4
Via Patrono d'Italia 48, 06081
Tel *075 80 40 867*
A cosy autumnal décor, a menu
of Italian pasta favourites and
an extensive selection of ice
creams, combine to make this
hotel trattoria a lively place.
There is also a special menu
for children.

**ASSISI: Trattoria degli
Orti** €€
Classic Umbrian   Map D4
Via Salita degli Orti, 06081
Tel *075 81 25 049*   **Closed** *Mon*
Housed in a stone building in a
quiet alley near the Piazza Santa
Chiara, this family-run eatery
offers innovative Umbrian
dishes like truffle omelette and
strangozzi orto (pasta with
cauliflower and tomatoes).

ASSISI: Trattoria Pallotta €€
Classic Umbrian   Map D4
*Vicolo della Volta Pinta 3/Via San
Rufino 4, 06081*
Tel *075 81 26 49*   **Closed** *Tue*
Reached via a particularly
beautiful alley with original
Renaissance frescoes, this pretty
eatery serves antipasti platters
designed to share. Typically, they
precede Umbrian classics like
strangozzi (handmade spaghetti
with olives).

DK Choice

**ASSISI: La Locanda Del
Cardinale** €€€
Gourmet   Map D4
Piazza del Vescovado 8, 06081
Tel *075 81 52 45*   **Closed** *Tue*
Favoured by celebs, this elegant
restaurant is known as much
for its menu as for its décor.
Tables stand on a glass floor
that covers the illuminated
remains of the Domus Romana
Palace of Assisi. The menu
encompasses Umbrian classics
with a gourmet twist,
accompanied by wine from a
cellar holding over one
thousand vintages.

ASSISI: San Francesco €€€
International   Map D4
Via San Francesco 52, 06081
Tel *075 81 23 29*
Carpaccio of *porcini* mushrooms,
home-made pâtés and steak
with truffles are highlights
on the menu at this classy
eatery, located right by the
Basilica in the heart of Assisi.
Upmarket wines sold by the
glass. Views from the terrace
are delightful.

The elegant La Locanda Del Cardinale is a favourite with celebs

**BETTONA: Il Poggio degli Olivi
La Veranda** €€
Gourmet   Map C4
Località Montebalacca, 06084
Tel *075 98 69 023*
This *agriturismo* restaurant,
housed in a 16th-century farm,
offers creative dishes that use
locally produced truffles, olive oil,
honey and beans. Try the risotto
with pigeon, followed by ragout
of rabbit flavoured with orange
and olive oil.

BETTONA: Osteria dell'Oca €€
Classic Umbrian   Map C4
Corso Marconi 3, 06084
Tel *075 98 85 019*   **Closed** *Mon*
Stylish, intimate restaurant
occupying the vaulted cellar of
a centuries-old building. Menu
includes the local *pasta
strangozzi*, lots of desserts and
good wine.

DK Choice

**BETTONA: La Taverna Del
Giullare** €€€
Gourmet   Map C4
Vicolo del Forte 11, 06084
Tel *075 98 72 54*   **Closed** *Sun eve*
Popular taverna set in a
beautifully restored olive oil
mill complete with stone
arches and a terrace for alfresco
dining. The menu is classic
Umbrian with a gourmet twist.
Typically omelette with black
truffle and asparagus cream
precedes pasta dishes and
mains of lemon-scented lamb
and roasted rabbit. Excellent
wine selection.

**CITTÀ DELLA PIEVE: Trattoria
Bruno Coppetta** €
Classic Umbrian   Map A4
Via Pietro Vannucci 90, 06062
Tel *057 82 98 108*   **Closed** *Mon*
Located near the Church of Santa
Maria dei Bianchi, this elegant

place with pretty frescoes
specializes in inexpensive char-
grilled meats, served between
starters like goose ragout and
home-made desserts.

**CITTÀ DI CASTELLO: Trattoria
da Noi** €
Classic Umbrian   Map B2
Via XI Settembre 12, 06012
Tel *075 372 0342*   **Closed** *Mon & Tue*
With tables outside on the road,
this popular trattoria has a
good wine list and makes its
own bread and pasta. Menu
includes *agnolotti al ragu* (mince
sauce), *beef tagliata*, salumi and
cheese platters, bruschetta pasta
and meats.

**CITTÀ DI CASTELLO: Amici
Miei** €€
Classic Umbrian   Map B2
Via del Monte 2, 06012
Tel *075 85 59 904*
Charming restaurant in the vaults
of a 16th-century palazzo. House
speciality is *cinghiale in umido
con fagioli*, a stew of wild boar
that is served with beans.

**CITTÀ DI CASTELLO: La Miniera
di Galparino** €€
Classic Umbrian   Map B2
*Vocabolo Galparino 34, Sansecondo,
06010*
Tel *075 85 40 784*
Serving Umbrian fare at wooden
tables in converted stables, this
local favourite is housed in an
agriturismo. It produces its own
honey, wine and olive oil.

DERUTA: L'Antico Forziere €€
Classic Umbrian   Map C4
Via della Rocca 2, Casalina, 06053
Tel *075 97 24 314*   **Closed** *Mon*
This elegant yet rustic Casalina
country house offers a creative
menu of char-grilled meat and
fish dishes, pasta, stews and
home-made desserts. Good
wine selection.

For more information on types of restaurants *see page 155*

DERUTA: Osteria Il Borghetto €€
Classic Umbrian Map C4
Via Garibaldi 102, 06053
Tel *075 97 24 264* **Closed** *Sun*
Attractive and informal family-run eatery serving classics including sheep-milk cheeses from their own farm, and stews of lamb and wild boar cooked to time-honoured recipes.

DERUTA: La Fontanina €€€
Gourmet Map C4
Via Solitaria 14, 06053
Tel *075 97 24 112*
Housed in a gorgeous 13th-century town house, this restaurant presents a contemporary take on Umbrian dishes. *Strangozzi* with wild boar sauce is a special. Good wine cellar and an attractive garden.

GUBBIO: Alcatraz €
Classic Umbrian Map D2
Località Santa Cristina 53, 06020
Tel *075 92 29 938*
Food prepared in the restaurant of this friendly *agriturismo* is healthy, colourful and mostly 100 per cent organic. Meals are served buffet-style.

GUBBIO: Del Lupo €€
Classic Umbrian Map D2
Via Ansidei 21, 06024
Tel *075 92 74 368*
With medieval stone walls and elegant décor, this charming restaurant offers an innovative Umbrian menu. *Tagliatelle* with truffles and guinea fowl with juniper are specials.

GUBBIO: Grotta Dell'Angelo €€
Pizza & Pasta Map D2
Via Gioia 47, 06024
Tel *075 92 71 747* **Closed** *Tue*
Wide choice of pizzas, from Neapolitan to seafood, as well as pasta and meat dishes are served at this traditional hotel trattoria set in 13th-century rooms. Terrace for alfresco dining.

GUBBIO: Locanda Del Cantiniere €€
Classic Umbrian Map D2
Via Dante 30, 06024
Tel *075 927 6851*
Friendly, old-fashioned crowd-pleaser, this elegant restaurant with exposed brick and wood beams even bakes its own bread and makes pasta by hand.

GUBBIO: Bosone Garden €€€
Gourmet Map D2
Via Galeotti 18, 06024
Tel *075 92 21 246*
Located in the beautiful Palazzo Raffaelli that was once home to a

Bosone Garden's entrance makes a very pretty picture

wealthy family, this refined restaurant serves exquisite Umbrian dishes, most of which feature truffles, with a modern twist.

DK Choice

GUBBIO: Villa Montegranelli €€€
Gourmet Map D2
Località Monteluiano, 06024
Tel *075 92 20 185*
Famous for its legendary truffle creations, the Villa Montegranelli uses Gubbio's white variety to prepare delicious pasta dishes and to flavour Umbrian *pecorino* or *formaggio di fossa* cheese which is served with *crostini* (toasts). Good wine cellar. The 18th-century villa offers great views of the rural countryside.

LAKE TRASIMENO – CASTIGLIONE DEL LAGO: La Cantina €
Fish & Seafood Map B3
Via Vittorio Emanuele 93, 06061
Tel *075 96 52 463*
An attractive *agriturismo* restaurant with outside dining, La Cantina has a creative menu of Umbrian lakewater fish dishes. Try the *tegamaccio*, a stew of fish from the lake.

LAKE TRASIMENO – CASTIGLIONE DEL LAGO: Antica Trattoria La Piazzetta €€
Fish & Seafood Map B3
Piazza Mazzini 8, 06061
Tel *075 95 11 57*
With fish dominating the menu and its garden dining terrace looking out over the lake, this hotel restaurant is a locals' favourite. Marinated perch served with polenta is outstanding.

LAKE TRASIMENO – CASTIGLIONE DEL LAGO: L'Acquario €€
Fish & Seafood Map B3
Via Vittorio Emanuele 69, 06061
Tel *075 96 52 432*
Said to be the town's oldest eatery, L'Acquario is located inside the city walls. Try the fish flavoured with herbs and flowers. Trasimeno caviar is a speciality. Good wine cellar.

LAKE TRASIMENO – CASTIGLIONE DEL LAGO: L'Essenza €€€
Gourmet Map B3
Località I Giorgi, Petrignano del Lago, 06061
Tel *075 96 89 008*
Serving both Umbrian and Tuscan cuisine accompanied by fine wines from the two regions, this elegant hotel restaurant inside Corte del Sole is a romantic spot amid medieval buildings.

DK Choice

LAKE TRASIMENO – ISOLA MAGGIORE: Da Sauro €€
Fish & Seafood Map B3
Via Guglielmi 1, 06060
Tel *075 82 61 68*
Part of the hotel with the same name Da Sauro is reachable only by boat, this is certainly a romantic restaurant. Fresh fish from the lake is transformed into creative dishes. Try the *Tartine di Pesce* (fish canapés) with chilled wine, before enjoying specials such as *Gnocchetti alla Trasimeno* (gnocchi with perch) or *lattarini fritti* (fried Atherines). There is also a delicious array of home-made desserts to choose from.

LAKE TRASIMENO – PASSIGNANO: Trattoria del Pescatore
Fish & Seafood   **Map** B3
Via San Bernardino 5, 06065
Tel 075 82 96 063
Enjoy fresh fish from the lake and interact with locals at this homely trattoria inside a hotel in the old town. Among the specials is the *tagliatelle alla crema di persico* (pasta with perch cream).

LAKE TRASIMENO – PASSIGNANO: Il Fischio del Merlo
Fish & Seafood   €€€
                            Map B3
Località Calcinaio 17a, 06065
Tel 075 82 92 83   **Closed** *Tue*
This homely restaurant overlooks its garden and the lake beyond. Trasimeno fish such as perch, eel and carp is the speciality here, each presented with imaginative sauces.

LISCIANO NICCONE: Ristorante da Gianna
Fish & Seafood   **Map** B3
Village centre, Lisciano Niccone, Via del Palazzo, 06060
Tel 075 84 43 58   **Closed** *Mon*
Popular family-run restaurant with home-made pasta dishes, crispy pizzas with a host of toppings, including seafood from nearby Lake Trasimeno.

MAGIONE: La Fattoria Di Montemelino
Classic Umbrian   **Map** B3
Via dei Montemelini 22, Località Montemelino, 06063
Tel 075 84 36 06
Refined yet informal, this *agriturismo* restaurant prepares its dishes using ingredients of its own produce, from steaks to vegetables. Old farm tools adorn the walls.

MAGIONE: Al Coccio
Classic Umbrian   €€
                            Map B3
Via del Quadrifoglio 12a/b, 06063
Tel 075 84 18 29
Maialino, a dish of oven-cooked suckling pig with herbs, accompanied by home-made pasta and desserts to finish is the draw at this popular restaurant in the heart of Magione.

MAGIONE: Rosso di Sera
Fish & Seafood   €€
                            Map B3
Via Fratelli Papini 81, 06063
Tel 075 84 76 277   **Closed** *Tue & Wed*
Tasteful décor and an imaginative menu that majors on fish from Lake Trasimeno ensure the restaurant's popularity. Try the ravioli stuffed with perch.

MONTELEONE DI SPOLETO: Trattoria da Gigetto
Classic Umbrian   €€
                            Map E5
Statale 471, Km 12,800, Ruscio, 06045
Tel 074 37 01 11
This traditional trattoria serves hearty soups, pasta and meat dishes from lunch to supper. *Agnello alla cacciatora*, an Umbrian lamb dish, is special.

MONTONE: Taverna del Verziere
Classic Umbrian   €€
                            Map C2
Via dell'Ospedale 25, 06014
Tel 075 93 06 512
Traditional tavern, with panoramic views from its terrace. Serves home-made *strangozzi* with truffles among other Umbrian dishes handed down through the generations.

NOCERA UMBRA: La Costa
Classic Umbrian   **Map** D3
Frazione Costa di Salmata, 06025
Tel 074 28 10 042
Traditional dishes such as *cinghiale alla cacciatore* (wild boar with red wine and herbs) are served at this *agriturismo* restaurant, a medieval farmhouse outside Nocera Umbra.

DK Choice

PACIANO: La Loggetta
Classic Umbrian   €€
                            Map B4
Via Guglielmo Marconi 36, 06060
Tel 075 83 0144   **Closed** *Tue*
Dine indoors or alfresco on the terrace. The recipes here have a Tuscan as well as Umbrian slant. Try the freshly made *pici* (pasta with choice sauces) that incorporate leek and pork cheek, amaretti and peach tart or choose between Chianian beef and guinea fowl stuffed with vegetables and cannelini beans flavoured with orange. Great wine selection.

PANICALE: Ristorante Pizzeria Il Tempo
Pizza & Pasta   **Map** B4
Via Perugia 27, 06068
Tel 075 868 1196   **Closed** *Mon*
This eatery with focus on high-quality local ingredients, has something for everyone and is very popular with locals. Faro salads, steaks, organic fresh pasta, risotto and even pizzas made with organic flour in a wood-fired oven. Eat indoors in the pretty room, at the tables outside or take away. They also have good desserts.

PANICALE: Lillo Tatini
Gourmet   €€€
                            Map B4
Piazza Umberto I 3, Panicale, 06064
Tel 075 83 7771   **Closed** *Mon*
Overlooking the medieval Panicale's village square, this supremely popular and elegant restaurant serves classics that major on pasta. Ravioli with truffle is the signature dish. Excellent wine list.

PANICALE: Villa Di Monte Solare
Gourmet   €€€
                            Map B4
Via Montali 7, 06068
Tel 075 83 23 76
Counted amongst the finest in the region, this restaurant is housed in a charming 18th-century villa standing in magnificent grounds. The menu is à la carte and comprises Umbrian dishes, each with a unique gourmet touch.

PERUGIA: Il Falchetto
Classic Umbrian   **Map** C3
Strada Fontana La Trinita 2/d, 06132
Tel 075 57 31775   **Closed** *Mon*
Falchetti verdi, a slow-cooked dish of spinach and ricotta gnocchi baked in tomato sauce and cheese, is the signature dish of this superb trattoria housed in a 14th-century palazzo.

View of the *agriturismo* restaurant, La Costa

For more information on types of restaurants *see page 155*

PERUGIA: Les Cre Fantastique €
Café & Patisserie **Map** C3
Via Volte della Pace 28, 06100
Tel 075 966 0392 **Closed** *Mon*
Serving savoury, sweet and
gluten-free crêpes as well as
piadine and pizza, this restaurant
with a rustic and relaxed vibe is
popular with locals and kids.

PERUGIA: Osteria Il Gufo €
Classic Umbrian **Map** C3
Via della Viola 18, 06122
Tel 075 57 34 126
Friendly restaurant with light
meat and vegetarian meals,
salads, cheeses and delicious
desserts. Offers a fixed menu too.

**PERUGIA: Pizzeria
Mediterranea** €
Pizza & Pasta **Map** C3
Via Guglielmo Marconi 11, 06121
Tel 075 57 24 021
A huge wood-fired oven
dominates the space in this lively
pizzeria. Choose from different
toppings, from Neapolitan to
versions with pepper and seafood.

**PERUGIA: Ristorante Dal
Mi'Cocco** €
Umbrian **Map** C3
Corso Garibaldi 12, 06123
Tel 075 57 32 511 **Closed** *Mon*
Locally sourced ingredients
served as imaginative starters,
main, side and dessert dishes as
per a set menu that changes
daily. Remarkable value.

PERUGIA: Ristorante Il Bacio €
Pizza & Pasta **Map** C3
Via Boncambi 6, 06123
Tel 075 57 20 909
With tables outside on the lovely
pedestrianized Corso Vanucci
and in the intimate dining room,
Il Bacio offers innovative pizzas,
freshly prepared and cooked in
its wood-fired oven. Great pasta
dishes, salads and desserts too.

PERUGIA: Ristorante Nana €
Classic Umbrian **Map** C3
Corso Cavour 202, 06121
Tel 075 573 35 71 **Closed** *Sun*
A favourite with the locals, this
lively eatery near San Domenico
is known for its authentic dishes.
Try the gnocchi (potato
dumplings) pasta and choose
from hearty soups.

PERUGIA: Altromondo €€
Classic Umbrian **Map** C3
Via Cesare Caporali 11, 06100
Tel 075 572 6157 **Closed** *Sun*
This city centre trattoria has a daily
changing menu with emphasis
on using only quality ingredients.
Try the *arrosto misto* (mix of roast
lamb and other meats).

PERUGIA: Caffè Di Perugia €€
Pizza & Pasta **Map** C3
Via Giuseppe Mazzini 10, 06121
Tel 075 57 31 863 **Closed** *Tue*
There's something for everyone
at this restaurant spread over
several floors. Mouthwatering
selection of pizzas and traditional
Umbrian fare. There is a café and
a bar too.

PERUGIA: Da Cesarino €€
Classic Umbrian **Map** C3
Piazza IV Novembre 4–5, 06123
Tel 075 57 28 974 **Closed** *Wed*
Old fashioned décor and alfresco
dining sets the tone for the
classic local cuisine served at Da
Cesarino.

**PERUGIA: Enone Enoteca
Cucina** €€
Gourmet **Map** C3
Corso Cavour 61, 06121
Tel 075 57 21 950 **Closed** *Mon*
A menu of imaginative dishes
at this trendy eaterie-cum-bar
is firing on all cylinders. Truffle
risotto, flavoured gnocchi and
sushi are popular specials.

PERUGIA: L'Opera €€
Fish & Seafood **Map** C3
*Via dell'Allodola 9, Ponte San
Giovanni, 06135*
Tel 075 393 337 **Closed** *Mon*
Run by a couple from Agrigento,
this eatery serves Sicilian fish
specialities typically followed by
delicious home-made Sicilian
desserts. Options for non-fish
eaters too. Excellent wine list.

PERUGIA: La Taverna €€
Classic Umbrian **Map** C3
Via delle Streghe 8, 06123
Tel 075 57 24 128
Home-made *tagliatelle* in a
duck ragout, followed by *baccalà*
(salt cod) with prunes, stand
out from among the signature
dishes of this popular restaurant.
Excellent choices for dessert.

A plateful of delicate crêpes served
with lemon slices

PERUGIA: Osteria a Priori €€
Classic Umbrian **Map** C3
Via dei Priori 39, 06123
Tel 075 57 27 098 **Closed** *Tue*
Housed in a stone building
near the Palazzo dei Priori, this
popular eatery specializes in
local fare. Be sure to try its
pumpkin ravioli with *torta al
testo* (bread) and the delicious
pastries.

**PERUGIA: Osteria del
Turreno** €
Classic Umbrian **Map** C3
Piazza Danti 16, 06122
Tel 075 57 26 397 **Closed** *Eve, Sat
all day*
Popular restaurant that serves
imaginative healthy food mostly
using Km0 ingredients. Freshly
made local dishes are laid out as
buffet in the pretty room or on
tables outside in the main
square near the fountain. .

> ## DK Choice
>
> **PERUGIA: Ristorante Del
> Sole** €€
> Gourmet **Map** C3
> *Via Rupe 1, 06121*
> **Tel** 075 57 35 031 **Closed** *Mon*
> Located in the heart of
> Perugia's medieval old town,
> this upmarket restaurant offers
> the chance to dine enjoying
> wonderful views of the city,
> both on its alfresco dining
> terrace and inside. Umbrian
> meat, fish and pasta dishes
> are given a modern twist
> with combinations like cheese
> ravioli with oranges, and
> lamb with figs. Excellent
> wine cellar.

PERUGIA: Ubu Re €€
Gourmet **Map** C3
Via Baldeschi 17, 06123
Tel 075 57 35 461 **Closed** *Mon eve,
Sat & Sun lunch*
A warm, rustic ambiance
and a menu of authentic
Umbrian cuisine combine to
make this upmarket eatery a
constant for gourmands. Try
the ravioli made with
caciocavallo cheese.

**PERUGIA: Antica Trattoria San
Lorenzo** €€€
Gourmet **Map** C3
Piazza Danti 19a, 06122
Tel 075 572 19 56 **Closed** *Sun*
Umbrian gourmet cuisine
featuring artful home-made
pasta and sauces at a lovely
location, right by the cathedral.
Choose from the excellent wine
selection and speciality ice
creams.

Key to Price Guide *see page 156*

Dining area at the very stylish Le Melograne in Torgiano

PERUGIA: Giò Arte e Vini   €€€
International   Map C3
Via Ruggero d'Andreotto 19, 06124
Tel *075 57 31 100*   **Closed** *Sun*
Beautifully prepared and
presented Umbrian dishes,
and a lengthy wine list to choose
from at this stylish and 'arty'
restaurant located inside the
Gio Jazz Hotel, a little way out
of Perugia.

PERUGIA: Il Postale   €€€
Gourmet   Map C3
*Strada Monteville 3, Residenza
d'Epoca Castello di Monterone,
06126*
Tel *075 85 21 356*
A Michelin-starred restaurant, the
Il Postale has rich décor and
an exciting menu of Umbrian
meat, fish and pasta dishes. It is
considered one of the best
dining options in town. Open
only in the evenings.

PERUGIA: La Rosetta   €€€
Gourmet   Map C3
Piazza Italia 19, 06123
Tel *075 57 20 841*
Delicious lamb, wild boar and
steak cooked in the red wine
Sagrantino di Montefalco are
among the dishes on the menu
at this elegant restaurant near
the Fontana Maggiore. Good
wine list.

**PETRIGNANO: Locanda ai
Cavalieri**   €€
International   Map D3
Via Matteotti 47, 06086
Tel *075 803 00 11*
The stylish restaurant of Hotel
Locanda ai Cavalieri makes
its own pasta and bread to
accompany its international
dishes. Taster menus, home-made
desserts and top wines too.

TORGIANO: Il Toscanino   €€
Classic Umbrian   Map C4
Località Signoria, Torgiano, 06089
Tel *075 98 24 47*   **Closed** *Sun*
The menu is a mix of Umbrian
and Tuscan cuisine at this

attractive eatery. *Antipasti* dishes
typically include *strangozzi*
(spaghetti) with sauces freshly
made and rich in taste, followed
by creative mains of game.
Speciality is the *fiorentina* steak.
Good pizzas too.

**TORGIANO: Le Delizie di
Monet**   €€
Gourmet   Map C4
Corso Vittorio Emanuele 19, 06089
Tel *075 98 80 788*   **Closed** *Tue*
Italian recipes handed down
through generations are given
a modern twist at Monet.
Signature dishes include risottos
flavoured with mushrooms or
asparagus and cheese, and hand-
made spaghetti.

TORGIANO: Osteria I Birbi   €€
Classic Umbrian   Map C4
*Località Vocabolo Casella,
Miralduolo, 06089*
Tel *075 98 89 041* **Closed** *Weekdays
for lunch*
The Osteria I Birbi is well-known
locally for its excellent steaks and
rich home-made pasta dishes. It
is housed in a rural farmhouse
that offers panoramic views from
its dining terrace.

TORGIANO: Ristorante Siro   €€
Classic Umbrian   Map C4
Via Giordano Bruno 16, 06089
Tel *075 98 20 10*
A cosy hotel restaurant that
has been thrilling diners for
several decades with *antipasti*
dishes featuring white truffles,
and mains cooked in authentic
Umbrian-style . It has a fine
wine selection.

TORGIANO: Le Melograne   €€€
Gourmet   Map C4
Via Giuseppe Garibaldi 48, 06089
Tel *075 98 80 447*
Try the mixed fish antipasti
platter followed by Catalan
lobster at this stylish eatery
inside the boutique-style Tre
Vaselle Hotel. A top-notch wine
list and the rural setting are a draw.

DK Choice
**UMBERTIDE: L'Abbazia Di
Montecorona**   €€
Gourmet   Map C2
Vocabolo Montecorona, 06019
Tel *075 94 13 501*   **Closed** *Mon*
A centuries-old stone abbey
has been carefully restored
to create a spectacular
setting for this upscale
restaurant. It lies in the rural
countryside on the outskirts
of Umbertide. Inside, its
decor comprises arches and
stone walls. Fish, such as perch
and trout from nearby Lake
Trasimeno, dominate the
menu. There is also an excellent
multi-label wine cellar.

UMBERTIDE: La Chiusa   €€
Classic Umbrian   Map C2
SS 146 del Niccone, near Umbertide
Tel *075 94 10 848*
La Chiusa is an organic restaurant
that uses meat from its own farm
and produce that has been
grown in its garden, to create
wholesome dishes. Wines are
from speciality vintners.

UMBERTIDE: La Rocca   €€
Fish & Seafood   Map C2
Piazza Caduti del Lavoro 4, 06019
Tel *075 94 11 828*   **Closed** *Mon*
Attractive little restaurant located
just across from Umbertide's
fortress. It specializes in fish.
Try the *carpaccio* of thinly
sliced fish followed by risotto
with prawns.

**UMBERTIDE: Locanda Di
Nonna Gelsa**   €€
Classic Umbrian   Map C2
*Via Caduti di Pentola 31, Niccone,
06019*
Tel *075 94 10 699*   **Closed** *Tue*
Elegant trattoria with a
traditional décor, crisp linens
and a menu of Umbrian dishes
that features game and rabbit.
Good choice of local and
Tuscan wines. Picturesque
countryside setting.

DK Choice

**UMBERTIDE:
Poggiomanente**   €€
Classic Umbrian   Map C2
*SS 219, E45 exit Umbertide/
Gubbio, 06019*
Tel *075 94 13 085*
Crispy pizzas fresh from the
oven, along with hearty soups,
stews and truffle-based mains
are served in this refined yet
rustic restaurant set in the cellar
of a 15th-century farmhouse.

For more information on types of restaurants *see page 155*

UMBERTIDE: Ristorante Albergo Capponi €€
Classic Umbrian   **Map** C2
Piazza XXV Aprile 19, 06019
Tel *075 941 3192*
Anatra in porchetta, an Umbrian dish of duck wrapped in bacon, roast lamb or game slow-cooked in wine are just some of the menu favourites at this popular restaurant.

UMBERTIDE: Taverna del Verziere €€
International   **Map** C2
Route Umbertide to Montone, Via Ospedale 25, 06014
Tel *075 93 06 512*   **Closed** *Mon*
The dining terrace looking out over the valley and a menu of both Umbrian and Sardinian dishes and wines, make this hilltop restaurant a big draw.

The rustic dining area at Ottavius in Bevagna

Southern Umbria

AMELIA: Anita €
Classic Umbrian   **Map** C6
Via Roma 31, 05022
Tel *074 49 82 146*   **Closed** *Mon*
A family-run restaurant with an exhaustive range of home-made pasta dishes, slow-cooked meat casseroles, roasts and desserts.

ARRONE: Il Grottino Del Nera €
Classic Umbrian   **Map** D6
SS Valnerina 209, Vocabolo Colleporto 21, 05031
Tel *074 43 89 104*   **Closed** *Wed*
One of the region's oldest eateries, this osteria serves classic Umbrian cuisine in the form of game, wild boar and trout. Tagliatelle with truffle is a special. Terrace for dining alfresco.

DK Choice

ARRONE: La Locanda €€
Gourmet   **Map** D6
Via Arrone 1, 05031 Arrone
Tel *074 43 89 961*   **Closed** *Mon*
Located in the Residence Fiocchi and offering spectacular views of the Parco Fluviale del Nera Valley, Locanda uses local produce to prepare trout truffles, risotto scented with Black crayfish, wild boar and venison sausages. Home-made desserts and pasta. Excellent wine list.

ARRONE: Rossi €€
Classic Umbrian   **Map** D6
Vocabolo Isola 7, 05031
Tel *074 43 88 372*   **Closed** *Fri &* Sun eve
A lengthy menu of *antipasti* dishes precede the char-grilled meats and pasta at Rossi. The Southern Umbrian crusted veal is a special. Located near the Cascata delle Marmore.

DK Choice

BASCHI: Vissani €€€
Gourmet   **Map** B6
Strada Statale 448, km 606, Todi-Baschi, 05020
Tel *074 49 50 206*   **Closed** *Mon: lunch; Wed; Thu: lunch; Sun: dinner*
Elegant, contemporary place with dark oak furniture teamed with vibrant orange. The Southern Umbrian cuisine specials served here include gourmet game and meat creations. The menus are devised by owner Gianfranco Vissani, a celebrity chef known throughout Italy for his exquisite cuisine.

BEVAGNA: Enoteca Onofri €€
Classic Umbrian   **Map** D4
Piazza Onofri 2, 06031
Tel *074 23 61 926*   **Closed** *Wed*
Housed in a 12th-century building with vaulted ceilings and an open fireplace, this trattoria specializes in local pasta dishes, cheese and fabulous wines. It has about 500 different vintages in its cellar.

BEVAGNA: Il Poggio Dei Pettirossi €€
Classic Umbrian   **Map** D4
Via del Poggio 1, 06031
Tel *074 23 61 744*   **Closed** *Tue*
Dishes such as *cinghiale alla cacciatore* (wild boar with red wine and herbs) are served to the loyal following that frequents this elegant restaurant. Wine is from Montefalco. Panoramic views of the rural countryside.

BEVAGNA: Osteria del Podestà €€
Classic Umbrian   **Map** D4
Corso Giacomo Matteotti 67, 06031
Tel *0742 360 222*   **Closed** *Tue*
Richly-decorated with antique-style furniture, this popular restaurant serves traditional Umbrian cuisine. The house speciality is the prized *gnocchi al Sagrantino* (in red wine sauce).

BEVAGNA: Ottavius €€
Classic Umbrian   **Map** D4
Via del Gonfalone 1, 06031
Tel *074 23 60 555*   **Closed** *Mon*
The seasonal menu always uses fresh local produce. Truffles are a special, along with home-made gnocchi. Good wine selection. Welcoming rustic décor.

BEVAGNA: Redibis €€€
Gourmet   **Map** D4
Via dell'Anfiteatro, 06031
Tel *074 23 60 130*   **Closed** *Tue*
Part of Bevagna's Roman theatre, Redibis is one of the few places in Umbria where you can find dishes cooked to authentic age-old recipes. Veal braised in Montefalco wine is a special.

DK Choice

CAMPELLO SUL CLITUNNO: Fonti Del Clitunno €
International   **Map** D5
Via Flaminia 7, Località Fonti Clitunno, 06042
Tel *074 32 75 057*   **Closed** *Tue*
Located in the Fonti del Clitunno Park, this restaurant serves meat, fish and vegetarian dishes from a menu that changes most days. Typically, it features antipasti of cold cuts, followed by *tagliatelle* with trout, juniper berry lamb and fresh fruit. Lengthy wine list. Alfresco dining on terrace.

CAMPELLO SUL CLITUNNO:
Trattoria Pettino   €€
Classic Umbrian   **Map** D5
Frazione Pettino 31, S.P. 458 (strada provinciale), Km 15.5, 06042
Tel *074 32 76 021*   **Closed** *Tue*
A local favourite, the Trattoria Pettino is a warmly decorated place in the mountains. The menu changes daily but, typically, features pasta and *agnello al tartufo* (lamb with truffles).

DK Choice

CAMPELLO SUL CLITUNNO:
Camesena   €€€
Gourmet   **Map** D5
Via del Castello 3, 06042
Tel *074 35 20 340* **Closed** *Mon; Mon & Tue in winters*
Located in the village of Lizori, near the Clitunno Springs, Camesena is an 'arty' place renowned for its creatively-presented dishes using fresh local produce. Its menu offers pasta in home-made sauces, and dishes of skewered pigeon or veal flavoured with truffle. Superb desserts such as lemon soufflé and tiramisu. Great wine selection.

CANNARA: Perbacco   €€
Classic Umbrian   **Map** D4
Via Umberto I 16, 06033
Tel *074 27 20 492* **Closed** *Sun eve*
Cannara is famous for a variety of red onion, which is used to good effect in the flavoursome Umbrian dishes served at Perbacco, a charming trattoria with traditional décor.

CIVITELLA DEL LAGO:
Trippini   €€€
Fish & Seafood   **Map** C5
Via Italia 14, 05023
Tel *0744 950 316* **Closed** *Sun eve*
An attractive restaurant with a cottage feel, Trippini changes its menu according to fresh local availability, but presents with considerable flair. Veal with mint gnocchi is the speciality here.

FABRO: La Bettola del
Buttero Fabro   €€
Classic Umbrian   **Map** B5
Via dei Pini 2, 05015
Tel *076 38 32 063* **Closed** *Sun eve*
The huge wood-fired oven and fireplace, on which meats flavoured with local herbs, potatoes and onions are cooked to order, dominates this idyllic country hotel restaurant. Alfresco dining in summers.

FERENTILLO: Il Cantico   €€
Pizza & Pasta   **Map** D6
Via Macenano 4, 06034
Tel *074 47 80 005* **Closed** *Mon & Tue lunch*
With the look of a traditional village trattoria, Il Cantico is part of a hotel created within a former Benedictine abbey. Pasta and pizzas are a speciality here, as are the classic dishes flavoured with truffles.

DK Choice

FERENTILLO: Piermarini   €€
Classic Umbrian   **Map** D6
23 Vosso Ancaiano, 05034
Tel *074 47 80 714* **Closed** *Sun eve, Mon*
The location of Piermarini in the Parco Fluviale del Nera, not far from the Marmore Waterfalls, along with its country house decor, charms its guests. Its lengthy menu of Umbrian dishes focuses on natural produce and vegetables from its own farm, including black truffles and olives. Dine inside or alfresco on its terrace that offers pleasing views of the countryside.

FOLIGNO: Basilicò   €
Pizza & Pasta   **Map** D4
Via Gramsci 60, Foligno, 06034
Tel *074 27 70 248* **Closed** *Sun & Mon*
This bright and breezy pizzeria excels in creating toppings from classic cheese and tomato to seafood and pepperoni. Its signature is Margherita with mozzarella and basil.

DK Choice

FOLIGNO: Ristorante Via
del Forno   €€
Gourmet   **Map** D4
Piazza Matteotti/Via Colomba Antonietti, 06034
Tel *074 235 0412*
This hotel restaurant tucked behind Foligno's pretty Palazzo Comunale has a pretty dining room in a noble old house. Serves fresh pasta, grilled meats, scrambled eggs with truffle, lamb from Colfiorito (a natural park nearby), pork in aromatic herbs, onion tart made with Cannara onions (an Umbrian speciality) and other upmarket versions of Foligno cuisine. A taste of the walnut and liquorice digestif are a great way to end the meal.

FOLIGNO: La Spagnola   €€
Classic Umbrian   **Map** D4
Via Rinaldi 14i, 06034
Tel *0742 351281*
Its vaulted stone building dating from the 1600s serving as backdrop, this elegant restaurant specializes in offering a wide variety such as *gnocchi al sagrantino*, wild boar medallions or lamb inn juniper, pizzas as well as fresh fish daily. The chef's Spanish origins ensure that the *paella alla valenciana* and *crème catalane* are also represented on the menu.

FOLIGNO: Villa Roncalli   €€€
Gourmet   **Map** D4
Via Roma 25, 06034 Foligno
Tel *074 23 91 091* **Closed** *Mon; lunch Tue–Sat*
The bread is home-made, the eggs and fresh produce come from the garden while the beef is the local-bred Chianina, at this refined restaurant set in a 17th-century palazzo.

DK Choice

MONTEFALCO: Coccorone €€
Classic Umbrian   **Map** D4
Largo Tempesti 11, Vicolo Fabbri 7, 06036
Tel *074 23 79 535* **Closed** *Wed*
Charming restaurant where traditional country recipes, that have been saved from being lost in time, have been given a modern twist. Menu favourites include home-made *strangozzi* (spaghetti) and *gnocchi*, meat cooked over charcoal as well as local dishes such as *cinghiale in umido con fagioli* (wild boar served with beans). Excellent Montefalco wines.

Fresh lobster risotto with lemon and herbs

MONTEFALCO: Villa Pambuffetti €€€
Gourmet **Map** D4
Via della Vittoria 20, Montefalco, 06036
Tel *074 23 79 417* **Closed** *Mon*
Olive oil and produce from its own farm as well as Montefalco wines are featured on the restaurant's gourmet menu. Quite popular with celebs, Pambuffetti is housed in a 19th-century mansion.

NARNI: Cavallino €
Classic Umbrian **Map** C6
Via Flaminia Romana 220, Località Testaccio, 05035
Tel *074 47 61 020* **Closed** *Tue*
Traditional trattoria where pasta creations and wholesome dishes of game, meat and fish are prepared to Umbrian recipes. The team prides itself on using only seasonal local produce.

NARNI: Il Feudo €€
Pizza & Pasta **Map** C6
Via del Forno 10, Montoro, 05035
Tel *074 47 35 168* **Closed** *Mon & Tue lunch*
The creamy décor and heavy wooden beams give this restaurant a welcoming feel. The à la carte menu offers excellent local pasta and pizza options, and dishes such as *scaloppine al limone* (veal escalope with lemon).

NARNI: Il Gattamelata €€
International **Map** C6
Via Pozzo della Comunità 4, 05035
Tel *074 47 17 245* **Closed** *Sun eve, Mon*
Located in Narni's main square, near the cathedral, this cosy eatery celebrates local cuisine. *Carpaccio d'anatra* (duck) and *tagliata di manzo di pura razza* (pure bred beef) are specials. Good wine list.

NORCIA: Dal Francese €
Classic Umbrian **Map** F5
Via Riguardati 16, 06046 Norcia
Tel *074 38 16 290* **Closed** *Wed*
Local delicacy *beccacce alla norcina* (woodcock stuffed with herbs, truffles and sausage) is one of the dishes on this rustic trattoria's popular truffle-based *menù degustazione* (tasting menu).

NORCIA: La Cucina del Casale €€
Classic Umbrian **Map** F5
Vocabolo Fontevena 8, 06046
Tel *074 38 16 481* **Closed** *Sun eve*
Family recipes prepared with organic vegetables, pulses and meat produced at its own farm, are served at this *agriturismo* set

deep in the country near Norcia. Norcia truffles and cheeses are from local gourmet outlets. Try the *coniglio alla cacciatore* (rabbit stew). Spectacular, heavily wood-beam dining hall.

DK Choice

NORCIA: Taverna De' Massari €€
Classic Umbrian **Map** F5
Via Roma 13, 06046
Tel *074 38 16 218* **Closed** *Tue*
Carpaccio di cinghiale del parco tartufato (wild boar carpaccio with mushrooms and truffles) and gnocchetti alla Norcina tartufato (potato gnocchi with cream and truffle) are just two of the exciting dishes served at this old town tavern. Beneath its dining hall is a Roman stone cellar where a wide selection of Italian wines are stored. The terrace has alfresco dining.

NORCIA: Il Granaro del Monte €€€
Classic Umbrian **Map** F5
Via Alfieri 6
Tel *074 38 17 551*
Perhaps the oldest Umbrian restaurant and part of the Hotel Grotta Azzurra, Il Granaro serves classic gastronomic dishes such as the *mazzafegati* (pig's liver sausage with raisons, nuts and orange peel). Superb desserts and wines. The dining room is beautiful and has a huge fireplace.

ORVIETO: Cantina Foresi €
Café & Patisserie **Map** B5
Piazza Duomo 2, 05018
Tel *076 33 41 611*
Popular with the trendy, this bistro-style place has over 110 wine labels from Umbria, Tuscany and Lazio, which it serves with a gourmet-standard selection of dipping olive oils, cheeses and

cold meats. Sip a glass gazing at the town's magnificent duomo.

ORVIETO: Charlie Pizzeria €
Pizza & Pasta **Map** B5
Via Loggia dei Mercanti, 14, 05018
Tel *076 33 44 766*
Renowned in Orvieto for its delicious pizzas, also serves fresh pasta and succulent meat dishes on offer with a fine range of local wines and artisan beers. Its pizzas made with sour dough and top seasonal ingredients such as fresh fungi makes this place very popular with locals and tourists alike. Pretty courtyard with tables outside. Centrally located.

ORVIETO: Duca Di Orvieto €€
Classic Umbrian **Map** B5
Via della Pace 5, 05018
Tel *076 33 44 663* **Closed** *Wed, Sun*
The theme of the menu at this cosy trattoria is 'our culture on a plate' and it draws from a stock of well-researched, old Orvieto recipes. Try the zucchini with ricotta, followed by fettuccine with Grappa and Gorgonzola cheese.

DK Choice

ORVIETO: I Sette Consoli €€
Umbrian **Map** B5
Piazza Sant'Angelo 1a, 05018
Tel *076 33 43 911* **Closed** *Wed, Sun eve*
I Sette Consoli sources top notch ingredients from Europe that come together as exquisite plates. *Ravioli di anatra* (duck-filled ravioli), Scottish salmon and pigeon in marsala sauce are specials. Dine inside in this cottage-style restaurant or outside on the canopied terrace. The wine cellar has over 800 labels from around the world, and over a hundred liquors.

The wine cellar at the cottage-style I Sette Consoli has over 800 labels

ORVIETO: Le Grotte del Funaro
€€
International   Map B5
Via Ripa Serancia 41, 05018
Tel *076 33 43 276*
Housed in the 12th-century workshop of a *funaro* (ropemaker), this cave-like restaurant has menus that typically feature beef with truffle and porcini mushrooms, and Umbrian game. Good fish and pasta selection, pizzas fresh from the wood-fired oven and an excellent wine list.

ORVIETO: Trattoria del Moro Aronne
€€
Classic Umbrian   Map B5
Via San Leonardo 7, 05018
Tel *076 33 42 763*   **Closed** *Tue*
This delightful trattoria, minutes from the duomo, welcomes diners with Umbrian-style home cooking. Try its signature dish *nidi di rondine*, *pecorino e miele caldo* (nest with pecorino cheese and warm honey). Very popular, reservations advised.

ORVIETO: Altarocca
€€€
Gourmet   Map B5
Località Rocca Ripesena 62, 05010
Tel *076 33 44 210*
The restaurant of this upscale wine resort, with its crisp linens and terraces that overlook vines and olives, is famous for its exquisite gourmet creations. Fish comes from the Lakes, meat is served in wine and desserts are home-made.

DK Choice

ORVIETO: La Badia
€€€
Gourmet   Map B5
Località Badia 8, 05019
Tel *076 33 01 959*   **Closed** *Mon & Tue lunch*
Housed in a gorgeous former abbey, that traces its origins back to the 6th century, this romantic restaurant tempts with Umbrian classics which have a gourmet twist. Dishes are artfully presented on the plate. Home-made *tagliolini* with black truffles and juniper-infused grilled meats are among the specials. Extensive wine list with Italian vintages.

ORVIETO: Villa Ciconia
€€€
Gourmet   Map B6
Via dei Tigli 69, 05018
Tel *076 33 05 582*   **Closed** *Wed*
A hotel restaurant housed in a delightful country palazzo dating from the 15th century, Villa Cinconia stands in magnificent grounds full of ancient trees.

The elegant Villa Ciconia is set in a 15th-century country palazzo

The dining room with wood panelling and a huge stone fireplace is as handsome as its menu of gastronomy-standard meat and fish dishes and upscale pizzas. Well-stocked wine cellar.

PORANO: Il Boccone del Prete
€€
Classic Umbrian   Map B5
Via Eugenio Bellini 12, 05010
Tel *076 33 74 772*
Located in the village of Porano, close to Orvieto, this trattoria serves Umbrian dishes such as *zuppa di fave con finocchio* (bean soup with fennel) and *strangozzi*. The cellar has over 300 labels. The dining rooms are a series of old Etruscan grottoes and the ground floor has tables outside.

DK Choice

PRECI: Al Porcello Felice
€€
Pizza & Pasta   Map E5
Frazione Castelvecchio, 06047
Tel *074 39 39 005*
Part of an agriturismo set in rolling countryside, the restaurant excels in home-cooked dishes that use vegetables and herbs from its gardens, olive and fruit from its groves and meat from its farm, all produced per organic traditions and methods. Dishes are traditional, including pasta with creative sauces and pizzas cooked in a wood-burning oven. Best to book during high season.

SAN GEMINI: Il Colle
€€
Pizza & Pasta   Map D6
Viale Garibaldi 6, 05029
Tel 074 630428
Gourmet-style pizzas from a wood-fired oven, along with meat and fish dishes, are served on the terrace of this superb restaurant set high on a hill over

San Gemini. Fine wine cellar. Popular party venue.

SCHEGGINO: Del Ponte
€€
Fish & Seafood   Map E5
Via di Borgo 11, 06040
Tel *074 36 12 53*
Located in the eponymous hotel, Del Porte serves a range of special dishes from the Valnerina valley. The emphasis is on fish, such as trout paired with local almonds, and black truffles with *tagliatelle* or used as a *crostini* topping.

DK Choice

SPELLO: Il Molino
€€
Classic Umbrian   Map D4
Hotel Palazzo Bocci, Piazza Giacomo Matteotti 6, 06038
Tel *074 26 51 305*   **Closed** *Tue*
Housed in a gorgeous 14th-century olive oil mill that has been tastefully converted while retaining its dramatic stone architecture, the Molino is a romantic place to dine and its passion about Umbrian cuisine shows clearly. Truffles and game dominate the menu, along with porcini mushrooms, wild asparagus and local herbs. The terrace is ideal for dining in summers.

SPELLO: La Bastiglia
€€€
Gourmet   Map D4
Via Salnitraria 1, 06049
Tel *074 26 51 823*
Modern upscale cuisine and an excellent wine selection has won over many a local afficionado at the elegant La Bastiglia. This gourmet restaurant is housed in a 17th-century antique-filled restored mill as its setting.

For more information on types of restaurants *see page 155*

Serene settings at the classic Le Casaline in Spoleto

SPOLETO: Il Panciolle €
Classic Umbrian   Map D5
Vicolo degli Ebri, Via del Duomo 3, 06049
Tel *074 34 56 77*
An attractive trattoria with a shaded terrace looking out over the city. Here, truffles give flavour to meat and pasta dishes as well as several fish options. Try the popular linguine pasta on creamed peppers.

SPOLETO: Al Palazzaccio Da Piero
Classic Umbrian   €€
Map D5
Località Palazzaccio 33, Poreta, 06049
Tel *074 35 20 168*   **Closed** *Mon*
Gnocchi al Sagrantino (dumplings in red wine) is just one of the delicious local dishes on the menu at this attractive, family-run stone eatery in Poreta, just outside Spoleto. Dine by a lovely log fire in winter and out on the terrace in summer.

SPOLETO: Il Capanno €€
Classic Umbrian   Map D5
Località Torrecola 6, 06049
Tel *074 35 41 19*   **Closed** *Mon*
Sitting amidst a garden full of mature trees in a rural setting, Il Capanno serves hearty steaks and game, and rich dishes such as home-made pasta in a pigeon sauce.

SPOLETO: Il Tartufo €€
Classic Umbrian   Map D5
Piazza Garibaldi 24, 06049
Tel *074 34 02 36*   **Closed** *Sun eve & Mon*
Il Tartufo opened in early 1900s and has been run by the same family ever since. It is best known for occupying a Roman building considered a national monument as much as it is known for its love of black and white truffles. Try the courgette flowers stuffed with truffle and cheese.

DK Choice
SPOLETO: Le Casaline €€
Classic Umbrian   Map D5
Località Poreta di Spoleto, Frazione Casaline, 06142
Tel *074 35 21 113*   **Closed** *Mon*
Cinghiale alla cacciatore (wild boar in a wine sauce) is just one dish to tempt at this elegant restaurant set in a mill dating from the 1700s. Ingredients ranging from the olive oil and vegetables from its garden to the lamb from the Campello mountains, are all organic. The meat is cooked in a wood-burning fireplace. Pasta and bread is home-made. Good local wine list.

SPOLETO: Sabatini €€
Classic Umbrian   Map D5
Corso Mazzini 54, 06049
Tel *074 347230*   **Closed** *Mon*
Sabatini is an elegant place known for its creative presentation of Umbrian dishes. *Strangozzi* with truffles, and home-made ravioli with ricotta and pistachios are specials. Good wine selection too.

DK Choice
SPOLETO: San Lorenzo €€
International   Map D5
Piazza Sordini 6, 06049
Tel *074 32 21 847*
An elegant cream with orange accent decor, crisp linens and a menu of top notch Umbrian dishes give this a la carte restaurant an edge. Try the exquisite *tagliata di Angus ai lemoni di Sorrento* (Angus beef with Sorrento lemon). Its wine list carries over 300 labels. San Lorenzo is located in central Spoleto, not too far from the San Domenico church.

SPOLETO: Trattoria del Festival €€
Pizza & Pasta   Map D5
Via Brignone 8, 06049
Tel *074 32 20 993*
Del Festival is a cosy trattoria set in a 16th-century building. Old photos adorn its walls and its menu features pizzas, hand-made pasta and plenty of local truffles.

SPOLETO: Apollinare €€€
International   Map D5
Via Santa Agata 14, 06049
Tel *074 32 23 256*   **Closed** *Tue in winters*
Housed in a historic building dating, in part, from Roman times, Apollinare excels in international and local cuisine. Choose from taster or à la carte menus. Fine wine selection.

DK Choice
SPOLETO: Il Tempio Del Gusto €€€
International   Map D5
Via Arco di Druso 9, 06049
Tel *074 34 71 21*   **Closed** *Thu*
Known as the Temple of Taste, this cosy eatery stands on architectural remains dating back to around 2,000 years. Its cellar, housing dozens of fine Umbrian wines along with labels from Italian regions, is thought to be much older. Its innovative menu majors on local recipes like home-made ravioli stuffed with foie gras, apple and truffle with herbs.

TERNI: Gelateria Gustoso €
Café & Patisserie   Map D6
Via Mazzini 17, 05100
Tel *033 56 43 61 93*
Very famous and popular, Gustoso is near the San Francesco Church. Its ice cream comes in dozens of flavours, including pistachio, almond and ricotta with cinnamon. Lactose-free options too.

TERNI: Lu Somaru €
Pizza & Pasta   Map D6
Viale Cesare Battisti 106, 05100
Tel *074 43 04 787*
Cosy pizzeria in central Terni, very well-known for its excellent pizzas. Toppings include the classic Margherita to the San Domenico with mozzarella.

TERNI: Oste della Mal'Ora €
Café & Patisserie   Map D6
Via Tre Archi 5, 05100
Tel *074 44 06 683*   **Closed** *Sun*
This historic yet trendy café is a place where locals meet, drink and dine on simple yet

flavoursome food, typically *crostini* with truffle and soups like *vellutata di ceci* (chickpea).

TERNI: Pizzeria Le Fox €
Pizza & Pasta **Map** D6
Piazza Briccialdo 2, 05100
Tel *033 91 89 05 98*
Relax on the terrace with views of the park or use the take-away option at this very popular city centre 'the fox' pizzeria. Along with pizzas, which come with 30 or more different toppings, there are pasta meals too.

TERNI: Trattoria Da Carlino €
Classic Umbrian **Map** D6
Via Piemonte 1, 05100
Tel *074 44 20 163*
Popular with locals and located near the Terni railway station, this eatery has a menu of local dishes like *crostini* (toasts) and tagliatelle with truffles.

TERNI: Osteria Garibaldi €€
Classic Umbrian **Map** D6
Via Garibaldi 27, 05100
Tel *074 44 29 511*
Lively spot where locals go for authentic Umbrian cuisine. There is no menu and the owner offers specials of the day according to what's in season.

TERNI: Taverna di Porta Nova €€
Classic Umbrian **Map** D6
Via di Porta Nuova 1, Stroncone
Tel *074 46 04 96*
Atmospheric restaurant occupying a converted convent in Stroncone. *Strangozzi alla montanara* (pasta with vegetables and chilli peppers) is a special.

DK Choice

TERNI: Il Ritratto €€€
Gourmet **Map** D6
Via Santa Croce 2, 05100 Terni
Tel *074 44 22 966* **Closed** *Lunch, Wed eve, Sun*
This attractive restaurant in the historic centre is justly proud of the traditional tastes and imaginative presentation. Menu includes delicious pasta dishes, charcoal-grilled meats and other Umbrian specialities. Try the *scaloppine al limone* (veal escalope in lemon sauce). Fabulous desserts and fine wines.

TERNI: Lu Pilottu €€€
Fish & Seafood **Map** D6
Strada delle Grazie 5, 05100
Tel *074 42 74 412* **Closed** *Sun eve, Mon*

This tasteful, family-run restaurant specialises in pasta, fish and pastry creations. Its *tonnarelli* (pasta) with seafood or a wild boar sauce are signature dishes.

TERNI: Nascostoposto €€€
International **Map** D6
Via di Portanuova 8, Stroncone
Tel *074 46 08 309* **Closed** *Sun eve, Mon*
The ultra-contemporary décor goes hand-in-hand with the modern menu at this Stroncone restaurant. Specials include ravioli with clams and sea asparagus, and lobster with gazpacho.

TODI: Dige's Pizza €
Pizza & Pasta **Map** C5
Piazza Jacopone 7, 06059
Tel *075 89 42 307* **Closed** *Wed*
Great place for a quick bite or takeaway. Pizza and focaccia with a choice of toppings, paninis and pastries plus lots of delicious fruit tarts.

TODI: La Mulinella €
Classic Umbrian **Map** C5
Località Pontenaia 29, 06059
Tel *075 89 44 779* **Closed** *Sun*
Stone farmhouse with a chic country décor serving fresh bread baked in a wood-burning oven, pasta that is made by hand and succulent grilled meats.

DK Choice

TODI: Le Roi de la Crepe €
Café & Patisserie **Map** C5
Corso Cavour 37, 06059
Tel *075 89 45 297* **Closed** *Tue*
Host of snacks are cooked fresh to order and be eaten at its counter or taken away. Savory and sweet crepes top the menu favourites, along with paninis and hamburgers. Drinks and small bottles of wine too.

The cosy La Vecchia Posta in Trevi serves a fine selection of Umbrian wine

TODI: Pizzeria Pozzo Beccaro €
Pizza & Pasta **Map** C5
Via Menecali Abdon 6, 06059
Tel *075 89 48 473* **Closed** *Wed*
Lingua di bue (ox tongue) is a speciality and used imaginatively in pasta dishes and for topping pizzas at this popular pizzeria.

TODI: Antica Osteria della Valle €€
Classic Umbrian **Map** C5
Via Ciuffelli 19, 06059
Tel *075 89 44 848* **Closed** *Mon*
Cosy osteria, not far from the duomo, known for its hearty, top quality dishes, home-made pasta. Try the ravioli with truffle. The desserts here are works of art.

TODI: Pane e Vino €€
Classic Umbrian **Map** C5
Via Augusto Ciuffelli 33, Todi, 06059
Tel *075 89 45 448* **Closed** *Wed*
Generous *antipasti* platters of cold meats, followed by pasta dishes and meats such as *regina in porchetta* (suckling pig) cooked on the fire are favourites. Nice wine bar.

TODI: Ristorante Umbria €€
Classic Umbrian **Map** C5
Via San Bonaventura 13, 06059
Tel *075 89 42 737* **Closed** *Tue*
A 500-year-old town centre mansion with beamed ceilings and a dramatic décor is the setting for this lovely eatery. The terrace has a panoramic view.

DK Choice

TODI: Bramante €€€
Gourmet **Map** C5
Via Orvietana 48, 06059
Tel *075 89 48 381*
Housed in an elegant room of a restored 12th-century convent, the restaurant of the Hotel Bramante has a huge terrace for serving their exquisite gourmet creations. Seasonal menu with vegetarian, vegan and gluten-free options. Breakfast through to dinner. Excellent wine cellar.

TREVI: La Vecchia Posta €€
Classic Umbrian **Map** D5
Piazza Mazzini 14, 06039
Tel *074 23 81 690* **Closed** *Eve*
Truffle-stuffed *cappelletti* and wild boar *sagrantino* (in red wine) feature on the menu at this cosy, family-run osteria. La Vecchia Posta also offers a fine selection of Umbrian wine.

SHOPPING IN UMBRIA

The small shops lining the narrow streets of the historic centres of Umbria's towns and the craft workshops seen in small Umbrian villages make the region a wonderful place for shopping. It is not simply a question of buying traditional furniture, ceramics or textiles: it is also possible to track down workshops producing new and modern interpretations of ancient crafts, created by real masters of their art. Their fame is such that there are many schools for artisans in Umbria, which are attended by students from all over the world. The street markets, which may be permanent or weekly, are often excellent places to find good handicrafts, as well as more everyday items. Shops are, in general, open in the morning from 9am to 1pm and in the afternoon from 3 to 8pm. In the major tourist centres, such as Perugia and Assisi, shops are often open on Sunday as well.

Pottery shop in Deruta, a town famous for its ceramics

Ceramics

The ancient art of making pottery is one of the most traditional of Umbrian crafts. It was practised by the Etruscans and then resumed in the Middle Ages.

The ceramics of Deruta are among the most famous in Umbria, for their sheer quality and their bright colours. Today, the introduction of new styles and designs has breathed fresh life into a series of workshops run by artist-potters, whose work can be seen in Perugia, Orvieto, Deruta, Gubbio and Umbertide.

Wood

The woodworkers of Umbria are not simply carpenters or restorers. Umbrian artisans working in wood, though famous for their solid and traditional furniture, have also introduced some individual lines, such as wooden models (Perugia), sculpture (Orvieto) and modern furniture (Assisi). Most carpentry workshops are keen to produce furniture and other items for individual customers. However, these custom-made pieces can be very costly.

Textiles and Embroidery

For some years now in Umbria the tradition of hand-weaving fabric, using methods and designs dating back as far as the Middle Ages, has been making a comeback. Rugs, bedspreads and household linens, all with an antique feel, are regaining popularity in the shops of many Umbrian towns.

Worker with a hand loom used in the production of typical Umbrian textiles

Another well-known tradition is that of *"punto Assisi"*, or Assisi embroidery. Less widespread but equally fine is embroidery on tulle, originating from Panicale, south of Lake Trasimeno.

Antiques

Traditional Umbrian taste, a sense of the past, and increasing numbers of visitors have helped antiques shops and galleries to prosper. Items on sale range from antique books and other printed material to statues, furniture, jewellery, carpets and even icons. There are, in addition, regular antiques markets, such as those held in Assisi, Todi and Perugia.

Wine and Olive Oil

Umbrian wine companies vary considerably in size, from the small vineyard owner to large modern industrial units. Wine is a serious matter in Umbria and the quality of its red and white wines now rivals the world's best.

Vineyards can often be visited, and wines tasted and purchased on site. In some cases the wine tasting, with sampling of cheeses and salami included, commands a fee and must be booked in advance. Apart from the traditional wine cooperatives, the most famous places to go to are the Lungarotti company in Torgiano; Antinori, not far from Orvieto; and Decugnano dei Barbi, near Corbara.

In Umbria, the production of olive

oil is an ancient and much-respected tradition. A good proportion of the oil made in Umbria is bottled with the quality mark DOP (Denominazione di Origine Protetta – or protected denomination of origin), which guarantees the origin of the olives used and the method of pressing. The best places to buy oil are at the olive presses (frantoi), which can be visited in November and December; here you can see how the olives are made into olive oil in a matter of hours. The price of a good-quality oil bought on site will be at least twice that of any everyday extra-virgin oil bought in an ordinary shop. Trevi, in particular, is known to produce very high-quality olive oil. **Museo della Civiltà dell'Ulivo**, the olive oil museum here, is worth a visit. Trevi also celebrates the harvest of olive oil every autumn with a wonderful festival, Festa dell Olio Nuovo.

Delicatessen in Norcia, a typical shop selling local produce

Gastronomy

Another popular buy is the traditional produce of the region. The cured meats – especially those from Norcia, although they can be found almost everywhere – are one of the top delicacies. The variety is impressive: salami, hams and sausages, cured or fresh. Bottled vegetables in oil or brine are widely available, as are locally made jams. Focaccia with cheese (which is traditional at Easter) is particularly good in southern Umbria, and Umbrian sheep's milk cheeses, both mature and fresh, are also excellent.

Cereals and vegetables are another important and popular Umbrian staple, and are often grown organically. In addition to the lentils of Castelluccio, look for spelt (farro) and chickling (cicerchia), a type of pea.

DIRECTORY

Crafts

L'Antica Deruta (ceramics)
SS E45, Deruta.
[w] anticaderuta.com

Artigianato Ferro Artistico (ironwork)
Via Baldassini 22, Gubbio.

Bottega del Legno di Gualverio Michelangeli (woodwork)
Via Michelangeli 3, Orvieto.
[w] mich.it

Ceramiche Artigianali (ceramics)
Via Storelli 42, Gualdo Tadino.

Ceramiche Rometti (ceramics)
Via Canavelle 5.

Duca di Montefeltro (ceramics)
Via dei Consoli 33, Gubbio.

La Fucina (metalwork)
Via dei Muratori, Orvieto.

Laboratorio Tela Umbra (textiles)
Via Sant'Antonio 3, Città di Castello.
[w] telaumbra.it

Mastri Cartai Editori (paper)
Via dei Priori 77, Perugia.

Officina Libris (leather-bound goods)
Via dei Consoli 39, Gubbio.

La Spola (general crafts)
Via Garibaldi 66, Torgiano.

Tele Umbre (tapestry)
Via Piccotti 1, Gubbio.

Tessuto Artistico Umbro (textiles)
Piazza del Comune 1, Montefalco.

Antiques Fairs

Assisi Antiquariato (end Apr–May)
Centro Umbriafiere Bastia Umbria.
[w] assisiantiquariato.it

Rassegna Antiquaria (end Oct–early Nov)
Rocca Paolina, Perugia.

Rassegna Antiquaria d'Italia (mid-end Apr)
Palazzo Vignola, Todi.

Gastronomy

L'Agricola Goretti
Strada Pino 4, Pila (nr Perugia).

Bartolini (porcini, truffles, oils etc.)
33 Via XX Settembre, Gubbio.

Bottega Barbanera
Piazza della Repubblica 34, Foligno.

Cantina Terre de' Trinci
Via Fiammenga 57, Foligno.

Fratelli Ansuini (cured meats)
Viale della Stazione, Norcia.

Giò Arte e Vini (wine)
Via Ruggero d'Andreotto 19, Perugia.

Macelleria Giulietti (meat products)
Corso Cavour 13, Città di Castello.

Pasticceria Muzzi (cakes and biscuits)
Via Roma 38, Foligno.

Pasticceria Sandri (cakes, biscuits and chocolates)
Corso Vannucci 32, Perugia.

La Spezieria Bavicchi (spices)
Piazza Matteotti 37, Perugia.

Urbani Tartufi (truffles)
SS Valnerina, 31.3 km, Santa Anatolia di Narco.

What to Buy in Umbria

The varied crafts of Umbria, derived from tradition but still open to new ideas, can be found either in shops or actually at the artists' own workshops. Old-fashioned ceramics sit side by side with works by great contemporary artists such as Cagli and Leonardi. Antique linen, lovingly produced by hand on a loom, is piled up next to more up-to-date and fashionable knitwear produced by Umbrian factories. It would also be impossible to ignore the delicious food of the region. Salami, of course, but also preserves, lentils, black truffles and chocolate, enabling visitors to take home something of the flavour of Umbria.

Potter at work in his studio

Ceramics

Ceramics production – of which Deruta is the capital – is inspired by techniques and designs from a centuries-old tradition. An interesting new and flourishing trend is for new artists to make modern pieces, which have been inspired by their own imagination and by the study of new production methods.

Whistle from Ficulle

Vases and jars in painted majolica

Basket and lid

Basket for fruit

Baskets

The reeds that grow around Lake Trasimeno are gathered for use today, as they were in centuries past. A sturdy but flexible plant material, the reed is used to make all kinds of objects. Baskets, mats and traps for fishing on the lake are on sale in the towns of Passignano, Castiglione del Lago and Tuoro.

Textiles and Embroidery

In several studios in Perugia, and in a few other towns, it is possible to buy household linen, fabrics and carpets, woven on a loom according to ancient methods. Umbrian embroidery and lace (made in Assisi, Panicale and Orvieto) are still widely available.

Detail from antique fabric

Cashmere wool is used to make high-quality garments. The most famous company name is that of Brunello Cucinelli.

Ars panicalensis is the name given to the technique of embroidering on tulle, originating in Panicale and now done throughout Umbria. The pieces have the delicacy of lace.

Knitwear

Umbria is a region with a series of small but dedicated knitwear companies producing garments using different types of wool. Clothes made from cashmere wool are particularly desirable.

Bookbinding

The old traditions of bookselling, bookbinding and book restoration are by no means dead in Umbria. Bookplates, diaries, notebooks, and albums are made with paper that reproduces the designs and colours of the Renaissance, a tradition that began with the followers of St Francis.

Book plate

Wood

A man called Michelangeli launched the trend for good-quality woodwork in Orvieto. There is now a small but flourishing trade in wooden statues and animals, as well as garden sculptures. Items made from olive wood are now a tourist attraction in Assisi.

Hand-made wooden aeroplane

Pork Sausages and Salami

The meat and salami of Norcia are superb. You can choose from hams (made from pig or wild boar), fresh sausages, cured pork sausage, *capocollo* (made with neck of pig), and wild boar salami among many other delicacies. Good salami from small producers is found all over the region.

Shop selling a selection of fine hams, sausages and salamis

The prized black truffle

White truffle

Truffles

The world's most prized type of black truffle *(tartufo nero)* grows in the Valnerina, especially around Norcia, and is gathered from November to March. The white truffle, gathered from October to December, is rare, prized and expensive.

Chocolate and Sweets

The manufacture of chocolate in the city of Perugia dates back to the early 1900s. Traditional sweets can be found all over the region, and a chocolate festival is held in Perugia every October.

Perugina

Baci Perugina, individually wrapped hazelnut chocolates, are the bestselling line of a business established in 1907. Their introduction led to a fresh appreciation of Italian confectionery. "*Baci*" means kisses and each sweet wrapper contains a little quotation about love, in four languages. Historic Perugina adverts are on display in Perugia's Museo Storico.

SURVIVAL
GUIDE

PRACTICAL INFORMATION

Along with an exceptional variety of landscapes, museums and places of historical and artistic interest, Umbria can offer a good range of services. The distances between the main centres are not great, making this, therefore, an ideal place for visitors eager to explore. The museums and galleries are, in general, modern, well run, welcoming and accessible to all (an increasing number have access for people with disabilities). The regional authority, Regione dell'Umbria, can offer a wide range of maps and lists of events through the various tourist offices. Banks and medical services are widely available throughout the region.

Mountain biking in the hills around Gubbio

When to Visit

Umbria is one of the richest regions in Italy in terms of its attractions (natural and man-made) and its calendar of traditional, cultural and religious events. As a result, Umbria attracts large numbers of visitors between May and September. If you have the option, it is certainly best to arrange to visit either in May and June or September and October, thereby avoiding the crowded peak summer months. In summer, Umbria can also be exceedingly hot. In winter, when snow falls in the mountains, temperatures are low and the winds cold.

Tourist Information

The two provinces that form Umbria – Perugia and Terni – each have their own **Azienda di Promozione Turistica** (APT), responsible for the promotion of tourism in that particular province.

There is a tourist office in every town of a decent size. In smaller centres, offices called Pro Loco are able to supply historical or cultural information, in addition to information about restaurants and lodgings. Specialist tour guides providing individual attention are available in some towns, too. In addition, there are numerous organizations which deal with all kinds of sporting events and activities *(see pp26–7)*. For those planning a cycling holiday, and for lovers of mountain biking, the APT provides a booklet called *Umbria in bicicletta* (Umbria by bicycle).

AZIENDA PROMOZIONE TURISTICA

Tourist office (APT) sign

Informa Giovani, set up by the Comune di Perugia (the Perugia town council), is aimed at young people, and can provide suggestions as well as addresses relating to culture, sport, music, wildlife, holidays, work opportunities and youth associations.

Sightseeing

Museums in Umbria are run either by the local town council or by the Italian government. In general, state museums are open from 9am to 7pm, and often close on Monday and on Sunday afternoon. Winter hours tend to be shorter. Museums run by the local authority have more varied timetables, and may even close over lunch. The use of a flash or a tripod is forbidden in most museums.

Church opening hours are unpredictable, but many close between noon and 3 or 4pm. When visiting churches, you should dress suitably. Tourists are discouraged from touring churches during services, and may be excluded from special religious festivals.

Communications

Post offices can be found in all towns and there is often more than one branch. Main post offices are usually open from 8:30am to 7:30pm Monday to Saturday. Smaller offices, however, are often open in the morning only, from 8:30am to 1:30pm; on Saturday and the last day of the month, these post offices close at noon.

If all you want is stamps *(francobolli)* for postcards and normal letters, you can buy these at any tobacconist *(tabacchi)* with the black and white "T" sign.

The number of public telephones has fallen in tandem with the rise of the mobile phone. Those that remain use telephone cards, available from tobacconists and some newspaper kiosks.

Telephone company logo

◄ Hikers look over Piano Grande near Palazzo Borghese Mountain in Sibillini Mountain National Park

Dialling Codes

- To phone another number in Italy, you must include the full area code.
- For international calls, country codes are: UK & Ireland 00 39; USA & Canada 0 11 39; Australia 00 11 39.
- For reverse charge calls, dial 170.
- For directory enquiries, dial 1240 (for Italy) or 176 (international).
- For the British Operator, dial 17200 44.
- US Operators: 172 10 11 (AT&T); 172 10 22 (MG Worldphone); 172 18 77 (Sprint).
- Australian Operators: 1225 (Telstra); 172 11 61 (Opus).

Tax Exemption

Value added tax (IVA in Italy) ranges from 12 to 35 per cent. Non-EU citizens can claim an IVA rebate, provided the total expenditure is over €155. It is easiest to get a refund if you shop where you see the "Euro Free Tax" sign. Show your passport, complete a form, and the IVA will be deducted from your bill. Or show your purchases and their receipts at customs upon departure; they will stamp the receipts. Send these to the vendor and a refund should then be sent to you.

Student Information

An International Student Identity Card (ISIC) can be used to get a reduction on admission charges to many museums and other tourist attractions. The ISIC card also gives access to a 24-hour phone helpline. For discount travel and information, visit any branch of the **Centro Turistico tudentesco** (CTS).

Electrical Adaptors

The voltage in Italy is 220 volts, with two-pin round-pronged plugs. It is worth buying adaptor plugs before you leave as they are difficult to find in Italy. Most hotels with three or more stars have hairdryers and shaving points in all bedrooms, but check the voltage first, to be safe.

Italian Time

Italy is 1 hour ahead of Greenwich Mean Time (GMT). The time difference is: London: –1 hour; New York: –6 hours; Perth: +7 hours; Auckland: +11 hours. These figures may vary briefly in summer with local time changes. Italy uses the 24-hour clock (e.g. 10pm = 22:00).

Conversion Chart

Imperial to Metric
1 inch = 2.54 centimetres
1 foot = 30 centimetres
1 mile = 1.6 kilometres
1 ounce = 28 grams
1 pound = 454 grams
1 pint = 0.57 litre
1 gallon = 4.6 litres

Metric to Imperial
1 centimetre = 0.4 inch
1 metre = 3 feet 3 inches
1 kilometre = 0.6 mile
1 gram = 0.04 ounce
1 kilogram = 2.2 pounds
1 litre = 1.8 pints

DIRECTORY

Italian State Tourist Offices Abroad

Canada
110 Yonge Street, Toronto MSC 1T4.
Tel 416-925-4882.

Ireland & United Kingdom
1 Princes St, London W1B 2AY.
Tel 020 7408 1254.

United States
630 Fifth Avenue, Suite 1565, New York, NY 10111. **Tel** 212-245-4822.

State Tourist Offices in Umbria

Regional Tourist Office (APT)
Via Mazzini 21, Perugia.
Tel 075 572 8937.

Assisi
Tel 075 812 534
info@iat.assisi.pg.it

Orvieto
Tel 0763 341 772.
info@iat.orvieto.tr.it

Perugia
Tel 075 573 6458.
info@iat.perugia.it

Spoleto
Tel 0743 238 920.
info@iat.spoleto.pg.it

Trasimeno
Tel 075 965 2738.
info@iat.castiglione dellago.pg.it

Other Tourist Information

Associazione Guide Turistiche (tour guides)
Via Dono Doni 18, Assisi.
Tel 075 815 228.
w assoguide.it

Centro Turistico Studentesco (CTS)
Viale Sempione 6, Città di Castello. **Tel** 075 855 3353. **w** cts.it

Informa Giovani
Piazza del Melo, Perugia.
Tel 075 577 2496.
w comune.perugia.it/ informagiovani

Embassies and Consulates

Canada
Via Salaria 243, Rome.
Tel 06 854 441.

Ireland
Villa Spada, Via Giacomo Medici, Rome.
Tel 06 581 3336.

United Kingdom
Via XX Settembre 80a, Rome. **Tel** 06 4220 0001.

United States
Via Vittorio Veneto 121a, Rome. **Tel** 06 46 741.

Websites

Regione Umbria
w regioneumbria.eu
w italian touristboard. co.uk
w italiantourism.com

Emergencies

General emergencies
Tel 113.

Carabinieri (police)
Tel 112.

Fire service
Tel 115.

Car breakdown
Tel 116.

Ambulance
Tel 118.

Hospital
Via Bonacci Brunamonti 51, Perugia.
Tel 075 57 81.

Health and Safety

Umbria is a safe region. However, if you are in diffculties, each town has a police headquarters, open 24 hours a day. Medical care in Umbria can be excellent, but be sure to take out medical insurance.

Police vehicle, equipped for off-road use

Vehicle used by the Vigili del Fuoco for smaller fires

Hospitals and Pharmacies

Pharmacy sign

Pharmacies are open 9am–1pm and 4–8pm, Monday to Friday, and mornings only on Saturdays.

Every Umbrian city has its own hospital. In emergencies, go to the *Pronto Soccorso* (Casualty) or telephone for help. EU citizens are entitled to free treatment if they have a European Health Insurance Card (EHIC), but making a claim is a bureaucratic process. Always ensure that your travel insurance includes medical cover.

Police

In Italy the forces of law and order are organized into two divisions: the *Carabinieri* and the police (*Polizia*), to which can be added, at urban level, the municipal police, including traffic police (*Vigili Urbani*). Traffic police can also deal with minor matters and can provide information and deal with emergency situations. They wear a dark uniform in winter and a light one in summer, with the city coat of arms usually on the pocket. *Carabinieri* are responsible for public order. They wear black trousers with a red stripe down the side, and a white band across the body. Patrols are often seen on the streets. The duties of the *Polizia* are more

A team of *carabinieri* in traffic police uniform

wide-ranging and are, in general, concerned with criminal investigations. The uniform is blue, with a white belt and hat. To report a theft or other serious problem, go to the nearest police station or dial 113.

Firefighters

In such a green and wooded region as Umbria, problems with fires are perhaps inevitable, even if the fairly damp climate and the scarcity of winds do not favour the spread of fire. Even so, particularly if you are planning an outdoor holiday, be sure to observe all the standard countryside code practices, especially with regard to not lighting a fire outside the designated areas and making sure cigarettes are completely extinguished.

Municipal policeman

The region has many fire stations, and fire engines respond rapidly to alarm calls. Firefighters also attend to other kinds of emergencies.

Personal Safety

Use common sense to keep safe. Do not carry large sums in cash and, if you have valuables, leave them in the safe at your hotel if possible. Pickpockets frequent main railway stations and crowded tourist sights. If travelling by car, lock the vehicle and don't leave any items in view.

It is essential to arrange full insurance cover before you travel, and you may wish to keep a separate photocopy of personal documents so that you can request duplicates in the event of theft.

In Umbria, there are no areas that need to be avoided. It is safe to walk around town streets in the evenings, and even late at night; of course, make sure you are always aware of your surroundings and use your common sense if you feel any unease.

Banking and Local Currency

Foreigners arriving in Umbria may change currency in a number of ways, but it is still wise to arrive with euros in your pocket. Credit cards are widely accepted for purchases and can be used to withdraw money.

Sign at a cash machine, useful for withdrawing cash with a debit card

Banks and Currency Exchange

In the larger towns there are bureaux de change as well as currency-converting machines. It is also possible to change money in hotels and in travel agencies, but you'll get a better exchange rate in the banks. Commission charges can be hefty, so it's worth shopping around.

Italian banks are normally open from 8:30am to 1:30pm, and then from 3pm to 4pm, from Monday to Friday, but these hours may vary from place to place; banks often close early the day before a public holiday. Your hotel reception or the tourist office should be able to help with information. Opening hours of bureaux de change and other places are much more variable. Some form of identification will be needed for all kinds of money transactions.

All towns have cashpoint (ATM) machines (bancomat), which allow you to take money out with a debit card or a credit card and a PIN number.

VISA, American Express, MasterCard and Diners Club are the most commonly seen credit cards and there should be no problems getting them accepted.

The Euro

The euro (€) is the common currency of the European Union. It went into general circulation on 1 January 2002, initially for 12 participating countries. Italy was one of those 12 countries, and the lira was phased out in February 2002. EU members using the Euro as their sole official currency are known as the Eurozone. Several EU members have opted out of joining this common currency.

Euro notes are identical throughout the Eurozone, each one including designs of fictional architectural structures and monuments. The coins, however, have one side identical (the value side) and one side with an image unique to each country. Both notes and coins are exchangeable in each participating country.

When travelling, it is best not to carry euro notes of large denominations, since not all businesses have large amounts of change.

Logo of the Banca dell'Umbria

Banknotes and Coins

Banknotes come in seven denominations. The €5 note is grey, €10 is pink, €20 is blue, €50 is orange, €100 is green, €200 is yellow and €500 is purple. There are eight different coins. The €1 and €2 coins are silver and gold; those worth 50, 20 and 10 cents are gold, while the 5-, 2- and 1-cent coins are bronze.

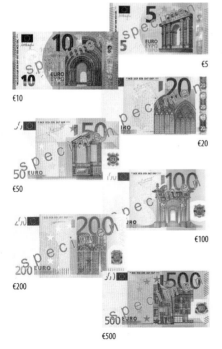

€10
€5
€20
€50
€100
€200
€500

€2 coin

€1 coin

50 cents

20 cents

10 cents

5 cents

2 cents

1 cent

TRAVEL INFORMATION

Umbria lies at the geographical heart of Italy. Despite the hills and the mountains of the Apennines, road and rail infrastructures are well maintained and well organized; this, combined with the relatively small size of the region, makes it easy and straightforward to travel from one place to another by car. Road and tourist signs are helpful and up-to-date. Driving and parking can be difficult in towns, but buses and taxis are plentiful, and most towns are small enough to be explored easily on foot. The railway network has few branch lines but there are frequent and reliable connections by coach where there are no trains. Umbria itself is easily reached by air or coach. Ferries link the villages on the shores of Lake Trasimeno as well as the lake islands.

Hiring a car, a practical and convenient way of getting around Umbria

Arriving by Air

The Umbrian Regional Airport of Sant'Egidio is 12 km (7 miles) from both Perugia and Assisi. Scheduled Alitalia flights arrive here from Milan Malpensa and the main Italian international airports; in high season there are also some charter flights. Ryanair flies to Perugia daily from London Stansted. Buses between the airport and the centre of Perugia are timed to coincide with the arrival of scheduled flights. Taxis are also available at the airport, as is car hire: the major companies (**Avis**, **Europcar** and **Hertz**) offer pre-booked fly-drive arrangements.

One option is to fly to Rome or another nearby airport, such as Ancona, Pisa or Florence, and take the train or drive from there. Rome to Perugia by car, for example, takes 2 hours.

Travelling by Car

The Autostrada del Sole (A1) from Milan, via Florence, skirts Umbria along the Tuscan border before continuing on to Rome.

At the Val di Chiana exit, a road runs east to Perugia. Other useful exit points are Chiusi Chianciano, Orvieto and Orte, from where a fast road runs to Terni and links up with the Via Flaminia. The latter is the most important state road in Umbria, running from north to south. The condition of the roads is good; only within the Apennines does driving become more challenging.

A car is by far the best way to explore Umbria, enabling you to reach the most remote villages and making it easier to enjoy the scenery.

Car hire is expensive and should be booked ahead. You must be over 21 and have held a licence for at least a year. Visitors from outside the EU may need to show an international licence.

A toll is payable for use of the motorways *(autostrade)*. Tolls are high, but you can usually pay by credit card.

Note that petrol stations may close at lunchtime and rarely stay open late.

Travelling by Train

Umbria has two railway lines: **Ferrovie dello Stato** (FS) and the private **Ferrovia Centrale Umbra** (FCU). FS operates the main routes, and its stations do not sell FCU tickets.

The FS Milan–Rome line stops at Orte, Orvieto and the rail junction at Terentola. From here there is another FS line running to Perugia and Foligno, stopping at a few places on Lake Trasimeno and passing close to Assisi. Two Eurostar (ES) and four regional trains provide a daily direct link between Perugia and Rome. Other useful FS lines are the one linking Florence to Perugia and the Rome–Ancona (stopping at Terni, Foligno, Spoleto and Orte).

The FCU Terni–Perugia line serves Todi and then goes on to Città di Castello and Sansepolcro, in Tuscany. Perugia has two stations: Sant'Anna and San Giovanni. The former is used only by FCU trains; the latter by both the FCU and FS.

Train stations may be some distance from the hill town after which they are named. Give yourself enough time to make your way back to the station to catch the return train.

You must buy tickets before departure. Be sure to validate both outward and return tickets

A train run by the state company Ferrovie dello Stato

in the machines provided on the platform, before boarding the train, or you will be fined. Always check before doing so that the train you plan to board stops at the station you want: InterCity and Eurostar trains stop only at major stations. Most InterCity and all Eurostar trains have a compulsory seat-reservation policy included in the fare.

Fares are still among the cheapest in Europe, but check in advance with **Rail Europe** for details of money-saving passes. Visit www. umbriamobilita.it for detailed information on trains and buses.

Travelling by Coach

Intercity coach travel can be faster than travelling by train. Perugia is the main hub for coach services. It has direct links to several Italian cities, with stops in various Umbrian towns en route. A daily service from Roma Tiburtina, Rome's main coach station, stops in Todi, Assisi and Deruta en route to Perugia. There are daily coaches between Rome and Gubbio and Città di Castello, as well as Norcia. Perugia is accessible by coach from Florence; many coaches also stop at Città di Castello (via Arezzo).

Coaches from Perugia to Assisi run six or seven times a day, while Todi has around five services a day and Gubbio ten. Coach services are often reduced at weekends, particularly on Sundays, and also vary between summer and winter.

Ferry logo

Town Buses

In Perugia the Azienda Perugina di Mobilità operates services within the city and out to the suburbs, among them buses linking the train terminal with the coach station. Tickets are valid for different lengths of time, and prices vary accordingly. Bus tickets can be purchased from newspaper kiosks and *tabacchi*. Season tickets are also available, including tourist tickets that are valid for 24 or 48 hours.

In Assisi, regular buses link the railway station, 5 km (3 miles) away at Santa Maria degli Angeli, to the centre. In Todi, too, the railway station is linked to the town by bus.

At Terni, buses run by the **Azienda Trasporti Pubblici** (ATC) serve the town and also travel as far as the Cascata delle Marmore.

Taxis

Hire a cab only from an official taxi stand or else reserve it by phone. If you telephone, the meter will run from the time of your call. Extra is charged for each piece of luggage put in the boot, for rides at night, on Sundays and public holidays, and for airport trips (fix a price before you set off).

Ferries

On Lake Trasimeno, ferries link Castiglione del Lago, the islands of Isola Polvese, Isola Maggiore and Isola Minore, as well as Tuoro sul Trasimeno and Passignano sul Trasimeno.

DIRECTORY

Airports

Perugia
Aeroporto Regionale Umbro di Sant'Egidio. **Tel** 075 592 141.
W airport.umbria.it

Rail Information

Umbria Mobilità
Tel 075 963 7637.
W umbriamobilita.it

Ferrovia Centrale Umbra (FCU)
Tel 075 575 401. W fcu.it

Ferrovie dello Stato (FS)
Tel 892 021. W trenitalia.it

Rail Europe
Tel 08448 485 848 (UK).
W uk.voyages-sncf.com
Tel 1-877-257-2887, 1-800-622-8600 (US). W raileurope.com

Coach Information

Società Umbro Laziale Gestione Autolinee
Tel 075 500 9641 or 800 099 661 (free from landlines). W sulga.it

Bus Information

ATC Terni
Tel 0744 492 711. W atcterni.it

Umbria Mobilità
Tel 075 963 7637.
W umbriamobilita.it.

Car Hire

Avis (Perugia)
Tel 075 500 0395. W avis.com

Europcar (Perugia)
Tel 075 501 8115. W europcar.it

Hertz (Perugia)
Tel 075 592 8115. W hertz.com

Taxis

Assisi	**Tel** 075 813 100.
Foligno	**Tel** 0742 344 280.
Orvieto	**Tel** 0763 301 903.
Perugia	**Tel** 075 500 4888.
Spoleto	**Tel** 0743 220 489.
Terni	**Tel** 0744 425 768.
Todi	**Tel** 075 894 2525.

One of the ferries linking the islands and towns on Lake Trasimeno

General Index

Acknowledgments

Dorling Kindersley would like to thank all those whose contribution and assistance have made the preparation of this book possible.

Special Thanks
Archivio Electa-Milano, Assessorato del Turismo Regione Umbria, APT di Perugia, APT di Assisi, APT di Foligno, APT di Spoleto, Consorzio del Parco del Lago Trasimeno, Consorzio del Parco del Monte Cucco, Ente Parco dei Monti Sibillini, Guido Stecchi for consultation and help with pages 154–5, and all the companies who have assisted with their products.

Photography
Ghigo Roli (Modena)

Translator
Fiona Wild

Editor
Emily Hatchwell

Revisions and Relaunch
Ashwin Raju Adimari, Beverley Ager, Marta Bescos Sanchez, Uma Bhattacharya, Gadi Farfour, Anna Freiberger, Carole French, Vinod Harish, Mohammad Hassan, Jasneet Kaur, Vincent Kurien, Sarah Lane, Leonie Loudon, Tanya Mahendru, Sam Merrell, Rebecca Milner, Deepak Mittal, Helen Partington, Sangita Patel, Gillian Price, Rada Radojicic, Ellen Root, Sands Publishing Solutions, Collette Sadler, Azeem Siddiqui, Ellie Smith, Susana Smith, Nikky Tywman, Conrad Van Dyk, Vinita Venugopal.

Additional Photography
John Heseltine, Ian O'Leary, Helena Smith, Christine Webb, Kate Whitaker.

Photography Permissions
The publisher would like to thank all the churches, museums, hotels, restaurants, art galleries, parks and all those who supplied material and contributed to the publication of this guide, too numerous to be named individually. While every effort has been made to contact the copyright holders, we apologize for any omissions and will be happy to include them in subsequent editions of this publication.

Picture Credits
t = top; tl = top left; tlc = top left centre; tc = top centre; tr = top right; cla = centre left above; ca = centre above; cra = centre right above; cl = centre left; c = centre; cr = centre right; clb = centre left below; cb = centre below; crb = centre right below;bl = bottom left; b = below; bc = bottom centre; bcl = bottom centre left; br = bottom right; (d) = detail.

Alamy Images: Bildagentur-online / Moreno 14t; Tibor Bognar 1c; Cubo Images srl/Enrico Caracciolo 155c; Domenico Farone 100; Norma Joseph 154cl, 155tl; Chuck Pefley 15tc; Unlisted Images, Inc. 11br; Christine Webb 13cr.

Fabrizio Ardito (Rome): 20tl, 37bl, 65tl, 65cr, 73tc, 75tr, 90br, 93clb, 96tr, 96bl, 135cr, 138cl, 139tc, 141cr.
The Art Archive: Galleria Nazionale dell'Umbria Perugia/Dagli Orti 92tr; Palazzo Trinci Foligno/Dagli Orti 106c.

AWL Images: Peter Adams 2-3, Francesco Iacobelli 18.

Adriano Bacchella (Milan): 20cl.
Bosone Garden: 158tr.

The Bridgeman Art Library: Galleria Nazionale dell'Umbria, Perugia, Italy Altarpiece: Annunciation; Madonna and Child with Saints; Miracles of St. Anthony, St. Francis and St. Elizabeth Piero della Francesca 92cl.

David Capasso (Modena): 46bl, 107cl, 108tl, 109cr.

Corbis: Elio Ciol 21b, Paul Harcourt Davies 172-173, JAI / Peter Adams 144-145.

Dreamstime.com: Eugene Bochkarev 163br, Claudio Giovanni Colombo 11crb, Steven Corton 12bl, Deniskelly 12tc, Flaviano Fabrizi 15br, Gkuna 10bc, Milla74 11tl, minnystock 13t, Patronestaff 10cl, Stevanzz 50-51.

Ferrovie Dello Stato: 178br; **Fondazione Festival dei Due Mondi:** 49bc; **Giovanni Francesio** (Mantua): 59cla, 59cr, 60 all photos, 61 all photos, 67tc, 67br, 68 all photos, 69 all photos, 70tr, 70bl, 71tl, 71cr, 71b, 86c, 86br, 87cl, 87cra, 98 all photos.

Getty Images: DEA / J. Ciganovic 128-129; Photodisc/Buena Vista Images 49cb.

I Sette Consoli: 164br.

Tim Jepson: 19b.

L'Antico Forziere: 156bl. **L'Orto degli Angeli:** 151bc. **La Costa:** 159br. **La Locanda Del Cardinale:** 157tr. **La Vecchia Posta:** 167bc. **Le Casaline:** 166tl. **Le Tre Vaselle:** 150tl, 161tl.

Marco Mandibola (Milan): 55b, 65bc, 82c, 104bl, 106tl, 109bl, 134b; **Guido Mannucci** (Florence): 37cr, 95clb; **Marka** (Milan): D. Donadoni 153br, R. Gropozzo 153tl.

Peter Noble: 176b.
Ottavius: 162tr. **Relais II:** 149tr.

Ristorante Le Mura: 152c.

Robert Harding Picture Library: T. Gervis 20br.

Anna Serrano (Rome): 22tr, 22crb, 23bl, 36cr.

Guido Stecchi (Milan): 154cra, 154bl. **SuperStock:** Tips Images 54. **Hotel Vannucci:** 148br. **Villa Ciconia:** 165tr.

Front End Paper
Alamy Images: Domenico Farone bl; **SuperStock:** Tips Images tr

Jacket
Front: **4Corners:** Giovanni Simeone main; **DK Images:** Rough Guides/ Chris Hutty bl.

All other images © Dorling Kindersley. For further information see: **www.dkimages.com**

Phrase Book

In an Emergency

Help!	Aiuto!	eye-yoo-toh
Stop!	Fermate!	fair-mah-teh
Call a doctor.	Chiama un medico.	kee-ah-mah oon meh-dee-koh
Call an ambulance.	Chiama un' ambulanza	kee-ah-mah oon am-boo-lan-tsa
Call the police.	Chiama la polizia.	kee-ah-mah lah pol-ee-tsee-ah
Call the fire brigade.	Chiama i pompieri.	kee-ah-mah ee pom-pee-air-ee
Where is the telephone?	Dov'è il telefono?	dov-eh eel teh-leh-foh-noh?
The nearest hospital?	L'ospedale più vicino?	loss-peh-dah-leh pee-oovee-chee-noh?

Communication Essentials

Yes/No	Si/No	see/noh
Please	Per favore	pair fah-vor-eh
Thank you	Grazie	grah-tsee-eh
Excuse me	Mi scusi	mee skoo-zee
Hello	Buon giorno	bwon jor-noh
Goodbye	Arrivederci	ah-ree-veh-dair-chee
Good evening	Buona sera	bwon-ah sair-ah
morning	la mattina	lah mah-tee-nah
afternoon	il pomeriggio	eel poh-meh-ree-joh
evening	la sera	lah sair-ah
yesterday	ieri	ee-air-ee
today	oggi	oh-jee
tomorrow	domani	doh-mah-nee
here	qui	kwee
there	la	lah
What?	Quale?	kwah-leh?
When?	Quando?	kwan-doh?
Why?	Perchè?	pair-keh?
Where?	Dove?	doh-veh

Useful Phrases

How are you?	Come sta?	koh-meh stah?
Very well, thank you.	Molto bene, grazie.	moll-toh beh-neh grah-tsee-eh
Pleased to meet you.	Piacere di conoscerla.	pee-ah-chair-eh dee coh-noh-shair-lah
See you soon.	A più tardi.	a pee-oo tar-dee
That's fine.	Va bene.	va beh-neh
Where is/are ...?	Dov'è/Dove sono ...?	dov-eh/doveh soh-noh?
How long does it take to get to ...?	Quanto tempo ci vuole per andare a ...?	kwan-toh tem-poh chee voo-oh-leh pair an-dar-eh ah...?
How do I get to ...?	Come faccio per arrivare a ...?	koh-meh fah-choh pair arri-var-eh ah...?
Do you speak English?	Parla inglese?	par-lah een-gleh-zeh?
I don't understand.	Non capisco.	non ka-pee-skoh
Could you speak more slowly, please?	Può parlare più lentamente, per favore?	pwoh par-lah-reh pee-oo len-ta-men-teh pair fah-vor-eh
I'm sorry.	Mi dispiace.	mee dee-spee-ah-cheh

Useful Words

big	grande	gran-deh
small	piccolo	pee-koh-loh
hot	caldo	kal-doh
cold	freddo	fred-doh
good	buono	bwoh-noh
bad	cattivo	kat-tee-voh
enough	basta	bas-tah
well	bene	beh-neh
open	aperto	ah-pair-toh
closed	chiuso	kee-oo-zoh
left	a sinistra	ah see-nee-strah
right	a destra	ah dess-trah
straight on	sempre dritto	sem-preh dree-toh
near	vicino	vee-chee-noh
far	lontano	lon-tah-noh
up	su	soo
down	giù	joo
early	presto	press-toh
late	tardi	tar-dee
entrance	entrata	en-trah-tah
exit	uscita	oo-shee-ta
toilet	il gabinetto	eel gah-bee-net-toh
free, unoccupied	libero	lee-bair-oh
free, no charge	gratuito	grah-too-ee-toh
out of order	guasto	gwass-to
strike (train etc.)	sciopero	sho-pay-ro

Making a Telephone Call

I'd like to place a long-distance call.	Vorrei fare una interurbana.	vor-ray far-eh oona in-tair-oor-bah-nah
I'd like to make a reverse-charge call.	Vorrei fare una telefonata a carico del destinatario.	vor-ray far-eh oona teh-leh-fon-ah-tah ah kar-ee-koh dell desstee-nah-tar-ree-oh
I'll try again later.	Ritelefono più tardi.	ree-teh-leh-foh-noh pee-oo tar-dee
Can I leave a message?	Posso lasciare un messaggio?	poss-oh lash-ah-reh oon mess-sah-joh?
Hold on.	Un attimo, per favore.	oon ah-tee-moh, pair fah-vor-eh
Could you speak up a little please?	Può parlare più forte, per favore?	pwoh par-lah-reh pee-oo for-teh, pair fah-vor-eh?
local call	la telefonata locale	lah teh-leh-fon-ah-ta loh-kah-leh

Shopping

How much does this cost?	Quant'è, per favore?	kwan-teh pair fah-vor-eh?
I would like ...	Vorrei...	vor-ray
Do you have ...?	Avete ...?	ah-veh-teh...?
I'm just looking.	Sto soltanto guardando.	stoh sol-tan-toh gwar-dan-doh
Do you take credit cards?	Accettate carte di credito?	ah-chet-tah-teh kar-teh dee creh-dee-toh?
What time do you open/close?	A che ora apre/ chiude?	ah keh or-ah ah-preh/keh-oo-deh?
this one	questo	kweh-stoh
that one	quello	kwell-oh
expensive	caro	kar-oh
cheap	a buon prezzo	ah bwon pret-soh
size, clothes	la taglia	lah tah-lee-ah
size, shoes	il numero	eel noo-mair-oh
white	bianco	bee-ang-koh
black	nero	neh-roh
red	rosso	ross-oh
yellow	giallo	jal-loh
green	verde	vair-deh
blue	blu/azzurro	bloo/at-zoo-row
brown	marrone	mar-roh-neh

Types of Shop

antique dealer	l'antiquario	lan-tee-kwah-ree-oh
bakery	la panetteria	lah pah-net-tair-ree-ah
bank	la banca	lah bang-kah
bookshop	la libreria	lah lee-breh-ree-ah
butcher's	la macelleria	lah mah-chell-eh-ree-ah
cake shop	la pasticceria	lah pas-tee-chair-ee-ah
chemist's	la farmacia	lah far-mah-chee-ah
delicatessen	la salumeria	lah sah-loo-meh-ree-ah
department store	il grande magazzino	eel gran-deh mag-gad-zee-noh
fishmonger's	la pescheria	lah pess-keh-ree-ah
florist	il fioraio	eel fee-or-eye-oh
greengrocer	il fruttivendolo	eel froo-tee-ven-doh-loh
grocery	alimentari	ah-lee-men-tah-ree
hairdresser	il parrucchiere	eel par-oo-kee-air-eh
ice-cream parlour	la gelateria	lah jel-lah-tair-ree-ah
market	il mercato	eel mair-kah-toh
news-stand	l'edicola	leh-dee-koh-lah
post office	l'ufficio postale	loo-fee-choh pos-tah-leh
shoe shop	il negozio di scarpe	eel neh-goh-tsioh dee skar-peh
supermarket	il supermercato	su-pair-mair-kah-toh
tobacconist	il tabaccaio	eel tah-bak-eye-oh
travel agency	l'agenzia di viaggi	lah-jen-tsee-ah dee vee-ad-jee

Sightseeing

art gallery	la pinacoteca	lah peena-koh-teh-kah
bus stop	la fermata dell'autobus	lah fair-mah-tah dell ow-toh-booss
church	la chiesa	lah kee-eh-zah
	la basilica	lah bah seel i kah
closed for the public holiday	chiuso per la festa	kee-oo-zoh pair lah fess-tah
garden	il giardino	eel jar-dee-no
library	la biblioteca	lah beeb-lee-oh-teh-kah
museum	il museo	eel moo-zeh-oh
railway station	la stazione	lah stah-tsee-oh-neh
tourist information	l'ufficio turistico	loo-fee-choh too-ree-stee-koh

Staying in a Hotel

Do you have any vacant rooms?	**Avete camere libere?**	ah-**veh**-teh **kah**-mair-eh **lee**-bair-eh?
double room	**una camera doppia**	oona **kah**-mair-ah **doh**-pee-ah
with double bed	**con letto matrimoniale**	kon **let**-toh mah-tree-moh-nee-**ah**-leh
twin room	**una camera con due letti**	oona **kah**-mair-ah kon **doo**-eh let-tee
single room	**una camera singola**	oona **kah**-mair-ah **sing**-goh-lah
room with a bath, shower	**una camera con bagno, con doccia**	oona **kah**-mair-ah kon **ban**-yoh, kon **dot**-chah
porter	**il facchino**	eel fah-**kee**-noh
key	**la chiave**	lah kee-**ah**-veh
I have a reservation.	**Ho fatto una prenotazione.**	oh **fat**-toh oona preh-noh-tah-tsee-**oh**-neh

Eating Out

Have you got a table for …?	**Avete una tavola per …?**	ah-**veh**-teh oona **tah**-voh-lah pair …?
I'd like to reserve a table.	**Vorrei riservare una tavola.**	vor-**ray** ree-sair-**vah**-reh oona **tah**-voh-lah
breakfast	**colazione**	koh-lah-tsee-**oh**-neh
lunch	**pranzo**	**pran**-tsoh
dinner	**cena**	**cheh**-nah
Enjoy your meal.	**Buon appetito.**	bwon ah-peh-**tee**-toh
The bill, please.	**Il conto, per favore.**	eel **kon**-toh pair fah-**vor**-eh
I am a vegetarian.	**Sono vegetariano/a.**	**soh**-noh veh-jeh-tar-ee-**ah**-noh/nah
waitress	**cameriera**	kah-mair-ee-**air**-ah
waiter	**cameriere**	kah-mair-ee-**air**-eh
fixed price menu	**il menù a prezzo fisso**	eel meh-**noo** ah **pret**-soh **fee**-soh
dish of the day	**piatto del giorno**	pee-**ah**-toh dell **jor**-no
starter	**antipasto**	an-tee-**pass**-toh
first course	**il primo**	eel **pree**-moh
main course	**il secondo**	eel seh-**kon**-doh
vegetables	**il contorno**	eel kon-**tor**-noh
dessert	**il dolce**	eel **doll**-cheh
cover charge	**il coperto**	eel koh-**pair**-toh
wine list	**la lista dei vini**	lah **lee**-stah day **vee**-nee
rare	**al sangue**	al **sang**-gweh
medium	**al puntino**	al poon-**tee**-noh
well done	**ben cotto**	ben **kot**-toh
glass	**il bicchiere**	eel bee-kee-**air**-eh
bottle	**la bottiglia**	lah bot-**teel**-yah
knife	**il coltello**	eel kol-**tell**-oh
fork	**la forchetta**	lah for-**ket**-tah
spoon	**il cucchiaio**	eel koo-kee-**eye**-oh

Menu Decoder

l'abbacchio	lah-**back**-kee-oh	lamb
l'aceto	lah-**cheh**-toh	vinegar
l'acqua	**lah**-kwah	water
l'acqua minerale gasata/naturale	**lah**-kwah mee-nair-**ah**-leh gah-**zah**-tah/ nah-too-**rah**-leh	mineral water fizzy/still
l'aglio	**lahl**-yoh	garlic
al forno	al **for**-noh	baked
alla griglia	ah-lah **greel**-yah	grilled
l'anatra	**lah**-nah-trah	duck
l'aragosta	lah-rah-**goss**-tah	lobster
l'arancia	lah-**ran**-chah	orange
arrosto	ar-**ross**-toh	roast
la birra	lah **beer**-rah	beer
la bistecca	lah bee-**stek**-kah	steak
il brodo	eel **broh**-doh	broth
il burro	eel **boor**-oh	butter
il caffè	eel kah-**feh**	coffee
il carciofo	eel kar-**choff**-oh	artichoke
la carne	la **kar**-neh	meat
carne di maiale	**kar**-neh dee mah-**yah**-leh	pork
la cipolla	lah chee-**poll**-ah	onion
i fagioli	ee fah-**joh**-lee	beans
il formaggio	eel for-**mad**-joh	cheese
le fragole	leh **frah**-goh-leh	strawberries
frutta fresca	**froo**-tah **fress**-kah	fresh fruit
frutti di mare	**froo**-tee dee **mah**-reh	seafood
i funghi	ee **foon**-gee	mushrooms
i gamberi	ee **gam**-bair-ee	prawns
il gelato	eel jel-**lah**-toh	ice cream
l'insalata	leen-sah-**lah**-tah	salad
il latte	eel **laht**-teh	milk
i legumi	ee leh-**goo**-mee	vegetables
lesso	**less**-oh	boiled
il manzo	eel **man**-tsoh	beef
la mela	lah **meh**-lah	apple

la melanzana	lah meh-lan-**tsah**-nah	aubergine
la minestra	lah mee-**ness**-trah	soup
l'olio	**loll**-yoh	oil
l'oliva	loh-**lee**-vah	olive
il pane	eel **pah**-neh	bread
il panino	eel pah-**nee**-noh	roll
le patate	leh pah-**tah**-teh	potatoes
patatine fritte	pah-tah-**teen**-eh **free**-teh	chips
il pepe	eel **peh**-peh	pepper
la pesca	lah **pess**-kah	peach
il pesce	eel **pesh**-eh	fish
il pollo	eel **poll**-oh	chicken
il pomodoro	eel poh-moh-**dor**-oh	tomato
il prosciutto cotto/crudo	eel pro-**shoo**-toh **kot**-toh/**kroo**-doh	ham cooked/cured
il riso	eel **ree**-zoh	rice
il sale	eel **sah**-leh	salt
la salsiccia	lah sal-**see**-chah	sausage
secco	**sek**-koh	dry
succo d'arancia/ di limone	**soo**-koh dah-ran-chah/ dee lee-**moh**-neh	orange/lemon juice
il tè	eel **teh**	tea
la tisana	lah tee-**zah**-nah	herb tea
il tonno	**ton**-noh	tuna
la torta	lah **tor**-tah	cake
l'uovo	loo-**oh**-voh	egg
l'uva	**loo**-vah	grapes
vino bianco	**vee**-noh bee-**ang**-koh	white wine
vino rosso	**vee**-noh **ross**-oh	red wine
il vitello	eel vee-**tell**-oh	veal
le vongole	leh **von**-goh-leh	baby clams
lo zucchero	loh **zoo**-kair-oh	sugar
gli zucchini	lyee dzo-**kee**-nee	courgettes
la zuppa	lah **tsoo**-pah	soup

Numbers

1	**uno**	**oo**-noh
2	**due**	**doo**-eh
3	**tre**	treh
4	**quattro**	**kwat**-roh
5	**cinque**	**ching**-kweh
6	**sei**	**say**-ee
7	**sette**	**set**-teh
8	**otto**	**ot**-toh
9	**nove**	**noh**-veh
10	**dieci**	dee-**eh**-chee
11	**undici**	**oon**-dee-chee
12	**dodici**	**doh**-dee-chee
13	**tredici**	**tray**-dee-chee
14	**quattordici**	kwat-**tor**-dee-chee
15	**quindici**	**kwin**-dee-chee
16	**sedici**	**say**-dee-chee
17	**diciassette**	dee-chah-**set**-teh
18	**diciotto**	dee-**chot**-toh
19	**diciannove**	dee-chah-**noh**-veh
20	**venti**	**ven**-tee
30	**trenta**	**tren**-tah
40	**quaranta**	kwah-**ran**-tah
50	**cinquanta**	ching-**kwan**-tah
60	**sessanta**	sess-**an**-tah
70	**settanta**	set-**tan**-tah
80	**ottanta**	ot-**tan**-tah
90	**novanta**	noh-**van**-tah
100	**cento**	**chen**-toh
1,000	**mille**	**mee**-leh
2,000	**duemila**	**doo**-eh **mee**-lah
5,000	**cinquemila**	**ching**-kweh **mee**-lah
1,000,000	**un milione**	oon meel-**yoh**-neh

Time

one minute	**un minuto**	oon mee-**noo**-toh
one hour	**un'ora**	oon or-ah
half an hour	**mezz'ora**	medz-**or**-ah
a day	**un giorno**	oon jor-noh
a week	**una settimana**	oona set-tee-**mah**-nah
Monday	**lunedì**	loo-neh-**dee**
Tuesday	**martedì**	mar-teh-**dee**
Wednesday	**mercoledì**	mair-koh-leh-**dee**
Thursday	**giovedì**	joh-veh-**dee**
Friday	**venerdì**	ven-air-**dee**
Saturday	**sabato**	**sah**-bah-toh
Sunday	**domenica**	doh-**meh**-nee-kah

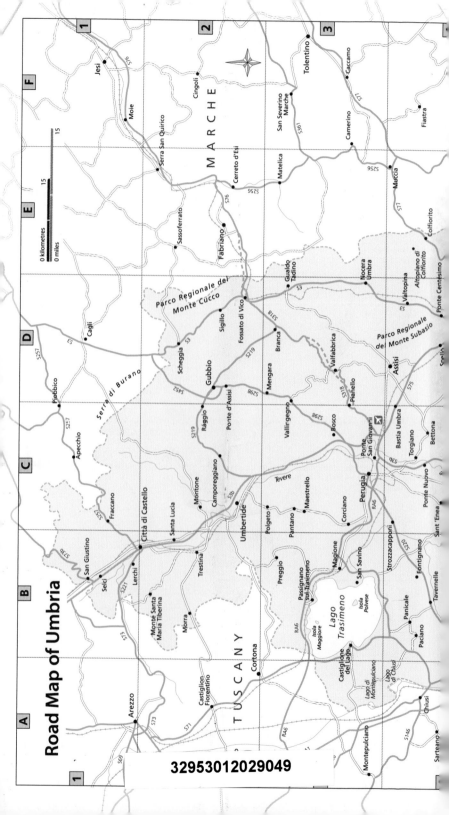

Road Map of Umbria